D1603399

# HEALING

The Three Great Classics on Divine Healing

# HEALING

The Three Great Classics on Divine Healing

Divine Healing
Andrew Murray

The Ministry of Healing
A.J. Gordon

The Gospel of Healing
A.B. Simpson

## Compiled and Edited
## by Jonathan L. Graf

CHRISTIAN PUBLICATIONS
CAMP HILL, PENNSYLVANIA

Christian Publications
3825 Hartzdale Drive
Camp Hill, PA 17011
www.cpi-horizon.com

*Faithful, biblical publishing since 1883*

ISBN: 0-87509-491-0
LOC Catalog Card Number: 92-90119
© 1992 by Christian Publications
All rights reserved
Printed in the United States of America

98 99 00 01 02  6 5 4 3 2

Unless otherwise noted, all Scripture is taken
from the King James Version of the Bible.

# CONTENTS

## THE MINISTRY OF HEALING

## THE GOSPEL OF HEALING

# PUBLISHER'S INTRODUCTION

For the past century, the subject of divine healing has caused debate, excitement and controversy in the evangelical church. Some don't believe in miraculous divine healing, others say they believe but in practice are skeptical. And still others believe in a "name-it-claim-it" doctrine that says if a person is not healed it's his or her fault—the person lacked faith. The continuing debate reveals a crying need for a Scripture-based doctrine that brings a balance.

Each of these views is flawed and damaging to the work of the Holy Spirit and the church. The first view denies; the second view causes frustration and doubt; and the third view can bring emotional stress and often permanent spiritual damage to those who are not healed, because it does not allow for the other reasons—besides a lack of faith—as to why a person was not be healed.

The works of Andrew Murray, A.J. Gordon and Albert Simpson provide solid, biblical teaching on the subject that today's church needs to hear. Each man was a pastor and theologian at the turn of the century who had a significant healing ministry. It is important to note, however, that none of the three allowed healing to be the central focus of his ministry. They did not go out gathering large crowds to witness miraculous healings. Rather, they preached the atoning work of Christ and the cross. Souls were saved and healings occurred—no hoopla. The healing ministry was just a matter-of-fact addition to their everyday pastoral duties.

As you read their works, remember the era in which they were living. The message of divine healing was just becoming known in the church so each had to convince his audience of the reality of that truth. Each started out by searching the Scriptures on the subject. Two of them, Murray and Simpson, experienced miraculous healings; Gordon did a detailed study of many experiences of divine healing. What resulted from their study and experience was three powerful books—books that provide practical, scriptural answers to such questions as:

- What is the role of faith in divine healing?
- Why are some healed and others are not?
- Can non-Christians experience divine healing?
- Does it show a lack of faith to see a doctor when we are sick?
- Is there a relationship between healing and faithful Christian service?
- What is the relationship of sin and sickness to divine healing?
- What is the relationship between Satan and sickness?
- Can Satan imitate divine healing?
- How do you detect the role of the adversary in supernatural healing?

We trust that your questions will be answered, your faith increased and your life and ministry enhanced as you put into practice the scriptural truths presented in these classics.

Jonathan Graf
Editorial Director
Christian Publications

# DIVINE HEALING

Andrew Murray

# PREFACE

The publication of this work may be regarded as a testimony of my faith in divine healing. After being stopped for more than two years in the exercise of my ministry, I was healed by the mercy of God in answer to the prayer of those who see in Him "the LORD that healeth thee" (Exodus 15:26).

This healing, granted to faith, has been the source of rich spiritual blessing to me. I have clearly seen that the Church possesses in Jesus, our divine Healer, an inestimable treasure, which she does not yet know how to appreciate. I have been convinced anew of that which the Word of God teaches us in this matter, and of what the Lord expects of us; and I am sure that if Christians learned to realize practically the presence of the Lord that healeth, their spiritual life would thereby be developed and sanctified. I can therefore no longer keep silence, and I publish here a series of meditations, with the view of showing, according to the Word of God, that "the prayer of faith" (James 5:15) is the means appointed by God for the cure of the sick, that this truth is in perfect accord with Holy Scripture, and that the study of this truth is essential for everyone who would see the Lord manifest His power and His glory in the midst of His children.

# CHAPTER

## 1

---

## *Pardon and Healing*

*But that ye may know that the Son of man hath power on earth to forgive sins, (then saith he to the sick of palsy,) Arise, take up thy bed, and go unto thine house. (Matthew 9:6)*

In man two natures are combined. He is at the same time spirit and matter, heaven and earth, soul and body. For this reason, on the one side he is the son of God, and on the other he is doomed to destruction because of the Fall. Sin in his soul and sickness in his body bear witness to the right which death has over him. It is the twofold nature which has been redeemed by divine grace. When the Psalmist calls upon all that is within him to bless the Lord for His benefits, he cries, "Bless the LORD, O my soul, . . . who forgiveth all thine iniquities, who healeth all thy diseases" (Psalm 103:1, 3). When Isaiah foretells the deliverance of his people, he adds, "The inhabitant shall not say, I am sick: the people that dwell therein shall be forgiven their iniquity" (Isaiah 33:24).

This prediction was accomplished beyond all anticipation when Jesus the Redeemer came down to this earth. How numerous were the healings wrought by Him who was come to establish upon earth the kingdom of heaven! Whether by His own acts or whether afterwards by the commands which He left for His disciples, does He not show us clearly that the preaching of the gospel and the healing of the sick went together in the salvation which He came to bring? Both are given as evident proof of His mission as the

Messiah. "The blind receive their sight, and the lame walk . . . and the poor have the gospel preached to them" (Matthew 11:5). Jesus, who took upon Him the soul and body of man, delivers both in equal measure for the consequences of sin.

This truth is nowhere more evident or better demonstrated than in the history of the paralytic. The Lord begins by saying to him, "Thy sins be forgiven thee," after which He adds, "Arise . . . and walk" (Mark 2:9). The pardon of sin and the healing of sickness complete each other, for in the eyes of God, who sees our entire nature, sin and sickness are as closely united as the body and the soul. In accordance with the Scriptures, our Lord Jesus has regarded sin and sickness in another light than we have. With us, sin belongs to the spiritual domain; we recognize that it is under God's just displeasure, justly condemned by Him, while sickness, on the contrary, seems only a part of the present condition of our nature, and to have nothing to do with God's condemnation and His righteousness. Some go so far as to say that sickness is a proof of the love and grace of God.

But neither the Scripture nor yet Jesus Christ Himself ever spoke of sickness in this light, nor do They ever present sickness as a blessing, as a proof of God's love which should be borne with patience. The Lord spoke to the disciples of divers sufferings which they should have to bear, but when He speaks of sickness, it is always as of an evil caused by sin and Satan, and from which we should be delivered. Very solemnly He declared that every disciple of His would have to bear his cross (Matthew 16:24), but He never taught one sick person to resign himself to be sick. Everywhere Jesus healed the sick, everywhere He dealt with healing as one of the graces belonging to the kingdom of heaven. Sin in the soul and sickness in the body both bear witness to the power of Satan, and "the Son of God was manifested, that he might destroy the works of the devil" (1 John 3:8).

Jesus came to deliver men from sin and sickness that He might make known the love of the Father. In His actions, in His teaching of the disciples, in the work of the apostles, pardon and healing are always to be found together. Either the one or the other may doubtless appear more in relief, according to the development, or the faith of those to whom they spoke. Sometimes it was healing which prepared the way for the acceptance of forgiveness; sometimes it was forgiveness which preceded the healing, which, coming afterwards, became a seal to it.

In the early part of His ministry, Jesus cured many of the sick, finding them ready to believe in the possibility of their healing. In this way He sought to influence hearts to receive Himself as the One who is able to pardon sin. When He saw that the paralytic could receive pardon at once, He began by that, which was of the greatest importance; after which came the healing which put a seal on the pardon which had been accorded to him.

We see, by the accounts given in the gospels, that it was more difficult for the Jews at that time to believe in the pardon of their sins than in divine healing. Now it is just the contrary. The Christian Church has heard so much of the preaching of the forgiveness of sins that the thirsty soul easily receives the message of grace. But it is not the same with divine healing. That is rarely spoken of. The believers who have experienced it are not as many. It is true that healing is not given in this day as in those times, to the multitudes whom Christ healed without any previous conversion. In order to receive it, it is necessary to begin by confession of sin and the purpose to live a holy life. This is without doubt the reason why people find more difficulty to believe in healing than in forgiveness; and this is also why those who receive healing receive at the same time new spiritual blessing, feel more closely united to the Lord Jesus, and learn to love and serve Him better. Unbelief may attempt to separate these two gifts, but they are always united in Christ. He is always the same Savior both of the soul and of the body, equally ready to grant pardon and healing. The redeemed may always cry: "Bless the LORD, O my soul . . . who forgiveth all thine iniquities; who healeth all thy diseases" (Psalm 103:1, 3).

# CHAPTER

## 2

---

# *Because of Your Unbelief*

*Then came the disciples to Jesus apart, and said, Why could we not cast him out? And Jesus said unto them, Because of your unbelief: for verily I say unto you, If ye have faith as a grain of mustard seed, ye shall say unto this mountain, Remove hence to yonder place; and it shall remove; and nothing shall be impossible unto you. (Matthew 17:19–20)*

When the Lord Jesus sent His disciples into different parts of Palestine, He endued them with a double power, that of casting out unclean spirits and that of healing all sickness and all infirmity (Matthew 10:1). He did the same for the 70 who came back to Him with joy, saying, "Lord, even the devils are subject unto us through thy name" (Luke 10:17).

On the day of the transfiguration, while the Lord was still upon the mountain, a father brought his son who was possessed with a demon to His disciples, beseeching them to cast out the evil spirit, but they could not. When, after Jesus had cured the child, the disciples asked Him why they had been unable to do it themselves as in other cases, He answered them, "because of your unbelief." It was, then, their unbelief, and not the will of God which had been the cause of their defeat.

In our days divine healing is very little believed in, because it has almost entirely disappeared from the Christian Church. One may ask the reason, and here are the two answers which have been given. The greater number think that miracles, the gift of healing included, should be limited to the time of the primitive Church, that their object was to establish the first foundation of Christianity; but from that time circumstances have altered. Other believers say unhesitatingly that if the Church has lost these gifts, it is by her own fault. It is because she has become worldly that the Spirit acts feebly in her. It is because she has not remained in direct and habitual relation with the full power of the unseen world. But that if she were to see anew springing up within her men and women who live the life of faith and of the Holy Spirit, entirely consecrated to their God, she would see again the manifestation of the same gifts as in former times. Which of these two opinions coincides the most with the Word of God? Is it by the will of God that the "gifts of healing" have been suppressed, or is it rather man who is responsible for it? Is it the will of God that miracles should not take place? Will He in consequence of this no longer give the faith which produces them? Or again, is it the Church which has been guilty of lacking faith?

## *What does the Scripture say?*

The Bible does not authorize us, either by the words of the Lord or His apostles, to believe that the gifts of healing were granted only to the early times of the Church. On the contrary, the promise which Jesus made to the apostles when He gave them instructions concerning their mission, shortly before His ascension, appears to us applicable to all times (Mark 16:15–18).

Paul places the gift of healing among the operations of the Holy Spirit. James gives a precise command on this matter without any restriction of time. The entire Scriptures declare that these graces will be granted according to the measure of the Spirit and of faith.

It is also alleged that at the onset of each new dispensation God works miracles, that it is His ordinary course of action; but it is nothing of the kind.

Think of the people of God in the former dispensation, in the time of Abraham, all through the life of Moses, in the exodus from

Egypt, under Joshua, in the time of the Judges and of Samuel, under the reign of David and other godly kings up to David's time; during more than a thousand years miracles took place.

But, it is said, miracles were much more necessary in the early days of Christianity than later. But what about the power of heathenism even in this day, wherever the gospel seeks to combat it? It is impossible to admit that miracles should have been more needful for the heathen in Ephesus (Acts 19:11–12) than for the heathen of Africa in the present day. And if we think of the ignorance and unbelief which reign even in the midst of the Christian nations, are we not driven to conclude that there is a need for manifest acts of the power of God to sustain the testimony of believers and to prove that God is with them? Besides, among believers themselves, how much of doubt, how much of weakness there is! How their faith needs to be awakened and stimulated by some evident proof of the presence of the Lord in their midst! One part of our being consists of flesh and blood; it is therefore in flesh and blood that God wills to manifest His presence.

In order to prove that it is the Church's unbelief which has lost the gift of healing, let us see what the Bible says about it. Does it not often put us on our guard against unbelief, against all which can estrange and turn us from our God? Does not the history of the Church show us the necessity of these warnings? Does it not furnish us with numerous examples of backward steps, of world pleasing, in which faith grew weak in the exact measure in which the spirit of the world took the upper hand? For such faith is only possible to him who lives in the world invisible. Until the third century the healings by faith in Christ were numerous, but in the centuries following they became more infrequent. Do we not know from the Bible that it is always unbelief which hinders the mighty working of God?

Oh that we could learn to believe in the promises of God! God has not gone back from His promises; Jesus is still He who heals both soul and body; salvation offers us even now healing and holiness, and the Holy Spirit is always ready to give us some manifestations of His power. Even when we ask why this divine power is not more often seen, He answers us: "Because of your unbelief."

The more we give ourselves to experience personally sanctification by faith, the more we shall also experience healing by faith. These two doctrines walk abreast. The more the Spirit of God lives and acts in the soul of believers, the more will the miracles multiply by which He works in the body. Thereby the world can recognize what redemption means.

# CHAPTER

## 3

---

# *Jesus and the Doctors*

*And a certain woman, which had an issue of blood twelve years, and had suffered many things of many physicians, and had spent all that she had, and was nothing bettered, but rather grew worse, when she had heard of Jesus, came in the press behind, and touched his garment. For she said, If I may touch but his clothes, I shall be whole. And straightway the fountain of her blood was dried up; and she felt in her body that she was healed of that plague. And Jesus, immediately knowing in himself that virtue had gone out of him, turned him about in the press, and said, Who touched my clothes? And his disciples said unto him, Thou seest the multitude thronging thee, and sayest thou, Who touched me? And he looked round about to see her that had done this thing. But the woman fearing and trembling, knowing what was done in her, came and fell down before him, and told him all the truth. And he said unto her, Daughter, thy faith hath made thee whole; go in peace, and be whole of thy plague. (Mark 5:25–34)*

We may be thankful to God for having given us doctors. Their vocation is one of the most noble, for a large number of them seek truly to do, with love and compassion, all they are able to alleviate the evils and sufferings which burden humanity as a result of sin. There are even some who are zealous servants of

Jesus Christ, and who seek also the good of their patients' souls. Nevertheless, it is Jesus Himself who is always the first, the best, the greatest Physician.

Jesus heals diseases for which earthly physicians can do nothing, for the Father gave Him this power when He charged Him with the work of our redemption. Jesus, in taking upon Him our human body, delivered it from the dominion of sin and Satan. He has made our bodies temples of the Holy Ghost and members of His own body (1 Corinthians 6:15, 19), and even in our day how many have been given up by the doctors as incurable, how many cases of consumption, of gangrene, of paralysis, of dropsy, of blindness and of deafness have been healed by Him! Is it not then astonishing that so small a number of the sick apply to Him?

The method of Jesus is quite another than that of earthly physicians. They seek to serve God in making use of remedies which are found in the natural world, and God makes use of these remedies according to natural law, according to the natural properties of each, while the healing which proceeds from Jesus is of a totally different order; it is by divine power, the power of the Holy Ghost, that Jesus heals. Thus the difference between these two modes of healing is very marked.

That we may understand it better, let us take an example. Here is a physician who is an unbeliever, but extremely clever in his profession; many sick people owe their healing to him. God gives the result by means of the prescribed remedies, and the physician's knowledge of them. Here is another physician who is a believer, and who prays God's blessing on the remedies which he employs. In this case also a large number are healed, but neither in the one case nor the other does the healing bring with it any spiritual blessing. They will be preoccupied, even the believing among them, with the remedies which they use, much more than with what the Lord may be doing with them, and in such a case their healing will be more hurtful than beneficial. On the contrary, when it is Jesus only to whom the sick person applies for healing, he learns to reckon no longer upon remedies, but to put himself into direct relation with His love and His almightiness. In order to obtain such healing, he must commence by confessing and renouncing his sins, and exercising a living faith. Then healing will come directly from the Lord, who takes possession of the sick body, and it thus becomes a blessing for the soul as well as for the body.

But is it not God who has given remedies to man? it is asked. Does not their power come from Him? Without doubt! But on the other hand, is it not God who has given us His Son with all power to heal? Shall we follow the way of natural law with all those who do not yet know Christ, and also with those of His children whose faith is still too weak to abandon themselves to His almightiness; or rather do we choose the way of faith, receiving healing from the Lord and from the Holy Spirit, seeing therein the result and proof of our redemption?

The healing which is wrought by our Lord Jesus brings with it and leaves behind it more real blessing than the healing which is obtained through physicians. Healing has been a misfortune to more persons than one. On a bed of sickness serious thoughts had taken possession, but from the time of his healing how often has a sick man been found anew far from the Lord! It is not thus when it is Jesus who heals. Healing is granted after confession of sin; therefore it brings the sufferer nearer to Jesus, and establishes a new link between him and the Lord; it causes him to experience His love and power; it brings within him a new life of faith and holiness. When the woman who had touched the hem of Christ's garment felt that she was healed, she learned something of what divine love means. She went away with the words: "Daughter, thy faith hath made thee whole; go in peace" (Mark 5:34).

O you who are suffering from some sickness, know that Jesus the sovereign Healer is yet in our midst. He is close to us, and He is giving anew to His Church manifest proofs of His presence. Are you ready to break with the world, to abandon yourself to Him with faith and confidence? Then fear not, remember that divine healing is a part of the life of faith. If nobody around you can help you in prayer, if no "elder" is at hand to pray the prayer of faith, fear not to go yourself to the Lord in the silence of solitude, like the woman who touched the hem of His garment. Commit to

Him the care of your body. Get quiet before Him and, like the poor woman, say, "I will be healed." Perhaps it may take some time to break the chains of your unbelief, but assuredly none that wait on Him shall be ashamed (Psalm 25:3).

CHAPTER

4

---

# *Health and Salvation by the Name of Jesus*

*And his name through faith in his name hath made this man strong, whom ye see and know: yea, the faith which is by him hath given him this perfect soundness in the presence of you all. (Acts 3:16)*

*Be it known unto you all, and to all the people of Israel, that by the name of Jesus Christ of Nazareth, whom ye crucified, whom God raised from the dead, even by him doth this man stand here before you whole. (4:10)*

*Neither is there salvation in any other: for there is none other name under heaven given among men, whereby we must be saved. (4:12)*

When after Pentecost, the paralytic was healed through Peter and John at the gate of the temple, it was "in the name of Jesus Christ of Nazareth" that they said to him, "Rise up and walk," and as soon as the people in their amazement ran together to them, Peter declared that it was the name of Jesus which had so completely healed the man.

As the result of this miracle and of Peter's discourse, many people which had heard the word believed (Acts 4:4). On the morrow Peter repeated these words before the Sanhedrin, "By the name of Jesus Christ of Nazareth . . . doth this man stand here before you whole"; and then he added, "There is none other name under heaven . . . whereby we must be saved." This statement of Peter's declares to us that the name of Jesus both heals and saves. We have here a teaching of the highest import for divine healing.

We see that healing and health form part of Christ's salvation. Does not Peter clearly state this in his discourse to the Sanhedrin where, having spoken of healing, he immediately goes on to speak of salvation by Christ (4:10, 12)? In heaven, even our bodies will have their part in salvation; salvation will not be complete for us until our bodies shall enjoy the full redemption of Christ. Why then should we not believe in this work of redemption here below? Even already here on earth, the health of our bodies is a fruit of the salvation which Jesus has acquired for us.

We see also that health as well as salvation is to be obtained by faith. The tendency of man by nature is to bring about his salvation by his works, and it is only with difficulty that he comes to receive it by faith; but when it is a question of the healing of the body, he has still more difficulty in seizing it. As to salvation, he ends up accepting it because by no other means can he open the door of heaven; while for the body, he makes use of well-known remedies. Why then should he seek for divine healing? Happy is he who comes to understand that it is the will of God; that God wills to manifest the power of Jesus, and also to reveal to us His Fatherly love; to exercise and to confirm our faith, and to make us prove the power of redemption in the body as well as the soul. The body is part of our being; even the body has been saved by Christ, therefore it is in our body that our Father wills to manifest the power of redemption, and to let men see that Jesus lives. Oh, let us believe in the name of Jesus! Was it not in the name of Jesus that perfect health was given to the impotent man? And were not these words: "Thy faith hath saved thee" (Luke 7:50; 18:42), pronounced when the body was healed? Then let us seek to obtain divine healing.

Wherever the Spirit acts with power, there He works divine healings. Would it not seem that if ever miracles were superfluous, it was at Pentecost, for then the word of the apostles worked mightily, and the pouring out of the Holy Spirit was abundant? Well, it is precisely because the Spirit acted powerfully that His working must needs be visible in the body. If divine healing is seen but rarely in our day, we can attribute it to no other cause than that the Spirit does not act with power. The unbelief of worldlings and the want of zeal among believers stop His working. The healings which God is giving here and there are the precursory signs of all the spiritual graces which are promised to us, and it is only the Holy Spirit who reveals the almightiness of the name of Jesus to operate such healings. Let us pray earnestly for the Holy Spirit, let us place ourselves unreservedly under His direction, and let us seek to be firm in our faith in the name of Jesus, whether for preaching salvation or for the work of healing.

God grants healing to glorify the name of Jesus. Let us seek to be healed by Jesus that His name may be glorified. It is sad to see how little the power of His name is recognized, how little it is the end of preaching and of prayer. Treasures of divine grace, of which Christians deprive themselves by their lack of faith and zeal, are hidden in the name of Jesus. It is the will of God to glorify His Son in the Church; and He will do it wherever He finds faith. Whether among believers, or whether among the heathen, He is ready with virtue from on high to awaken consciences, and to bring hearts to obedience. God is ready to manifest the all-power of His Son, and to do it in a striking way in body as well as in soul. Let us believe it for ourselves, let us believe it for others, for the circle of believers around us, and also for the Church in the whole world. Let us give ourselves to believe with firm faith in the power of the name of Jesus. Let us ask great things in His name, counting on His promise, and we shall see God still do wonders by the name of His holy Son.

# CHAPTER
## 5

---

## *Not by Our Own Power*

*And when Peter saw it, he answered unto the people, Ye men of Israel, why marvel ye at this? or why look ye so earnestly on us, as though by our own power or holiness we had made this man to walk? (Acts 3:12)*

As soon as the impotent man had been healed at the gate of the temple, through Peter and John, the people ran together unto them. Peter, seeing this miracle was attributed to their power and holiness, loses no time in setting them right by telling them that all the glory of this miracle belongs to Jesus, and that it is He in whom we must believe.

Peter and John were undoubtedly full of faith and holiness; perhaps even they may have been the most holy and zealous servants of God in their time, otherwise God might not have chosen them as instruments in this case of healing. But they knew that their holiness of life was not of themselves, that it was of God through the Holy Spirit. They think so little of themselves that they ignore their own holiness and know only one thing, that all power belongs to their Master. They hasten then to declare that in this thing they count for nothing, that it is the work of the Lord alone.

This is the object of divine healing; to be a proof of the power of Jesus, a witness in the eyes of men of what He is, proclaiming His divine intervention, and attracting hearts to Him. "Not by our own power or holiness." Thus it becomes those to speak whom the Lord is pleased to use in helping others by their faith.

It is necessary to insist on this because of the tendency of believers to think the contrary. Those who have recovered their health in answer to "the prayer of faith," "the supplication of a righteous man availeth much in its working" (James 5:16, R.V.), are in danger of being too much occupied with the human instrument which God is pleased to employ, and to think that the power lies in man's piety.

Doubtless the prayer of faith is the result of real godliness, but those who possess it will be the first to acknowledge that it does not come from themselves, nor from any effort of their own. They fear to rob the Lord of the least particle of the glory which belongs to Him, and they know that if they do so, they will compel Him to withdraw His grace from them. It is their great desire to see the souls which God has blest through them enter into a direct and increasingly intimate communion with the Lord Jesus Christ Himself, since that is the result which their healing should produce. Thus they insist that it is not caused by their own power or holiness.

Such testimony on their part is necessary to reply to the erroneous accusations of unbelievers. The Church of Christ needs to hear clearly announced that it is on account of her worldliness and unbelief that she has lost these spiritual gifts of healing (1 Corinthians 12:9) and that the Lord restores these gifts to those who, with faith and obedience, have consecrated their lives to Him. This grace cannot reappear without being preceded by a renewal of faith and of holiness. But then, says the world, and with it a large number of Christians, "You are laying claim to the possession of a higher order of faith and holiness; you consider yourselves holier than others." To such accusations this word of Peter is the only reply before God and before man, confirmed by a life of deep and real humility; "Not unto us, O LORD, not unto us, but unto thy name give glory, for thy mercy, and for thy truth's sake" (Psalm 115:1).

Such a testimony is also necessary in view of our own heart and of the wiles of Satan. As long as, through the Church's unfaithfulness, the gifts of healing are but rarely given, those children of God who have received these gifts are in danger of priding themselves upon them, and of imagining that they have in themselves something exceptionally meritorious. The enemy does not forget to persecute them by such insinuations, and woe unto them if they listen to him. They are not ignorant of his devices (2 Corinthians 2:11), therefore, they need to pray continually to the Lord to keep them in humility, the true means of obtaining continually more grace. If they persevere in humility, they will recognize that the more God makes use of them, the more also will they be penetrated with the conviction that it is God alone who works by them, and that all the glory belongs to Him. "Not I, but the grace of God which was with me" (1 Corinthians 15:10). Such is their watchword.

Finally, this testimony is useful for the feeble ones who long for salvation, and who desire to receive Christ as their Healer. They hear of full consecration and entire obedience, but they form a false idea of it. They think they must in themselves attain to a high degree of knowledge and of perfection, and they fall a prey to discouragement. No, no! It is not by our own power or holiness that we obtain these graces, but by a faith quite simple, a childlike faith, which knows that it has no power nor holiness of its own, and which commits itself completely to Him who is faithful, and whose almightiness can fulfill His promise. Oh, let us not seek to do or to be anything of ourselves! It is only as we feel our own powerlessness, and expect all from God and His Word that we realize the glorious way in which the Lord heals sickness "by faith in his name."

# CHAPTER

## 6

---

## *According to the Measure of Faith*

*And Jesus said unto the centurion, Go thy way; and as thou hast believed, so be it done unto thee. And his servant was healed in the selfsame hour. (Matthew 8:13)*

This passage of Scripture brings before us one of the principal laws of the kingdom of heaven. In order to understand God's ways with His people, and our relations with the Lord, it is needful to understand this law thoroughly and not to deviate from it. Not only does God give or withhold His grace according to the faith or unbelief of each, but they are granted in greater or lesser measure, only in proportion to the faith which receives them. God respects the right to decide which He has conferred on man. Therefore, He can only bless us in the measure in which each yields himself up to His divine working, and opens all his heart to Him. Faith in God is nothing else than the full opening of the heart to receive everything from God; therefore man can only receive divine grace according to his faith; and this applies as much to divine healing as to any other grace of God.

This truth is confirmed by the spiritual blessings which may result from sickness. Two questions are often asked: (1) Is it not God's will that His children should sometimes remain in a prolonged state of sickness? (2) Since it is a recognized thing that divine healing brings with it greater spiritual blessing than the sickness itself, why does God allow certain of His children to continue sick through many years, and while in this condition give them blessing in sanctification, and in communion with Himself?

The answer to these two questions is that God gives to His children according to their faith. We have already had occasion to remark that in the same degree in which the Church has become worldly, her faith in divine healing has diminished until at last it has disappeared. Believers do not seem to be aware that they may ask God for the healing of their sickness, and that thereby they may be sanctified and fitted for His service. They have come to seek only submission to His will and to regard sickness as a means to be separate from the world. In such conditions the Lord gives them what they ask. He would have been ready to give them yet more, to grant them healing in answer to the prayer of faith, but they lacked the faith to receive it. God always meets His children where they are, however weak they may be. The sick ones, therefore, who have desired to receive Him with their whole heart, will have received from Him the fruit of the sickness in their desire that their will should be conformed to the will of God. They might have been able to receive healing, in addition, as a proof that God accepted their submission; if this has not been so, it is because faith has failed them to ask for it.

"As thou hast believed, so be it done unto thee." These words give the reply to yet another question: How can you say that divine healing brings with it so much of spiritual blessing, when one sees that the greater number of those who were healed by the Lord Jesus received nothing more than a deliverance from their present sufferings, without giving any proof that they were also spiritually blest? Here again, as they believed, so was it done unto them.

A good number of sick people, having witnessed the healing of others, gained confidence in Jesus just far enough to be healed, and Jesus granted them their request, without adding other blessings for their souls. Before His ascension the Lord had not as free an entrance as He now has into the heart of man, because "the Holy Ghost was not yet given" (John 7:39). The healing of the sick was then hardly more than a blessing for the body. It was only later, in the dispensation of the Spirit, that the conviction and confession of sin have become for the believer the first grace to be received, the essential condition for obtaining healing, as St. Paul tells us in his epistle to the Corinthians, and James in his to the 12 tribes scattered abroad (1 Corinthians 11:31–32; James 5:16). Thus the degrees of spiritual grace, which it is possible for us to receive, depend upon the measure of our faith, whether it be for its external manifestation, or especially whether for its influence upon our inner life.

We commend then, to every suffering one who is looking for divine healing and seeks to know Jesus as His divine Healer, not to let himself be hindered by his unbelief, not to doubt the promises of God, and thus be made "strong in faith giving glory to God" as is His due. "As thou hast believed so be it done unto thee." If with all your heart you trust in the living God you will be abundantly blest; do not doubt it.

The part of faith is always to lay hold on just that which appears impossible or strange to human eyes. Let us be willing to be considered fools for Christ's sake (1 Corinthians 4:10). Let us not fear to pass for weak minded in the eyes of the world and of such Christians as are ignorant of these things, because, on the authority of the Word of God, we believe that which others cannot yet admit. Do not, then, let yourself be discouraged in your expectation even though God should delay to answer you, or if your sickness be aggravated. Once having placed your foot firmly on the immovable rock of God's own Word, and having prayed the Lord to manifest His almightiness in your body because you are one of the members of His Body, and the temple of the Holy Ghost, persevere in believing in Him with the firm assurance that He has undertaken for you, that He has made Himself responsible for your body, and that His healing virtue will come to glorify Him in you.

# CHAPTER

# 7

---

# *The Way of Faith*

*And straightway the father of the child cried out, and said
with tears, Lord, I believe; help thou mine unbelief. (Mark
9:24)*

These words have been a help and strength to thousands of
souls in their pursuit of salvation and the gifts of God. Notice
that it is in relation to an afflicted child that they were pronounced,
in the fight of faith when seeking healing from the Lord Jesus. In
them we see that in one and the same soul there can arise a struggle
between faith and unbelief, and that it is not without a struggle
that we come to believe in Jesus and in His all-power to heal the
sick. In this we find the needful encouragement for realizing the
Savior's power.

I speak here especially to sufferers who do not doubt the power
or the will of the Lord Jesus to heal in this day without the use of
earthly remedies, but who lack the boldness to accept healing for
themselves. They believe in the divine power of Christ; they believe
in a general manner His good will to heal. They have acquired,
either by the Scriptures, or by facts of healing by the Lord alone
which have taken place in our days, the intellectual persuasion that
the Lord can help even them, but they shrink from saying with
faith, "The Lord has heard me; I know that He is healing me."

Take notice first that without faith no one can be healed. When
the father of the afflicted child said to Jesus, "If thou canst do

anything, have compassion on us, and help us," Jesus replied: "If *thou* canst believe" (Mark 9:22–23). Jesus had the power to heal and He was ready to do it, but He casts the responsibility on the man. "If thou canst. All things are possible to him that believeth" (R.V.).

In order to obtain your healing from Jesus, it is not enough to pray. Prayer without faith is powerless. It is "the prayer of faith" which saves the sick (James 5:15). If you have already asked for healing from the Lord, or if others have asked it for you, you must, before you are conscious of any change, be able to say with faith, "On the authority of God's Word I have the assurance that He hears me and that I shall be healed." To have faith means in your case to surrender your body absolutely into the Lord's hands, and to leave yourself entirely to Him. Faith receives healing as a spiritual grace which proceeds from the Lord even while there is no conscious change in the body. Faith can glorify God and say, "Bless the LORD, O my soul . . . who healeth all [my] diseases" (Psalm 103:1–3). The Lord requires this faith that He may heal.

But how is such faith to be obtained? Tell God the unbelief which you find in your heart, and count on Him for deliverance from it. Faith is not money by which your healing can be purchased from the Lord. It is He who desires to awaken and develop in you the necessary faith. "Help my unbelief," cried the father of the child. It was his ardent desire that his faith should not come short. Confess to the Lord all the difficulty you have to believe Him on the ground of His Word; tell Him you want to be rid of this unbelief, that you bring it to Him with a will to harken only to His Word. Do not lose time in deploring your unbelief, but look to Jesus. The light of His countenance will enable you to find the power to believe in Him (Psalm 44:3).

He calls on you to trust in Him; listen to Him, and by His grace faith will triumph in you. Say to Him, "Lord, I am still aware of the unbelief which is in me. I find it difficult to believe that I am sure of my healing because I possess Him who works it. And, nevertheless, I want to conquer this unbelief. Thou, Lord, will give me the victory. I desire to believe; I will believe; by Thy grace I dare to say I can believe. Yes, Lord, I believe, for Thou comest to the help of my unbelief." It is when we are in intimate communion with the Lord, and when our heart responds to His, that unbelief is overcome and conquered.

It is needful also to testify to the faith one has. Be resolved to believe that which the Lord says to you—to believe, above all, that which He is. Lean wholly upon His promises. "The prayer of faith shall save the sick." "I am the LORD that healeth thee" (Exodus 15:26). Look to Jesus, who "bare our sickness" (Matthew 8:17), and who healed all who came to Him; count on the Holy Spirit to manifest in your heart the presence of Jesus who is also now in heaven, and to work also in your body the power of His grace. Praise the Lord without waiting to feel better, or to have more faith. Praise Him, and say with David, "O LORD, my God, I cried unto thee, and thou hast healed me" (Psalm 30:2).

Divine healing is a spiritual grace which can only be received spiritually and by faith, before feeling its effects on the body. Accept it, then, and give glory to God. When the Lord Jesus had commanded the unclean spirit to come out of the child, he rent him sore, so that he was as one dead, inasmuch as many said, "He is dead." If, therefore, your sickness does not yield at once, if Satan and your own unbelief attempt to get the upper hand, do not heed them. Cling closely to Jesus your Healer, and He will surely heal you.

# CHAPTER

## 8

---

## *Your Body Is the Temple of the Holy Ghost*

*Know ye not that your bodies are the members of Christ?
Shall I then take the members of Christ, and make them
the members of an harlot? God forbid. (1 Corinthians
6:15)*

*What? know ye not that your body is the temple of the Holy
Ghost which is in you, which ye have of God, and ye are
not your own? For ye are bought with a price: therefore
glorify God in your body, and in your spirit, which are
God's. (19–20)*

The Bible teaches us that the Body of Christ is the company
of the faithful. These words are taken generally in their
spiritual sense, while the Bible asks us positively whether we know
not that our bodies are the members of Christ. In the same way,
when the Bible speaks of the indwelling of the Holy Spirit or of
Christ, we limit their presence to the spiritual part of our being:
our soul, or our heart. Nevertheless the Bible says expressly, "Know
ye not that your body is the temple of the Holy [Spirit]?"

When the Church understands that the body also has part in the
redemption which is by Christ, by which it ought to be brought
back to its original destiny, to be the dwelling place of the Holy
Spirit, to serve as His instrument, to be sanctified by His presence,
she will also recognize all the place which divine healing has in the

Bible and in the counsels of God.

The account of the creation tells us that man is composed of three parts. God first formed the body from the dust of the earth, after which He breathed into it "the breath of life" (Genesis 2:7). He caused His own life, His Spirit, to enter into it. By this union of the Spirit with matter, the man became a "living soul." The soul, which is essentially the man, finds its place between the body and the spirit; it is the link that binds them together. By the body the soul finds itself in relation to the external world; by the spirit, with the world invisible and with God. By means of the soul, the spirit can subject the body to the action of the heavenly powers and thus spiritualize it; by means of the soul, the body also can act upon the spirit and attract it earthwards. The soul, subject to the solicitations of both spirit and body, is in a position to choose between the voice of God, speaking by the spirit, or the voice of the world, speaking through the senses.

This union of spirit and body forms a combination which is unique in the creation; it makes man to be the jewel of God's work. Other creatures had existed already, some were like angels, all spirit, without any material body, and others, like the animals, were only flesh, possessing a body animated with a living soul, but devoid of spirit. Man was destined to show that the material body, governed by the spirit, was capable of being transformed by the power of the Spirit of God, and of being thus led to participate in heavenly glory.

We know what sin and Satan have done with this possibility of gradual transformation. By means of the body, the spirit was tempted, seduced, and became a slave of sense. We know also what God has done to destroy the work of Satan and to accomplish the purpose of creation. "The Son of God was manifested, that he might destroy the works of the devil" (1 John 3:8). God prepared a body for His Son (Hebrews 10:5). "The Word was made flesh" (John 1:14). "In him dwelleth all the fullness of the Godhead bodily" (Colossians 2:9). "Who his own self bare our sins in his own body on the tree" (1 Peter 2:24). And now Jesus, raised up from the dead with a body as free from sin as His spirit and His soul, communicates to our body the virtue of His glorified body. The Lord's Supper is "the communion of the body of Christ"; and our bodies are "the members of Christ" (1 Corinthians 10:16; 6:15; 12:27).

Faith puts us in possession of all that the death of Christ and His resurrection have procured for us, and it is not only in our spirit and our soul that the life of the risen Jesus manifests its presence here below, it is in the body also that it would act according to the measure of our faith.

"Know ye not that your body is the temple of the Holy [Spirit]?" Many believers represent to themselves that the Holy Spirit comes to dwell in our body as we dwell in a house. Nothing of the kind. I can dwell in a house without it becoming part of my being. I may leave it without suffering; no vital union exists between my house and me. It is not thus with the presence of our soul and spirit in our body. The life of a plant lives and animates every part of it; and our soul is not limited to dwell in such or such part of the body, the heart or the head for instance, but penetrates throughout, even to the end of the lowest members. The life of the soul pervades the whole body; the life throughout proves the presence of the soul. It is in like manner that the Holy Ghost comes to dwell in our body. He penetrates it entirely. He animates and possesses us infinitely more than we can imagine.

In the same way in which the Holy Spirit brings to our soul and spirit the life of Jesus—His holiness, His joy, His strength—He comes also to impart to the sick body all the vigorous vitality of Christ as soon as the hand of faith is stretched out to receive it. When the body is fully subject to Christ, crucified with Him, renouncing all self-will and independence, desiring nothing but to be the Lord's temple, it is then that the Holy Spirit manifests the power of the risen Savior in the body. Then only can we glorify God in our body, leaving Him full freedom to manifest therein His power, to show that He knows how to set His temple free from the domination of sickness, sin and Satan.

# The Body for the Lord

*Meats for the belly, and the belly for meats: but God shall
destroy both it and them. Now the body is not for fornication, but for the Lord; and the Lord for the body. (1
Corinthians 6:13)*

O ne of the most learned of theologians has said that corporiety
is the end of the ways of God. As we have already seen, this
is indeed what God has accomplished in creating man. It is this
which makes the inhabitants of heaven wonder and admire when
they contemplate the glory of the Son. Clothed with a human
body, Jesus has taken His place forever upon the throne of God,
to partake of His glory. It is this which God has willed. It shall be
recognized in that day when regenerated humanity, forming the
body of Christ, shall be truly and visibly the temple of the living
God (2 Corinthians 6:16), and when all creation in the new
heavens and new earth shall share the glory of the children of God.
The material body shall then be wholly sanctified, glorified by the
Spirit; and this body, thus spiritualized, shall be the highest glory
of the Lord Jesus Christ and of His redeemed.

It is in anticipation of this new condition of things that the Lord
attaches a great importance to the indwelling and sanctification of
our bodies, down here, by His Spirit. So little is this truth understood by believers that less still do they seek for the power of the
Holy Spirit in their bodies. Many of them also, believing that this

body belongs to them, use it as it pleases them. Not understanding how much the sanctification of the soul and spirit depends upon the body, they do not grasp all the meaning of the words, "The body is for the Lord," in such a way as to receive them in obedience.

"The body is for the Lord." What does this mean? The apostle has just said, "Meats for the belly, and the belly for meats: but God shall destroy both it and them." Eating and drinking afford the Christian an opportunity of carrying out this truth, "The body is for the Lord." He must indeed learn to eat and drink to the glory of God. By eating, sin and the Fall came about. It was also through eating that the devil sought to tempt our Lord. Thus Jesus Himself sanctified His body in eating only according to the will of His Father (Matthew 4:4). Many believers fail to watch over their bodies, to observe a holy sobriety through the fear of rendering it unfit for the service of God. Eating and drinking should never impede communion with God; its end is, on the contrary, to facilitate it in maintaining the body in its normal condition.

The apostle speaks also of fornication, this sin which defiles the body, and which is in direct opposition to the words, "The body is for the Lord." It is not simply incontinence outside the married state, but in that state also, which is meant here; all voluptuousness, all want of sobriety of whatever kind is condemned in these words: "Your body is the temple of the Holy Ghost" (1 Corinthians 6:19). In the same way, all of what goes to maintain the body—to clothe it, strengthen it, rest it in sleep, or afford it enjoyment—should be placed under the control of the Holy Spirit. As under the Old Covenant, the temple was constructed solely for God, and for His service, even so our body has been created for the Lord and for Him alone.

One of the chief benefits then of divine healing will be to teach us that our body ought to be set free from the yoke of our own will to become the Lord's property. God does not grant healing in answer to our prayers until He has attained the end for which He had permitted the sickness. He wills that this discipline should bring us into a more intimate communion with Him; He would make us understand that we have regarded our body as our own property, whilst it belonged to the Lord; and that the Holy Spirit seeks to sanctify all its actions. He leads us to understand that if we yield our body unreservedly to the influence of the Holy Spirit, we shall experience His power in us, and He will heal us by bringing into our body the very life of Jesus; He leads us, in short, to say with full conviction, "The body is for the Lord."

There are believers who seek after holiness, but only for the soul and spirit. In their ignorance they forget that the body and all its systems of nerves—that the hand, the ear, the eyes, the mouth—are called to testify directly to the presence and the grace of God in them. They have not sufficiently taken in these words: "Your bodies are the members of Christ" (1 Corinthians 6:15). "If by the Spirit ye make to die the deeds of the body, ye shall live" (Romans 8:13, R.V. margin). "And the very God of peace sanctify you wholly; and I pray God your whole spirit and soul and body be preserved blameless unto the coming of our Lord Jesus Christ" (1 Thessalonians 5:23). Oh, what a renewing takes place in us when, by His own touch, the Lord heals our bodies, when He takes possession of them, and when by His Spirit He becomes life and health to them! It is with an indescribable consciousness of holiness, of fear and of joy that the believer can then offer his body a living sacrifice to receive healing, and to have for his motto these words: "The body is for the Lord."

# CHAPTER

## 10

---

# *The Lord for the Body*

*Meats for the belly, and the belly for meats: but God shall destroy both it and them. Now the body is not for fornication, but for the Lord; and the Lord for the body. (1 Corinthians 6:13)*

There is reciprocity in God's relations with man. That which God has been for me, I ought in my turn to be for Him. And that which I am for Him, He desires again to be for me. If, in His love, He gives Himself fully to me, it is in order that I may lovingly give myself fully to Him. In the measure in which I more or less really surrender to Him all my being, in that measure also He gives Himself more really to me.

God thus leads the believer to understand that this abandonment of Himself comprises the body, and the more our life bears witness that that body is for the Lord, the more also we experience that the Lord is for the body. In saying, "The body is for the Lord," we express the desire to regard our body as wholly consecrated, offered in sacrifice to the Lord, and sanctified by Him. In saying, "The Lord is for the body," we express the precious certainty that our offering has been accepted, and that by His Spirit, the Lord will impart to our body His own strength and holiness, and that henceforth He will strengthen and keep us.

This is a matter of faith. Our body is material, weak, feeble, sinful, mortal. Therefore it is difficult to grasp all at once the full extent of the words, "The Lord is for the body." It is the Word of God which explains to us the way to assimilate this. The body was created by the Lord and for the Lord. Jesus took upon Him an earthly body. In His body He bore ours sins on the cross, and thereby set our body free from the power of sin. In Christ the body has been raised again, and seated on the throne of God. The body is the habitation of the Holy Spirit; it is called to eternal partnership in the glory of heaven. Therefore, with certainty, and in a wide and universal sense, we can say, "Yes, the Lord Jesus, our Savior, is for the body."

This truth has divers applications. In the first place, it is a great help in practical holiness. More than one sin derives its strength from some physical tendency. The converted drunkard has a horror of intoxicating drinks, but, notwithstanding, his appetites are sometimes a snare to him, gaining victory over his new convictions. If, however, in the conflict he gives over his body with confidence to the Lord, all physical appetite, all desire to drink will be overcome. Our temper also often results from our physical constitution. A nervous, irritable system produces words which are sharp, harsh and wanting in love. But let the body with this physical tendency be taken to the Lord, and it will soon be experienced that the Holy Spirit can mortify the risings of impatience, and sanctify the body, rendering it blameless.

These words, "The Lord for the body," are applicable also to the physical strength which the Lord's service demands of us. When David cries, "It is God that girdeth me with strength, and maketh my way perfect. He maketh my feet like hinds' feet, . . . a bow of steel is broken by mine arms" (Psalm 18:32–34). Again in these words: "The LORD is the strength of my life" (27:1). It does not mean only the spiritual man but the entire man. Many believers have experienced that the promise: "They that wait upon the LORD shall renew their strength" (Isaiah 40:31), touches the body, and the Holy Spirit increases the physical strength.

But it is especially in divine healing that we see the truth of these words: "The Lord is for the body." Yes, Jesus, the sovereign and merciful Healer, is always ready to save and cure.

There was in Switzerland, some years ago, a young girl in consumption and near death. The doctor had advised a milder climate, but she was too weak to take the journey. She learned that Jesus is the Healer of the sick. She believed the good news, and one night when she was thinking of this subject it seemed to her that the body of the Lord drew near to her, and that she ought to take these words literally, "His body for our body." From this moment she began to improve. Some time after she began to hold Bible readings, and later on she became a zealous and much-blest worker for the Lord among women. She had learned to understand that the Lord is for the body.

Dear sick one, the Lord has shown you by sickness what power sin has over the body. By your healing He would also show you the power of the redemption of the body. He calls you to show that which you have not understood hitherto, that "the body is for the Lord." Therefore, give Him your body. Give it to Him with your sickness and with the sin, which is the original source of sickness. Believe always that the Lord has taken charge of this body, and He will manifest with power that He really is the Lord, who is for the body. The Lord, who has Himself taken upon Him a body here on earth and regenerated it, from the highest heaven where He now is, clothed with His glorified body, sends us His divine strength, willing thus to manifest His power in our body.

CHAPTER

**11**

---

## *Do Not Consider Your Body*

*I speak after the manner of men because of the infirmity of
your flesh: for as ye have yielded your members servants to
uncleanness and to iniquity unto iniquity; even so now
yield your members servants to righteousness unto holiness.
For when ye were the servants of sin, ye were free from
righteousness. What fruit had ye then in those things
whereof ye are now ashamed? for the end of those things is
death. (Romans 6:19–21)*

When God promised Abraham to give him a son, the
patriarch would never have been able to believe in this
promise if he had considered his own body, already aged and worn
out. He would see nothing but God and His promise, the power
and faithfulness of God who guaranteed him the fulfillment of His
promise.

This enables us to lay hold of all the difference there is between
the healing which is expected from earthly remedies and the
healing which is looked for from God only. When we have
recourse to remedies for healing, all the attention of the sick one
is upon the body, considering the body, while divine healing calls
us to turn away our attention from the body, and to abandon
ourselves, soul and body, to the Lord's care, occupying ourselves
with Him alone.

This truth equally enables us to see the difference between the sickness retained for blessing and the healing received from the Lord. Some are afraid to take the promise in James 5 in its literal sense, because they say sickness is more profitable to the soul than health. It is true that in the case of healing obtained by earthly remedies, many people would be more blest in remaining ill than in recovering health, but it is quite otherwise when healing comes directly from the hand of God. In order to receive divine healing, sin must be so truly confessed and renounced, one must be completely surrendered to the Lord, self must be so really yielded up to be wholly in His hands, and the will of Jesus to take charge of the body must be so firmly counted on that the healing becomes the commencement of a new life of intimate communion with the Lord.

Thus we learn to give up to Him entirely the care of the health, and the smallest indication of the return of the evil is regarded as a warning not to consider our body, but to be occupied with the Lord only.

What a contrast this is from the greater number of sick people who look for healing from remedies. If some few of them have been sanctified by the sickness, having learned to lose sight of themselves, how many more are there who are drawn by the sickness itself to be constantly occupied with themselves and with the condition of their body. What infinite care they exercise in observing the least symptom, favorable or unfavorable! What a constant preoccupation to them is their eating and drinking, the anxiety to avoid this or that! How much they are taken up with what they consider due to them from others, whether they are sufficiently thought of, whether well enough nursed, whether visited often enough! How much time is thus devoted to considering the body and what it exacts, rather than the Lord and the relations which He seeks to establish with their souls! Oh, how many are they who, through sickness, are occupied almost exclusively with themselves!

All this is totally different when healing is looked for in faith from the loving God. Then the first thing to learn is: Cease to be anxious about the state of your body, you have trusted it to the

Lord and He has taken the responsibility. If you do not see a rapid improvement immediately, but on the contrary the symptoms appear to be more serious, remember that you have entered on a path of faith, and therefore you ought not to consider the body, but cling only to the living God. The commandment of Christ, "Take no thought . . . for your body" (Matthew 6:25), appears here in a new light. When God called Abraham not to consider his own body, it was that He might call him to the greatest exercise of faith which could be, that he might learn to see only God and His promise. Sustained by his faith, he gave glory to God, convinced that God would do what He had promised. Divine healing is a marvelous tie to bind us to the Lord. At first, one may fear to believe that the Lord will stretch forth His mighty hand and touch the body; but in studying the Word of God the soul takes courage and confidence. At last one decides, saying, I yield up my body into the hands of God; and I leave the care of it to Him. Then the body and its sensations are lost sight of, and only the Lord and His promise are in view.

Will you also enter upon this way of faith, very superior to that which it is the habit to call natural? Walk in the steps of Abraham. Learn from him not to consider your own body , and not to doubt through unbelief. To consider the body gives birth to doubts, while clinging to the promise of God and being occupied with Him alone gives entrance into the way of faith, the way of divine healing, which glorifies God.

# CHAPTER

## 12

---

# *Discipline and Sanctification*

*For [our human fathers] for a few days chastened us after their own pleasure; but [God] for our profit, that we might be partakers of his holiness. (Hebrews 12:10)*

*If a man therefore purge himself from these, he shall be a vessel unto honour, sanctified, and meet for the master's use, and prepared unto every good work. (2 Timothy 2:21)*

To sanctify anything is to set it apart, to consecrate it to God and to His service. The temple at Jerusalem was holy, that is to say, it was consecrated, dedicated to God that it might serve Him as a dwelling place. The vessels of the temple were holy, because they were devoted to the service of the temple; the priests were holy, chosen to serve God and ready to work for Him. In the same way the Christian ought also to be sanctified, at the Lord's disposal, "ready to do every good work."

When the people of Israel went out of Egypt, the Lord reclaimed them for His service as a holy people. "Let my people go that they may serve me" (Exodus 7:16), He said to Pharaoh. Set free from their hard bondage, the children of Israel were debtors to enter at once upon the service of God, and to become His happy servants. Their deliverance was the road that led to their sanctification.

Again in this day, God is forming for Himself a holy people, and it is that we may form part of them that Jesus sets us free. He "gave himself for us, that he might redeem us from all iniquity, and purify unto himself a peculiar people, zealous of good works" (Titus 2:14). It is the Lord who breaks the chains by which Satan would hold us in bondage. He would have us free, wholly free to serve Him. He wills us to save, to deliver both the soul and the body, that each of the members of the body may be consecrated to Him and placed unreservedly at His disposal.

A large number of Christians do not yet understand all this, they do not know how to take in that the purpose of their deliverance is that they may be sanctified, prepared to serve their God. They make use of their lives and their members to procure their own sanctification; consequently they do not feel at liberty to ask for healing with faith. It is therefore to chasten them—that they may be brought to desire sanctification—that the Lord permits Satan to inflict sickness upon them, and by it keeps them chained and prisoners (Luke 13:11, 16). God chastens us "for our profit, that we might be partakers of his holiness" (Hebrews 12:10), and that we may be sanctified, "meet for the master's use" (2 Timothy 2:21).

The discipline which inflicts the sickness brings great blessings with it. It is a call to the sick one to reflect; it leads him to see that God is occupied with him, and seeks to show him what there is which still separates him from Himself. God speaks to him; He calls him to examine His ways, to acknowledge that he has lacked holiness, and that the purpose of the chastisement is to make him partaker of His holiness. He awakens within him the desire to be enlightened by the Holy Spirit down into the inmost recesses of his heart, that he may be enabled to get a clear idea of what his life has been up to the present time, a life of self-will, very unlike the holy life which God requires of him. He leads him to confess his sins, to entrust them to the Lord Jesus, to believe that the Savior can deliver him from them. He urges him to yield to Him, to consecrate his life to Him, to die to himself that he may be able to live unto God.

Sanctification is not something which you can accomplish yourself; it cannot even be produced by God in you as something which you can possess and contemplate in yourself. No, it is the Holy

Spirit, the Spirit of holiness alone who can communicate His holiness to you and renew it continually. Therefore, it is by faith you have become "partakers of his holiness." Having understood that Jesus has been made, unto you of God, sanctification (1 Corinthians 1:30), and that it is the Holy Spirit's work to impart to you His holiness which was manifested in His life on earth. Surrender yourself to Him by faith that He may enable you to live that life from hour to hour. Believe that the Lord will, by His Spirit, lead you into, and keep you in this life of holiness and of consecration to God's service. Live thus in obedience of faith, always attentive to His voice, and the guidance of His Spirit.

From the time that this Fatherly discipline has led the sick one to a life of holiness, God has attained His purpose, and He will heal him who asks it in faith. Our earthly parents "for a few days chastened us . . . All chastening seemeth for the present to be not joyous, but grievous, yet afterward it yieldeth the peaceable fruit of righteousness unto them that have been exercised thereby" (Hebrews 12:10–11, R.V.). Yes, it is when the believer realizes this "peaceable fruit of righteousness," that he is in a condition to be delivered from the chastisement.

Oh, it is because believers still understand so little that sanctification means an entire consecration to God that they cannot really believe that healing will quickly follow the sanctification of the sick one. Good health is too often for them only a matter of personal comfort and enjoyment which they may dispose of at their will, but God cannot thus minister to their selfishness. If they understood better that God requires of His children that they should be "sanctified and meet for the master's use," they would not be surprised to see Him giving healing and renewed strength to those who have learned to place all their members at His disposal, willing to be sanctified and employed in His service by the Holy Spirit. The Spirit of healing is also the Spirit of sanctification.

# CHAPTER

## 13

---

## *Sickness and Death*

*Surely he shall deliver thee from the snare of the fowler, and from the noisome pestilence.*

*Nor for the pestilence that walketh in darkness; nor for the destruction that wasteth at noonday.*

*With long life will I satisfy him, and shew him my salvation. (Psalm 91:3, 6, 16)*

*To shew that the LORD is upright: he is my rock, and there is no unrighteousness in him. (92:15)*

This objection is often made to the words of the Apostle James, "The prayer of faith shall save the sick" (5:15). If we have the promise of being always healed in answer to prayer, how can it be possible to die? And some add: How can a sick person know whether God, who fixes the time of our life, has not decided that we shall die by such a sickness? In such a case, would it not be a sin to ask for healing?

Before replying, we would remark that this objection touches not such as believe in Jesus as the Healer of the sick, but the Word of God itself, and the promise so clearly declared in the epistle of James and elsewhere. We are not at liberty to change or to limit the promises of God whenever they present some difficulty to us;

neither can we insist that they shall be clearly explained to us before
we can bring ourselves to believe what they state. It is for us to
begin by receiving them without resistance; then only can the
Spirit of God find us in the state of mind in which we can be taught
and enlightened.

Furthermore, we would remark that in considering a divine truth
which has been for a long time neglected in the Church, it can
hardly be understood at the outset. It is only little by little that its
importance and bearing are discerned. In measure as it revives,
after it has been accepted by faith, the Holy Spirit will accompany
it with new light. Let us remember that it is by the unbelief of the
Church that divine healing has left her. It is not on the answers of
such or such an one that faith in Bible truths should be made to
depend. "There ariseth light in the darkness" (Psalm 112:4) for
the "upright" who are ready to submit themselves to the Word of
God.

1. To the first objection it is easy to reply. Scripture fixes 70 or
80 years as the ordinary measure of human life. The believer who
receives Jesus as the Healer of the sick will rest satisfied then with
the declaration of the Word of God. He will feel at liberty to expect
a life of 70 years, but not longer. Besides, the man of faith places
himself under the direction of the Spirit, which will enable him to
discern the will of God regarding him if something should prevent
his attaining the age of 70. Every rule has its exceptions, in the
things of heaven as in the things of earth. Of this, therefore, we
are sure according to the Word of God, whether by the words of
Jesus or by those of James, that our heavenly Father wills, as a rule,
to see His children in good health that they may labor in His
service.

For the same reason He wills to set them free from sickness as
soon as they have made confession of sin and prayed with faith for
their healing. For the believer who has walked with his Savior,
strong with the strength which proceeds from divine healing, and
whose body is consequently under the influence of the Holy Spirit,
it is not necessary that when his time comes to die, he should die
of sickness. To "fall asleep in Jesus Christ," such is the death of the

believer when the end of his life is come. For him death is only sleep after fatigue, the entering into rest. The promise, "that it may be well with thee, and thou mayest live long on the earth" (Ephesians 6:3) is addressed to us who live under the New Covenant. The more the believer has learned to see in the Savior Him who "took our infirmities," the more he has the liberty to claim the literal fulfillment of the promises: "With long life will I satisfy him"; "They shall bring forth fruit in old age; they shall be fat and flourishing" (Psalm 92:14).

2. The same text applies to the second objection. The sick one sees in God's Word that it is His will to heal His children after the confession of their sins, and in answer to the prayer of faith. It does not follow that they shall be exempt from other trials; but as for sickness, they are healed of it because it attacks the body, which has become the dwelling place of the Holy Spirit. The sick one should then desire healing that the power of God may be made manifest in him, and that he may serve Him in accomplishing His will. In this he clings to the revealed will of God, and for that which is not revealed, he knows that God will make known His mind to His servants who walk with Him. We would insist here that faith is not a logical reasoning which ought in some way to oblige God to act according to His promises. It is rather the confiding attitude of the child who honors his Father—who counts upon His love to see Him fulfilling His promises, and who knows that He is faithful to communicate to the body as well as to the soul the new strength which flows from the redemption, until the moment of departure is come.

# CHAPTER

## 14

---

## *The Holy Spirit, The Spirit of Healing*

*Now there are diversities of gifts, but the same Spirit.*

*To another faith by the same Spirit; to another the gifts of healing by the same Spirit.*

*But all these worketh that one and the selfsame Spirit, dividing to every man severally as he will. (1 Corinthians 12:4, 9, 11)*

What is it which distinguishes the children of God? What is their glory? It is that God dwells in the midst of them and reveals Himself to them in power (Exodus 33:16; 34:9–10). Under the New Covenant, this dwelling of God in the believer is still more manifest than in former times. God sends the Holy Spirit to His Church, which is the Body of Christ, to act in her with power, and her life and her prosperity depend on Him. The Spirit must find in her unreserved, full liberty, that she may be recognized as the Church of Christ, the Lord's Body. In every age the Church may look for manifestations of the Spirit, for they form our indissoluble unity: "There is one body, and one Spirit" (Ephesians 4:4).

The Spirit operates variously in such or such a member of the Church. It is possible to be filled with the Spirit for one special work and not for another. There are also times in the history of the Church when certain gifts of the Spirit are given with power, while at the same time ignorance or unbelief may hinder other gifts. Wherever the life more abundant of the Spirit is to be found, we may expect Him to manifest all His gifts.

The gift of healing is one of the most beautiful manifestations of the Spirit. It is recorded of Jesus, "how God anointed Jesus of Nazareth with the Holy Ghost and with power: who went about doing good, and healing all that were oppressed of the devil; for God was with him" (Acts 10:38). The Holy Spirit in Him was a healing Spirit, and He was the same in the disciples after Pentecost. Thus the words of our text express what was the continuous experience of the early churches (compare attentively Acts 3:7; 4:30; 5:12, 15–16; 6:8; 8:7; 9:41; 14:9–10; 16:18–19; 11:12; 28:8–9). The abundant pouring out of the Spirit produced abundant healings. What a lesson for the Church in our days!

Divine healing is the work of the Holy Spirit. Christ's redemption extends its powerful working to the body, and the Holy Spirit has in charge both to transmit it to and maintain it in us. Our body shares in the benefit of the redemption, and even now it can receive the pledge of it by divine healing. It is Jesus who heals, Jesus who anoints and baptizes with the Holy Spirit. Jesus who baptized His disciples with the same Spirit, is He who sends us the Holy Spirit here on earth, whether to take away sickness for us, or whether to restore us to health when sickness has taken hold upon us.

Divine healing accompanies the sanctification by the Spirit. It is to make us holy that the Holy Spirit makes us partakers of Christ's redemption. Hence His name Holy. Therefore, the healing which He works is an intrinsic part of His divine mission, and He bestows it, whether to lead the sick one to be converted and to believe (Acts 4:29–30; 5:12, 14; 6:7–8; 8:6, 8; 9:42) or to confirm his faith if he is already converted. He constrains him thus to renounce sin, and to consecrate himself entirely to God and to His service (1 Corinthians 11:31; James 5:15–16; Hebrews 12:10).

Divine healing tends to glorify Jesus. It is God's will that His Son should be glorified, and the Holy Spirit does this when He comes to show us what the redemption of Christ does for us. The redemption of the mortal body appears almost more marvelous than that of the immortal soul. In these two ways God wills to dwell in us through Christ, and thus to triumph over the flesh. As soon as our body becomes the temple of God through the Spirit, Jesus is glorified.

Divine healing takes place wherever the Spirit of God works in power. Proofs of this are to be found in the lives of the Reformers, and in those of certain Moravians in their best times. But there are yet other promises touching the pouring out of the Holy Spirit which have not been fulfilled up to this time. Let us live in a holy expectation, praying the Lord to accomplish them in us.

# CHAPTER
## 15

---

## *Persevering Prayer*

*. . . men ought always to pray, and not faint.*

*I tell you that [God] will avenge them speedily. Nevertheless when the Son of man cometh, shall he find faith on the earth? (Luke 18:1, 8)*

The necessity of praying with perseverance is the secret of all spiritual life. What a blessing to be able to ask the Lord for such and such a grace until He gives it, knowing with certainty that it is His will to answer prayer; but what a mystery for us in the call to persevere in prayer, to knock in faith at His door, to remind Him of His promises, and to do so without wearying until He arises and grants us our petition! Is not the assurance that our prayer should obtain from the Lord that which He would not otherwise give, the evident proof that man has been created in the image of God, that he is His friend, that he is His fellow-worker, and that the believers who together form the Body of Christ partake in this manner His intercessory work? It is to Christ's intercession that the Father responds, and to which He grants His divine favors.

More than once the Bible explains to us the need for persevering prayer. There are many grounds, the chief of which is the justice of God. God has declared that sin must bear its consequences; sin therefore has rights over a world which welcomes and remains enslaved by it. When the child of God seeks to quit this order of things, it is necessary that the justice of God should consent to this; time, therefore, is needed that the privileges which Christ has procured for the believers should weigh before God's tribunal. Besides this, the opposition of Satan, who always seeks to prevent the answer to prayer, is a reason for it (Daniel 10:12–13). The only means by which this unseen enemy can be conquered is faith. Standing firmly on the promises of God, faith refuses to yield, and continues to pray, and wait for the answer, even when it is delayed, knowing that the victory is sure (Ephesians 6:12–13).

Finally, perseverance in prayer is needful for ourselves. Delay in the answer is intended to prove and strengthen our faith; it ought to develop in us the steadfast will which will no longer let go the promises of God, but which renounces its own side of things to trust on God alone. It is then that God, seeing our faith, finds us ready to receive His favor and grants it to us. He will avenge speedily, even though He tarry. Yes, notwithstanding all the needful delays, He will not make us wait a moment too long. If we cry unto Him day and night, He will avenge us speedily.

This perseverance in prayer will become easy to us as soon as we fully understand what faith is. Jesus teaches us in these words, "And all things, whatsoever ye shall ask in prayer, believing, ye shall receive" (Matthew 21:22). When the Word of God authorizes us to ask anything, we ought at once to believe that we receive it. God gives it us; this we know by faith, and we can say between God and us that we have received it, although it might be only later that we are permitted to realize the effects here on earth. It is before having seen or experienced anything whatsoever that faith rejoices in having received, perseveres in praying and waiting until the answer is manifest. It is then precisely in order to count upon the answer that it is sometimes useful to continue to pray; and even after having believed that we are heard, it is good to persevere until it has become an accomplished fact.

This is of great importance in obtaining divine healing. Some-times, it is true, that healing is immediate and complete; but it may happen that we have to wait, even when a sick person has been able to ask for it in faith. Sometimes also the first symptoms of healing are immediately manifest; but afterwards the progress is slow, and interrupted by times when it is arrested or when the evil returns. In either case it is important as much for the sick person as for those who pray with him, to believe in the efficacy of persevering prayer, even though they may not understand the mystery of it. That which God appears at first to refuse, He grants later to the prayer of the Canaanite woman, to the prayer of the "widow," to that of the friend who knocks at midnight (Matthew 15:22; Luke 18:3; 11:5). Without regarding either change or answer, the faith which is grounded on the Word of God, and which continues to pray with importunity, ends by gaining the victory. "And shall not God avenge his own elect, which cry out day and night unto him, though he bear long with them? I tell you that he will avenge them speedily" (Luke 18:7–8). God knows how to delay all the time which is necessary, and nevertheless to act speedily without waiting more than is needful. The same two things should belong to our faith. Let us lay hold with a holy promptitude of the grace which is promised us, as if we had already received it; let us await with untiring patience the answer which is slow to come. Such faith belongs to living in Him. It is in order to produce in us this faith that sickness is sent to us, and that the healing is granted to us, for such faith above all glorifies God.

CHAPTER

**16**

---

# *Let Him That Is Healed Glorify God*

*And immediately he received his sight, and followed him glorifying God: and all the people, when they saw it, gave praise unto God. (Luke 18:43)*

*And he leaping up stood, and walked, and entered with them into the temple, walking, and leaping, and praising God. (Acts 3:8)*

It is a prevalent idea that piety is easier in sickness than in health; that silence and suffering incline the soul to seek the Lord, and enter into communion with Him better than the distractions of active life; that, in fact, sickness throws us more upon God. For these reasons sick people hesitate to ask for healing from the Lord; for they say to themselves, *How can we know whether sickness may not be better for us than health?* To think thus is to ignore that the healing and its fruits are divine. Let us try to understand that if the healing through ordinary means may at times run the risk of making God relax His hand, divine healing, on the contrary, binds us more closely to Him. Thus it comes to pass that in our day, as in the time of the early ministry of Jesus Christ, the believer who has been healed by Him can glorify Him far better than the one who remains sick. Sickness can only glorify God in the measure in which it gives occasion to manifest His power (John 9:3; 11:4).

The sufferer who is led by his sufferings to give glory to God, does it, so to speak, by constraint. If he had health and the liberty to choose, it is quite possible that his heart would turn back to the world. In such a case the Lord must keep him on one side; his piety depends on his sickly condition. This is why the world supposes that religion is hardly efficacious anywhere but in sick chambers or death beds, and for such as have no need to enter into the noise and stir of ordinary life. In order that the world may be convinced of the power of religion against temptation, it must see the believer who is in good health walking in calmness and holiness even in the midst of work and of active life. Doubtless very many sick people have glorified God by their patience in suffering, but He can be still more glorified by a health which He has sanctified.

Why then, we are asked, should those who have been healed in answer to the prayer of faith glorify the Lord more than such as have been healed through earthly remedies? Here is the reason. Healing by means of remedies shows us the power of God in nature, but it does not bring us into living and direct contact with Him; while divine healing is an act proceeding from God, without anything but the Holy Spirit.

In the latter, contact with God is the thing which is essential, and it is for this reason that examination of the conscience and the confession of sins should be the preparation for it (1 Corinthians 11:30–32; James 5:15–16). One who is so healed is called to consecrate himself quite anew and entirely to the Lord (1 Corinthians 6:13, 19). All this depends upon the act of faith which lays hold of the Lord's promise, which yields to Him, and which does not doubt that the Lord at once takes possession of what is consecrated to Him. This is why the continuance of health received depends on the holiness of life, and the obedience in seeking always the good pleasure of the divine Healer (Exodus 15:26).

Health obtained under such conditions ensures spiritual blessings much greater than the mere restoration to health by ordinary means. When the Lord heals the body it is that He may take possession of it and make it a temple that He may dwell in. The joy which then fills the soul is indescribable; it is not only the joy of being healed, it is joy mingled with humility, and a holy enthusiasm which realizes the touch of the Lord, and which receives a new life from Him. In the exuberance of his joy, the healed one exalts the Lord, he glorifies Him by word and deed, and all his life is consecrated to his God.

It is evident that these fruits of healing are not the same for all, and that sometimes there are steps made backwards. The life of the healed one has a solidarity with the lives of believers around him. Their doubts and their inconsistencies may in time tend to make his steps totter, although this generally results in a new beginning. Each day he discovers and recognizes afresh that his life is the Lord's life; he enters into a more intimate and more joyous communion with Him; he learns to live in habitual dependence upon Jesus, and receives from Him that strength which results from a more complete consecration.

Oh, what may not the Church become when she lives in this faith, when every sick person shall recognize in sickness a call to be holy, and shall expect from the Lord a manifestation of His presence, when healings shall be multiplied, producing in each a witness of the power of God, all ready to cry with the Psalmist, "Bless the LORD, O my soul . . . who healeth all thy diseases" (103:2–3).

CHAPTER

**17**

---

# *The Need of a Manifestation of God's Power*

*And now, Lord, behold their threatenings: and grant unto thy servants, that with all boldness they may speak thy word, By stretching forth thine hand to heal; and that signs and wonders may be done by the name of thy holy child Jesus.*

*And when they had prayed, the place was shaken where they were assembled together; and they were all filled with the Holy Ghost, and they spake the word of God with boldness. (Acts 4:29–31)*

Is it permissible to pray in this way now, to ask the Lord, "Grant thy servants to speak thy word with all boldness while thou stretchest out thy hand to heal" (R.V.)? Let us look into this question.

Does not the Word of God meet with as many difficulties in our days as then, and are not the needs now equally pressing? Let us picture to ourselves the apostles in the midst of Jerusalem and her unbelief; on the one hand the rulers of the people and their threatenings; on the other, the blinded multitude refusing to believe in the Crucified. Now the world is no longer so openly hostile to the Church because it has lost its fear of her, but its flattering words are more to be dreaded than its hatred. Dissimulation is sometimes worse than violence. Is not a Christianity of mere form, in the sleep of indifference, equally inaccessible with an openly resisting Judaism? God's servants need, even in the present day, in order that the Word may be preached with all boldness, that the power of God should be evidently manifested among them.

Is not the help of God as necessary now as then? The apostles knew well that it was not the eloquence of their preaching which caused the truth to triumph, but they knew then the need that the Holy Spirit should manifest His presence by miracles. It was needful that the living God should stretch forth His hand, that there might be healings, miracles and signs in the name of His holy Son Jesus. It was only thus that His servants rejoiced, and, strengthened by His presence, could speak His Word with boldness and teach the world to fear His name.

Do not the divine promises concern us also? The apostles counted on these words of the Lord before He ascended, "Go ye into all the world, and preach the gospel to every creature. . . . And these signs shall follow them that believe . . . they shall lay hands on the sick, and they shall recover" (Mark 16:15–18). This charge indicates the divine vocation of the Church; the promise which follows it shows us what is her armor, and proves to us that the Lord acts in concert with her. It was because the apostles counted on this promise that they prayed the Lord to grant them this proof of His presence. They had been filled with the Holy Ghost on the Day of Pentecost, but they still needed the supernatural signs which His power works. The same promise is as much for us, for the command to preach the gospel cannot be severed from the promise of divine healing with which it is accompanied. It is nowhere to be found in the Bible that this promise was not for future times. In all ages God's people greatly need to know that the Lord is with them, and to possess the irrefutable proof of it. Therefore this promise is for us; let us pray for its fulfillment.

Ought we to reckon on the same grace? We read in Acts that when the apostles had prayed, "they were all filled with the Holy Ghost, and they spake the word of God with boldness" (4:31). "And by the hands of the apostles were many signs and wonders wrought among the people; . . . And believers were the more added to the Lord, multitudes both of men and women" (5:12–14). Oh, what joy and what new strength would God's people receive today if anew the Lord should thus stretch forth His hand! How many wearied and discouraged laborers grieve that they do not see more result, more blessing on their labors! What life would come into their faith if signs of this kind should arise to prove to them that God is with them! Many who are indifferent would be led to reflect, more than one doubter would regain confidence, and all unbelievers would be reduced to silence. And the poor heathen! How he would awake if he saw by facts that which words had not enabled him to lay hold of, if he were forced to acknowledge that the Christian's God is the living God who doeth wonders, the God of love who blesses!

Awake, awake, put on your strength, Church of Christ! Although you have lost by your unfaithfulness the joy of seeing allied to the preaching of the Word, the hand of the Lord stretched out to heal, the Lord is ready to grant you this grace anew. Acknowledge that it is your own unbelief which has so long deprived you of it, and pray for pardon. Clothe yourself with the strength of prayer.

"Awake, awake, put on strength, O arm of the LORD; awake, as in the ancient days" (Isaiah 51:9).

# CHAPTER

## 18

---

# *Sin and Sickness*

*The prayer of faith shall save the sick, and the Lord shall raise him up; and if he have committed sins, they shall be forgiven him. Confess your faults one to another, and pray one for another, that ye may be healed. (James 5:15–16)*

Here, as in other Scriptures, the pardon of sins and the healing of sickness are closely united. James declares that pardon of sins will be granted with the healing; and for this reason he desires to see confession of sin accompany the prayer which claims healing. We know that confession of sin is indispensable to obtain from God the pardon of sin; it is not less so to obtain healing. Unconfessed sin presents an obstacle to the prayer of faith; in any case, the sickness may soon reappear and for this reason.

The first care of a physician, when he is called to treat a patient, is to diagnose the cause of the disease. If he succeeds he stands a better chance to combat it. Our God also goes back to the primary cause of all sickness—that is sin. It is their part to confess and God's to grant the pardon which removes this first cause, so that healing can take place. In seeking for healing by means of earthly remedies, the first thing to do is to find a clever physician, and then to follow his prescriptions exactly; but in having recourse to the prayer of faith, it is needful to fix our eyes, above all, upon the Lord, and to ascertain how we stand with Him. James therefore points out to us a condition which is essential to the recovery of our health;

namely, that we confess and forsake sin.

Sickness is a consequence of sin. It is because of sin that God permits it; it is in order to show us our faults, to chasten us, and purify us from them. Sickness is therefore a visible sign of God's judgment upon sin. It is not that the one who is sick is necessarily a greater sinner than another who is in health. On the contrary, it is often the most holy among the children of God whom He chastens, as we see from the example of Job. Neither is it always to check some fault which we can easily determine: it is especially to draw the attention of the sick one to that which remains in him of the egotism of the "old man" and of all which hinders him from a life entirely consecrated to his God. The first step which the sick one has to take in the path of divine healing will be therefore to let the Holy Spirit of God probe his heart and convince him of sin. After which will come, also, humiliation, decision to break with sin, and confession. To confess our sins is to lay them down, as Achan did before God (Joshua 7:23), to subject them to His judgment, with the fixed purpose to fall into them no more. A sincere confession will be followed by a new assurance of pardon.

"If he have committed sins they shall be forgiven him." When we have confessed our sins, we must receive also the promised pardon, believing that God gives it in very deed. Faith in God's pardon is often vague in the child of God. Either he is uncertain, or he returns to old impressions, to the time when he first received pardon; while the pardon which he now receives with confidence, in answer to the prayer of faith, will bring him new life and strength. The soul then rests under the efficacy of the blood of Christ, receives from the Holy Spirit the certainty of the pardon of sin, and that therefore nothing remains to hinder the Savior from filling him with His love and with His grace. God's pardon brings with it a divine life which acts powerfully upon him who receives it.

When the soul has consented to make a sincere confession and has obtained pardon, it is ready to lay hold of the promise of God; it is no longer difficult to believe that the Lord will raise up His sick one. It is when we keep far from God that it is difficult to believe; confession and pardon bring us quite near to Him. As soon as the cause of the sickness has been removed, the sickness itself can be arrested. Now it is easy for the sick one to believe that if the Lord necessarily subjected the body to the chastisement of the sins committed, He also wills that, the sin being pardoned, this same body should receive the grace which manifests His love. His presence is revealed; a ray of life, of His divine life, comes to quicken the body, and the sick one proves that as soon as he is no longer separated from the Lord, the prayer of faith does save the sick.

# CHAPTER

## 19

---

## *Jesus Bore Our Sickness*

*He took on him our sickness and bore our pains. (R. V.)*

*He shall see the travail of his soul, and shall be satisfied: by his knowledge shall my righteous servant justify many; for he shall bare their iniquities. Therefore will I divide him a portion with the great, and he shall divide the spoil with the strong; because he hath poured out his soul unto death: and he was numbered with the transgressors; and he bare the sin of many, and made intercession for the transgressors. (Isaiah 53:4, 11–12)*

Do you know this beautiful chapter, the 53rd of Isaiah—which has been declared the fifth Gospel—in the light of the Spirit of God, as well as the divine graces which should result from them?

The expression "to bear" could not but appear in this prophecy. It is, in fact, the word which must accompany the mention of sin, whether as committed directly by the sinner, or whether as transmitted to a substitute. The transgressor, the priest and the expiatory victim must all bear the sin. In the same way, it is because the Lamb of God has borne our sins, that God smote Him for the iniquity of us all. Sin was not found in Him, but it was put upon Him; He took it voluntarily upon Him. And it is because He bore it, and that, in bearing it, He put an end to it, that he has the power to save us. "By his knowledge shall my righteous servant justify many; for he shall bare their iniquities. . . . he shall divide the spoil with the strong; because . . . he bare the sin of many" (Isaiah 53:11–12). It is therefore, because our sins have been borne by Jesus Christ that we are delivered from them as soon as we believe this truth; consequently we have no longer to bear them ourselves.

In this same chapter, the expression "to bear" occurs twice, but in relation to two different things. It is not said only that the Lord's righteous Servant has borne our sins (v. 12), but also that He has borne our sicknesses (v. 4, R.V., margin). Thus His bearing our sicknesses forms an integral part of the Redeemer's work as well as bearing our sins. Although Himself without sin He has borne our sins, and He has done as much for our sicknesses. The human nature of Jesus could not be touched by sickness because it remained holy. We never find in the account of His life any mention of sickness. Participating in all the weaknesses of our human nature—hunger, thirst, fatigue and sleep—because all these things are not the consequences of sin, He still had no trace of sickness. As He was without sin, sickness had no hold on Him, and He could die only a violent death and that by His voluntary consent. Thus it is not in Him but on Him that we see sickness as well as sin; He took upon Him and bore them of His own free will. In bearing them and taking them upon Him, He has by the very fact triumphed over them, and has acquired the right of delivering His children from them.

Sin had attacked and ruined equally the soul and the body. Jesus came to save both. Having taken upon Him sickness as well as sin, He is in a position to set us free from the one as well as the other, and that He may accomplish this double deliverance, He expects from us only one thing: our faith.

As soon as a sick believer understands the purport of the words, Jesus has borne my sins, he does not need to fear to say also: "I need no longer bear my sins; they are upon me no longer." In the same way as soon as he has fully taken in and believed for himself that Jesus has borne our sicknesses, he does not fear to say: "I need no longer bear my sickness; Jesus in bearing sin bore also sickness which is its consequence; for both He has made propitiation, and He delivers me from both."

I have myself witnessed the blessed influence which this truth exercised one day upon a sick woman. For seven years she had almost entirely kept her bed. A sufferer from consumption, epilepsy and other sicknesses, she had been assured that no hope of cure remained for her. She was carried into the room where the late Mr. W.E. Boardman was holding a Sunday evening service for the sick, and was laid in a half-fainting condition on the sofa. She was too little conscious to remember anything of what took place until she heard the words, "himself took our infirmities and bare our sicknesses" (Matthew 8:17); and then she seemed to hear the words, "If He has borne your sicknesses, why then bear them yourself? Get up!" But she thought, *if I attempt to get up, and fall upon the ground, what will they think of me?* But the inward voice began again, "If He has borne my sins, why should I have to bear them?" To the astonishment of all who were present, she arose, and, although still feeble, sat down in a chair by the table. From that moment her healing made rapid progress. At the end of a few weeks she had no longer the appearance of an invalid, and later on her strength was such that she could spend many hours a day visiting the poor. With what joy and love she could then speak of Him who was "the strength of her life" (Psalm 27:1). She had believed that Jesus had borne her sicknesses as well as her sins, and her faith was not put to confusion. It is thus that Jesus reveals Himself as a perfect Savior to all those who will trust themselves unreservedly to Him.

# CHAPTER
## 20

---

## *Is Sickness a Chastisement?*

*For this cause many among you are weak and sickly, and not a few sleep. For if we discerned ourselves, we should not be judged. But when we are judged, we are chastened of the Lord, that we may not be condemned with the world. (1 Corinthians 11:30–32, R.V.)*

In writing to the Corinthians, the Apostle Paul must needs reprove them for the manner in which they observed the Lord's Supper, drawing upon themselves the chastisements of God. Here, therefore, we see sickness as a judgment of God, a chastisement for sin. Paul sees it to be a real chastisement since he afterward says: "chastened by the Lord," and he adds that it is in order to hinder them from falling yet deeper into sin, to prevent them from being "condemned with the world" that they are thus afflicted. He warns them that if they would be neither judged nor chastened by the Lord; that if by such examination they discovered the cause of the sickness and condemned their sins, the Lord would no longer need to exercise severity. Is it not evident that here sickness is a judgment of God, a chastisement of sin, and that we may avoid it in examining and condemning ourselves?

Yes, sickness is, more often than we believe it, a judgment, a chastisement for sin. God "doth not afflict willingly nor grieve the children of men" (Lamentations 3:33). It is not without a cause that He deprives us of health. Perhaps it may be to render us attentive to some sin which we can recognize; "sin no more, lest a worse thing come unto thee" (John 5:14); perhaps because God's child has got entangled in pride and worldliness; or it may be that self-confidence or caprice have been mixed with his service of God. It is again quite possible that the chastisement may not be directed against any particular sin, but that it may be the result of the preponderance of sin which weighs upon the entire human race. When in the case of the man born blind, the disciples asked the Lord, "Who did sin, this man, or his parents, that he was born blind" (9:2), and He answered, "Neither hath this man sinned, nor his parents" (9:3), He does not by any means say that there is no relation between sin and sickness, but He teaches us not to accuse every sick person of sin.

In any case, sickness is always a discipline which ought to awaken our attention to sin, and turn us from it. Therefore a sick person should begin by condemning or discerning himself (1 Corinthians 11:31), by placing himself before his heavenly Father with a sincere desire to see anything which could have grieved Him or could have rendered the chastisement necessary. So doing, he may count assuredly on the Holy Spirit's light, who will clearly show him his failure. Let him be ready at once to renounce what he may discern, and to place himself at the Lord's disposal to serve Him with perfect obedience; but let him not imagine that he can conquer sin by his own efforts. No, that is impossible to him. But let him, with all his power of will, be on God's side in renouncing what is sin in His sight, and let him believe that he is accepted of Him. In so doing he will be yielding himself, consecrating himself anew to God, willing to do only His holy will in all things.

Scripture assures us that if we thus examine ourselves, the Lord will not judge us. Our Father only chastens His child as far as needful. God seeks to deliver us from sin and self. As soon as we understand Him and break with these, sickness may cease; it has done its work. We must come to see what the sickness means, and recognize in it the discipline of God. One may recognize vaguely that he commits sins while scarcely attempting to define what they are; or if he does define them, he may not believe it is possible to give them up; and if he decides to renounce them, he may fail to count on God that He will put an end to the chastisement. And yet, how glorious is the assurance which Paul's words here give us!

Dear sick one, do you understand that your heavenly Father has something to reprove in you? He would have your sickness help you to discover it, and the Holy Spirit will guide you in the search. Then renounce at once what He may point out to you. You should not have the smallest shade remain between your Father and you. It is His will to pardon your sin and to heal your sickness. In Jesus we have both pardon and healing; they are two sides of His redemptive work. He calls you to live a life of dependence upon Him in a greater degree than hitherto. Abandon yourself then to Him in a complete obedience, and walk henceforth as a little child in following His steps. It is with joy that your heavenly Father will deliver you from chastisement, that He will reveal Himself to you as your Healer, that He will bring you nearer to Him by this new tie of His love, that He will make you obedient and faithful in serving Him. If, as a wise and faithful Father, He has been obliged to chasten you, it is also as a Father that He wills your healing, and that He desires to bless and keep you henceforth.

# CHAPTER

## 21

*God's Prescription for the Sick*

*Is any sick among you? let him call for the elders of the church; and let them pray over him, anointing him with oil in the name of the Lord: And the prayer of faith shall save the sick, and the Lord shall raise him up; and if he have committed sins, they shall be forgiven him. (James 5:14–15)*

This text, above all others, is that which most clearly declares to the sick what they have to do in order to be healed. Sickness and its consequences abound in the world. What joy, then, for the believer to learn from the Word of God the way of healing for the sick! The Bible teaches us that it is the will of God to see His children in good health. The Apostle James has no hesitation in saying that "the prayer of faith shall save the sick, and the Lord shall raise him up." May the Lord teach us to hearken and to receive with simplicity what His Word tells us!

Notice, first, that James here makes a distinction between affliction (or suffering) and sickness. He says "Is any among you afflicted? Let him pray" (v. 13). He does not specify what shall be requested in such a case; still less does he say that deliverance from suffering shall be asked. No, suffering which may arise from divers exterior causes is the portion of every Christian. Let us therefore understand that the object of James is to lead the tried believer to ask for deliverance only with a spirit of submission to the will of

God, and, above all, to ask the patience which he considers to be the privilege of the believer (James 1:2–4, 12; 5:7–8).

But in dealing with the words, "Is any sick among you?" James replies in quite another manner. Now he says with assurance that the sick one may ask for healing with confidence that he shall obtain it, and the Lord will hear him. There is therefore a great difference between suffering and sickness. The Lord Jesus spoke of suffering as being necessary, as being willed and blest of God; while He says of sickness that it ought to be cured. All other suffering comes to us from without, and will only cease when Jesus shall triumph over the sin and evil which are in the world; while sickness is an evil which is in the body itself—in this body saved by Christ that it may become the temple of the Holy Spirit, and which, consequently, ought to be healed as soon as the sick believer receives by faith the working of the Holy Spirit, the very life of Jesus in him.

What is the direction here given to the sick? Let him call for the elders of the church, and let the elders pray for him. In the time of James there were physicians, but it is not to them the sick believer must turn. The elders then were the pastors and leaders of the churches, called to the ministry not because they had passed through schools of theology, but because they were filled with the Holy Spirit, and well-known for their piety and for their faith. Why should their presence be needed by the sick one? Could he not have prayed for himself? Could not his friends have prayed? Yes, but it is not so easy for everybody to exercise the faith which obtains healing, and, doubtless, that is one reason why James desired that men should be called whose faith was firm and sure. Besides this, they were representatives to the sick one of the Church, the collective body of Christ, for it is the communion of believers which invites the Spirit to act with power. In short, they should, after the pattern of the great Shepherd of the sheep, care for the flock as He does, identify themselves with the sick one, understand his trouble, receive from God the necessary discernment to instruct him and encourage him to persevere in faith. It is, then, to the elders of the church that the healing of the sick is committed, and it is they, the servants of the God who pardons iniquities and heals diseases (Psalm 103:3), who are called to transmit to others the Lord's graces for soul and body.

Finally, there is the promise still more direct—that of healing. The apostle speaks of it as the certain consequence of the prayer of faith. "The prayer of faith shall save the sick, and the Lord shall raise him up." This promise ought to stimulate in every believer the desire and expectation of healing. Receiving these words with simplicity and as they are written, ought we not to see in them an unlimited promise, offering healing to whomsoever shall pray in faith? May the Lord teach us to study His Word with the faith of a truly believing heart!

---

# The Lord that Healeth Thee

*I will put none of these diseases upon thee, which I have brought upon the Egyptians: for I am the LORD that healeth thee. (Exodus 15:26)*

How often have we read these words without daring to take them for ourselves, and without expectation that the Lord would fulfill them to us! We have seen in them that the people of God ought to be exempt from the diseases inflicted upon the Egyptians, and we have believed that this promise applied only to the Old Testament, and that we who live under the economy of the New Testament cannot expect to be kept from, or healed of sickness by the direct intervention of the Lord! As, however, we were obliged to recognize the superiority of the New Covenant, we have come, in our ignorance, to allege that sickness often brings great blessings, and that consequently God had done well to withdraw what He had formerly promised, and to be no longer for us what He was for Israel, "The LORD that healeth thee."

But in our day we see the Church awakening and acknowledging her mistake. She sees that it is under the New Covenant that the Lord Jesus acquired the title of Healer by all His miraculous healings. She is beginning to see that in charging His Church to preach the gospel to every creature, He has promised to be with her "alway, even unto the end of the world" (Matthew 28:20), and as the proof of His presence, His disciples should have the power to lay hands on the sick, and they should be healed (Mark 16:15–18). She sees, moreover, that in the days of Pentecost, the miraculous pouring out of the Holy Spirit was accompanied by miraculous healings, which were evident proof of the blessings brought about by the power from on high (Acts 3:16; 5:12; 9:40). There is nothing in the Bible to make her believe that the promise made to Israel has been since retracted, and she hears from the mouth of the Apostle James this new promise: "The prayer of faith shall save (or heal) the sick" (5:14). She knows that at all times it has been unbelief which has limited (or set bounds to) the Holy One of Israel (Psalm 78:41), and she asks herself if it is not unbelief which hinders in these days this manifestation of the power of God. Who can doubt it? It is not God or His Word which are to blame here; it is our unbelief which prevents the miraculous power of the Lord, and which holds Him back from healing as in past times. Let our faith awake, let it recognize and adore in Christ the all-power of Him who says: "I am the LORD that healeth thee." It is by the works of God that we can best understand what His Word tells us; the healings which again are responding to the prayer of faith confirm, by gloriously illustrating, the truth of His promise.

Let us learn to see in the risen Jesus the divine Healer, and let us receive Him as such. In order that I may recognize in Jesus my justification, my strength and my wisdom, I must grasp by faith that He is really all this to me; and equally when the Bible tells me that Jesus is the sovereign Healer, I must myself appropriate this truth, and say, "Yes, Lord, it is Thou who art my Healer." And why may I hold Him as such? It is because He gives Himself to me, that I am "one plant with him" (Romans 6:5, French version), and that, inseparably united to Him, I thus possess His healing power; it is because His love is pleased to load His beloved with His favors, to communicate Himself with all His heart to all who desire to receive Him. Let us believe that He is ready to extend the treasure of blessing, contained in the name, the Lord that healeth thee, to all who know and who can trust in this divine name. This is the treatment for the sick indicated by the law of His kingdom. When I bring my sickness to the Lord, I do not depend on what

I see, on what I feel or what I think, but on what He says. Even when everything appears contrary to the expected healing, even if it should not take place at the time or in the way that I had thought I should receive it, even when the symptoms seem only to be aggravated, my faith, strengthened by the very waiting, should cling immovably to this word which has gone out of the mouth of God, "I am the LORD that healeth thee." God is ever seeking to make us true believers. Healing and health are of little value if they do not glorify God, and serve to unite us more closely with Him; thus in the matter of healing our faith must always be put to the proof. He who counts on the name of his God, who can hear Jesus saying to him, "Said I not unto thee, that, if thou wouldest believe, thou shouldest see the glory of God?" (John 11:40) will have the joy of receiving from God Himself the healing of the body, and of seeing it take place in a manner worthy of God and conformably to His promises. When we read these words, "I am the LORD that healeth thee," let us not fear to answer eagerly, "Yes, Lord, You are the Lord that heals me."

# CHAPTER

## 23

---

# *Jesus Heals the Sick*

*[He] healed all that were sick: That it might be fulfilled which was spoken by Esaias the prophet, saying, Himself took our infirmities, and bare our sicknesses. (Matthew 8:16–17*

In the preceding chapter we have studied the words of the prophet Isaiah. If the reader has still any doubt as to the interpretation of it which has been given, we remind him of that which the Holy Spirit caused the evangelist St. Matthew to write about it. It is expressly said regarding all the sick ones whom Jesus healed, "That it might be fulfilled which was spoken by Esaias the prophet." It was because Jesus had taken on Him our sickness that He could, that He ought to heal them. If He had not done so, one part of His work of redemption would have remained powerless and fruitless.

This text of the Word of God is not generally understood in this way. It is the generally accepted view that the miraculous healings done by the Lord Jesus are to be looked upon only as the proof of His mercy, or as being the symbol of spiritual graces. They are not seen to be a necessary consequence of redemption, although that is what the Bible declares. The body and the soul have been created to serve together as a habitation of God; the sickly condition of the body is, as well as that of the soul, a consequence of sin, and that is what Jesus is to come to bear, to expiate and to conquer.

When the Lord Jesus was on earth, it was not in the character of the Son of God that He cured the sick, but as the Mediator who had taken upon Him and borne sickness, and this enables us to understand why Jesus gave so much time to His healing work, and why also the evangelists speak of it in a manner so detailed. Read for example what Matthew says about it:

> *And Jesus went about all Galilee, teaching in their synagogues, and preaching the gospel of the kingdom, and healing all manner of sickness and all manner of disease among the people. And his fame went throughout all Syria: and they brought unto him all sick people that were taken with divers diseases and torments, and those which were possessed with devils, and those which were lunatick, and those that had the palsy; and he healed them. (4:23–24)*

> *And Jesus went about all the cities and villages, teaching in their synagogues, and preaching the gospel of the kingdom, and healing every sickness and every disease among the people. (9:35)*

> *And when he had called unto him his twelve disciples, he gave them power against unclean spirits, to cast them out, and to heal all manner of sickness and all manner of disease. (10:1)*

When the disciples of John the Baptist came to ask Jesus if He were the Messiah, that He might prove it to them, He replied: "The blind receive their sight, and the lame walk, the lepers are cleansed, and the deaf hear, the dead are raised up, and the poor have the gospel preached to them" (11:5). After the cure of the withered hand, and the opposition of the Pharisees who sought to destroy Him, we read that "great multitudes followed him, and he healed them all" (12:15). When later, the multitude had followed Him into a desert place, it is said, "And Jesus went forth, and saw a great multitude, and was moved with compassion toward them, and he healed their sick" (14:14). Farther on: "they sent out into all that country round about, and brought unto him all that were diseased; And besought him that they might only touch the hem of his garment: and as many as touched were made perfectly whole" (14:35–36). It is said also of the sick which were among the multitudes that they "cast them down at Jesus' feet; and he healed them." And Matthew adds, "Insomuch that the multitude wondered, when they saw the dumb to speak, the maimed to be whole, the lame to walk, and the blind to see: and they glorified the God of Israel" (15:30–31). And finally when He came into the coasts of Judea beyond Jordan, "And great multitudes followed him; and he healed them there" (19:2).

Let us add to these divers texts those which give us in detail the account of healings wrought by Jesus, and let us ask ourselves if these healings afford us only the proof of His power during His life here on earth, or if they are not much rather the undoubted and continual result of His work of mercy and of love, the manifestation of His power of redemption which delivers the soul and body from the dominion of sin? Yes, that was in very deed the purpose of God. If, then, Jesus bore our sicknesses as an integral part of the redemption, if He has healed the sick "that he might be fulfilled which was spoken by Esaias," and if His Savior-heart is always full of mercy and of love, we can believe with certainty that to this very day it is the will of Jesus to heal the sick in answer to the prayer of faith.

# CHAPTER

## 24

---

# *Fervent and Effectual Prayer*

*Pray one for another, that ye may be healed. The effectual fervent prayer of a righteous man availeth much. [Elijah] was a man subject to like passions as we are, and he prayed earnestly that it might not rain: and it rained not on the earth by the space of three years and six months. And he prayed again, and the heaven gave rain, and the earth brought forth her fruit. (James 5:16–18)*

James knew that a faith which obtains healing is not the fruit of human nature; therefore he adds that the prayer must be "fervent." Only such can be efficacious. In this he stands upon the example of Elijah, a man of the same nature ("subject to like passions") as we are, drawing therefore the inference that our prayer can be and ought to be of the same nature as his. How then did Elijah pray? This will throw some light upon what the prayer of faith should be.

Elijah had received from God the promise that rain was about to fall upon the earth (1 Kings 18:1), and he had declared this to Ahab. Strong in the promise of his God, he mounts Carmel to pray (1 Kings 18:42; James 5:18). He knows, he believes that God's will is to send rain; nevertheless he must pray, or the rain will not come. His prayer is no empty form; it is a real power, the efficacy of which is about to make itself felt in heaven. God wills that it shall rain, but the rain will only come at Elijah's request, a request repeated with faith and perseverance until the appearance of the first cloud in the sky. In order that the will of God shall be accomplished, this will must on one side be expressed by a promise, and on the other it must be received and laid hold of by the believer who prays. He therefore must persevere in prayer that he may show his God that his faith expects an answer, and will not grow weary until it is obtained.

This is how prayer must be made for the sick. The promise of God, "The Lord will raise him up," must be rested on, and His will to heal recognized. Jesus Himself teaches us to pray with faith which counts on the answer of God; He says to us: "All things whatsoever ye pray for, and ask for, believe that ye have received them and ye shall have them" (Mark 11:24, R.V.). After the prayer of faith which receives beforehand that which God has promised, comes the prayer of perseverance, which does not lose sight of that which has been asked until God has fulfilled His promise (1 Kings 18:43).

There may be some obstacle which hinders the fulfillment of the promise; whether on the side of God and His righteousness (Deuteronomy 9:18), or on the side of Satan, and his constant opposition to the plans of God, something which may still impede the answer to the prayer (Daniel 10:12–13). It may also be that our faith needs to be purified (Matthew 15:22–28). Whatever it may be, our faith is called to persevere until the answer comes. He who prays six times fervently and stops there, when he ought to have prayed seven times (2 Kings 13:18–19), deprives himself of the answer to his prayer.

Perseverance in prayer, a perseverance which strengthens the faith of the believer against all which may seem opposed to answer, is a real miracle; it is one of the impenetrable mysteries of the life of faith. Does it not say to us, the Savior's redeemed, one is in very deed His friend, a member of His body, and that the government of the world and the gifts of divine grace depend in some sense upon his prayers? Prayer, therefore, is no vain form. It is the work of the Holy Spirit, who intercedes here on earth in us and by us; and as such, it is as efficacious, as indispensable as the work of the

Son interceding for us before the throne of God. It might seem strange that after having prayed with the certainty of being heard, and having seen therein the will of God, we should still need to continue in prayer. Nevertheless it is so. In Gethsemane, Jesus prayed three times in succession. On Carmel Elijah prayed seven times; and we, if we believe the promise of God without doubting, shall pray until we receive the answer. Both the importunate friend at midnight and the widow who besieged the unjust judge are examples of perseverance in seeking the end in view.

Let us learn from Elijah's prayer to humble ourselves, to recognize why the power of God cannot be more manifest in the Church, whether in the healing of the sick, or in conversion, or sanctification. "Ye have not, because ye ask not" (James 4:2). Let it also teach us patience. In the cases where healing is delayed, let us remember that obstacles may exist over which only perseverance in prayer can triumph. Faith which ceases to pray, or which is allowed to relax in its fervor, cannot appropriate that which God has nevertheless given. Let not our faith in the promises of Scripture be shaken by those things which are as yet beyond our reach. God's promise remains the same: "The prayer of faith shall save the sick." May the prayer of Elijah strengthen our faith. Let us remember that we have to imitate them who through faith and patience inherit the promises (Hebrews 6:12). If we learn to persevere in prayer, its fruit will be always more abundant, always more evident, and we shall obtain, as Jesus obtained when He was on earth, healing of the sick, often immediate healing, which shall bring glory to God.

# CHAPTER

## 25

---

# *Intercessory Prayer*

*Confess therefore your sins to one another, and pray one for another that ye may be healed. The supplication of a righteous man availeth much in its working. (James 5:16, R.V.)*

James begins by speaking to us of the prayers of the elders of the church; but here he addresses all believers in saying: "Pray for one another that ye may be healed." Having already spoken of confession and of pardon, he still adds: "Confess your sins one to another."

This shows us that the prayer of faith which asks for healing is not the prayer of one isolated believer, but that it ought to unite the members of the body of Christ in the communion of the Spirit. God certainly hears the prayer of each one of His children as soon as it is presented to Him with living faith, but the sick one does not always possess such faith as this; and that the Holy Spirit may come to act with power, there must be the union of several members of the body of Christ unitedly claiming His presence. We need one another.

This dependence on our brethren should be exercised in two ways. First of all, we must confess our faults to any whom we may have wronged, and receive pardon from them. But besides this, if one who is sick has been brought to see in such or such a sin which he has committed the cause of his sickness, and to recognize in it a chastening of God, he ought in such a case to acknowledge his sin before the elders, or brethren in Christ who pray for him, and who are thus enabled to do so with more light and more faith. Such confession will be also a touchstone which tests the sincerity of his repentance, for it is easier to confess our sins to God than to man. Before he will do it, his humiliation must needs be real and his repentance sincere. The result will be a closer communion between the sick one and those who intercede for him, and their faith will be quickened anew.

"Pray one for another that ye may be healed." Does not this clearly answer that which one so often hears said: What is the use in going to M. Zeller in Switzerland, Dr. Cullis in America, or Bethshan in London? [Editor's note: These were all individuals or places during the late 19th and early 20th centuries where miraculous healings took place. You will read more about this in A.J. Gordon's book *The Ministry of Healing*.] Does not the Lord hear prayer in whatsoever place it is offered? Yes, without any doubt. Wherever a prayer in living faith rises up to God, it finds Him ready to grant healing; but the Church has so neglected to believe in this truth that it is a rare thing in the present day to find Christians capable of praying in this manner. Thus we cannot be too grateful to the Lord that He has inspired certain believers with the desire to consecrate their lives, in part, to witness to the truth of divine healing. Their words and their faith awakens faith in the hearts of many sick ones who, without their help, would never arrive at it. It is precisely these very people who always say to everybody: "The Lord is everywhere to be found." Let Christians learn not to neglect the least part of the marvelous power of their God, and He will be able to manifest to all that He is always "the LORD that healeth thee" (Exodus 15:26). Let us take heed to obey the Word of God, to confess to one another and to pray one for another that we may be healed.

James notes here still another essential condition to successful prayer: it must be the prayer of the righteous. "The supplication of a righteous man availeth much in its working." The Scripture tells us that "every man that hath this hope in him purifieth himself, even as he [Christ] is pure" (1 John 3:3). James himself was surnamed "The Just," on account of his piety and the tenderness of his conscience. Whether an "elder" or a simple believer, it is only after one is wholly surrendered to God and living in obedience to His will, that one can pray effectually for the brethren. John says as much: "And whatsoever we ask, we receive of him, because we keep his commandments, and do those things that are pleasing in his sight" (3:22). It is therefore the prayer of one who lives in intimate communion with God which "availeth much." It is to such prayer that God will grant the answer, which He would not be able to give to such other of His children.

We often hear these words quoted: "The prayer of a righteous man availeth much," but very rarely is it taken in connection with its context, or remembered that it is most especially divine healing which is in question here. Oh, may the Lord raise up in His Church many of these righteous men, animated with living faith, whom He can use to glorify Jesus as the divine Healer of the sick!

# CHAPTER
## 26

---

# *The Will of God*

*Thy will be done. (Matthew 6:10)*

*If the Lord will. (James 4:15)*

In days of sickness, when doctors and medicines fail, recourse is generally had to the words we have here quoted, and they may easily become a stumbling block in the way of divine healing. How may I know, it is asked, whether it is not God's will that I should remain ill? And as long as this is an open question, how can I believe for healing, how can I pray for it with faith?

Here truth and error seem to touch. It is indeed impossible to pray with faith when we are not sure that we are asking according to the will of God. "I can," one may say, "pray fervently in asking God to do the best for me, believing that He will cure me if it is possible." As long as one prays thus, one is indeed praying with submission, but this is not the prayer of faith. That is only possible when we are certain that we are asking according to the will of God. The question then resolves itself into making sure of what is the will of God. It is a great mistake to think that the child of God cannot know what is His will about healing.

## *Part of our salvation*

In order to know His divine will, we must be guided by the

Word of God. It is His Word which promises us healing. The promise of James 5 is so absolute that it is impossible to deny it. This promise only confirms other passages, equally strong, which tell us that Jesus Christ has obtained for us the healing of our diseases, because He has borne our sicknesses. According to this promise, we have a right to healing, because it is a part of the salvation which we have in Christ, and therefore we may expect it with certainty. Scripture tells us that sickness is, in God's hands, the means of chastening His children for their sins, but that this discipline ceases to be exercised as soon as His suffering child acknowledges and turns from the sin. Is it not as much as to say clearly that God desires only to make use of sickness to bring back His children when they are straying?

Sick Christian, open your Bible, study it and see in its pages that sickness is a warning to renounce sin, but that whoever acknowledges and forsakes his sins finds in Jesus pardon and healing. Such is God's promise in His Word. If the Lord had in view some other dispensation for such of His children whom He was about to call home to Him, He would make known to them His will, giving them by the Holy Spirit a desire to depart; in other special cases, He would awaken some special conviction; but as a general rule, the Word of God promises us healing in answer to the prayer of faith.

"Nevertheless," some might say, "is it not better in all things to leave it to the will of God?" And they quote the instance of such and such Christians who would have, so to speak, forced the hand of God by their praying without adding, "Thy will be done," and who would not have experienced blessing in the answer to their prayers. And these would say, "How do we know whether sickness would not be better for us than health?" Notice here that this is no case of forcing the hand of God, since it is His Word which tells us that it is His will to heal us. "The prayer of faith shall save the sick." God wills that the health of the soul should have a blessed reflex influence on the health of the body, that the presence of Jesus in the soul should have its confirmation in the good condition of the body. And when you know that such is His will you cannot, when speaking in such a way, say truthfully that you are in all things leaving it to Him. It is not leaving it to Him when you make use of all possible remedies to get healing, instead of laying hold of His promise. Your submission is nothing else than spiritual sloth in view of that which God commands you to do.

## The fruit of holiness

As to knowing whether sickness is not better than health, we do not hesitate to reply that the return of health which is the fruit of giving up sin, of consecration to God, is infinitely better than sickness. "For this is the will of God, even your sanctification" (1 Thessalonians 4:3), and it is by healing that God confirms the reality of this. When Jesus comes to take possession of our body, and cures it miraculously, when it follows that the health received must be maintained from day to day by an uninterrupted communion with Him, the experience which we thus make of the Savior's power and of His love is a result very superior to any which sickness has to offer. Doubtless sickness may teach us submission, but healing received directly from God makes us better acquainted with our Lord, and teaches us to confide in Him better. Besides which, it prepares the believer to accomplish better the service of God.

Sick Christian, if you will really seek to know what is the will of God in this thing, do not let yourself be influenced by the opinions of others, nor by your own former prejudices, but listen to and study what the Word of God has to say. Examine whether it does not tell you that divine healing is a part of the redemption of Jesus, and that God wills that every believer should have the right to claim it. See whether it does not promise that the prayer of every child of God for this thing shall be heard, and whether health restored by the power of the Holy Spirit does not manifest the glory of God in the eyes of the Church and of the world. Inquire of it; it will answer you, that, according to the will of God, sickness is a discipline occasioned by sin (or shortcoming), and that healing, granted to the prayer of faith, bears witness to His grace which pardons, which sanctifies, and which takes away sin.

# CHAPTER

## 27

---

# *Obedience and Health*

*There he made for them a statute and an ordinance, and there he proved them, and said, If thou wilt diligently harken to the voice of the LORD thy God, and wilt do that which is right in his sight, and wilt give ear to his commandments, and keep all his statutes, I will put none of these diseases upon thee, which I have brought upon the Egyptians: for I am the LORD that healeth thee. (Exodus 15:25–26)*

It was at Marah that the Lord gave to His people this ordinance. Israel was just released from the yoke of Egypt when their faith was put to the proof in the desert by the waters of Marah. It was after He had sweetened the bitter waters that the Lord promised He would not put upon the children of Israel any of the diseases which He had brought upon the Egyptians so long as they would obey Him. They should be exposed to other trials, they might sometimes suffer the need of bread and of water, they would have to contend with mighty foes, and encounter great dangers; all these things might come upon them in spite of their obedience, but sickness might not touch them. In a world still under the power of Satan, they might be a butt for attacks coming from without, but their bodies should not be oppressed with sickness, for God had delivered them from it. Had He not said, "If thou wilt diligently harken to the voice of the LORD thy God, . . . I will put none of these diseases upon thee which I have brought upon the Egyptians, for I am the LORD that healeth thee"? Again elsewhere, "And ye shall serve the LORD your God, . . . and I will take sickness away from the midst of thee" (Exodus 23:25; read also Leviticus 26:14; Deuteronomy 7:15, 23; 28:15–61).

## Health of body and soul

This calls our attention to a truth of the greatest importance: the intimate relations which exist between obedience and health, between sanctification which is the health of the soul, and the divine healing which ensures the health of the body— both are comprised in the salvation that comes from God. It is noteworthy that in several languages these three words, salvation, healing and sanctification, are derived from the same root and present the same fundamental thought. (For instance, the German *Heil*, salvation, *Heilung*, healing, *Heilichung*, sanctification.) Salvation is the redemption which the Savior has obtained for us, health is the salvation of the body which also comes to us from the Divine Healer, and lastly, sanctification reminds us that true salvation and true health consist in being holy as God is holy. Thus, it is in giving health to the body and sanctification to the soul that Jesus is really the Savior of His people. Our text clearly declares the relation which exists between holiness of life and the healing of the body. The expressions which bear this out seem to be purposely multiplied: "If thou wilt diligently hearken . . . if thou wilt do that which is right . . . if thou wilt give ear . . . if thou wilt keep all his statutes, I will not send any sickness upon thee."

Here we have the key to all true obedience and holiness. We often think we know well the will of God revealed in His Word; but why does not this knowledge bring forth obedience? It is that in order to obey we must begin by hearkening. "If thou wilt diligently hearken to the voice of the LORD thy God, . . . and give ear . . ." As long as the will of God reaches me through the voice of man, or through the reading of a book, it may have but little power with me; while if I enter into direct communion with God, and listen to His voice, His commandment is quickened with living power to facilitate its accomplishment. Christ is the living Word and the Holy Spirit is His voice. Listening to His voice means to renounce all our own will and wisdom, to close the ear to every other voice so as to expect no other direction but that of the Holy Spirit. One who is redeemed is like a servant or child, who needs to be directed; he knows that he belongs entirely to God, and that all his being, spirit, soul and body, ought to glorify God.

But he is equally conscious that this is above his strength, and that he needs to receive, hour by hour, the direction which he needs. He knows also that the divine commandment, as long as it is a dead letter to him, cannot impart to him strength and wisdom, and that it is only as he attentively gives ear that he will obtain the desired strength; therefore, he listens and learns thus to observe the laws of God. The life of attention and action, of renouncement and of crucifixion, constitutes a holy life. The Lord brings us to it in the first place by sickness, and makes us understand that which we are lacking, and then also by the healing which calls the soul to this life of continual attention to the voice of God.

Most Christians see nothing more in divine healing than a temporal blessing for the body, while in the promise of our Holy God its end is to make us holy. The call to holiness sounds daily stronger and more clearly in the Church. More and more believers are coming to understand that God wants them to be like Christ; and the Lord is beginning again to make use of His healing virtue, seeking thereby to show us that still in our own days the Holy One of Israel is "The LORD that healeth thee," and that it is His will to keep His people both in health of body and in obedience.

Let him that looks for healing from the Lord receive it with joy. It is not a legal obedience which is required of him, an obedience depending upon his own strength. No, God asks of him, on the contrary, the abandonment of a little child, the attention which hearkens and consents to be led. This is what God expects of him; and the healing of the body will respond to this childlike faith. The Lord will reveal Himself to him as the mighty Savior who heals the body and sanctifies the soul.

---

# *Job's Sickness and Healing*

*So Satan went forth from the presence of the LORD, and smote Job with sore boils from the sole of his foot unto his crown. (Job 2:7)*

The veil which hides from us the unseen world is lifted for a moment in the mysterious history of Job; it discovers to us heaven and hell occupied with God's servants upon earth. We see in it the temptations peculiar to sickness, and how Satan makes use of them to dispute with God, and to seek the perdition of the soul of man; while God, on the contrary, seeks to sanctify it by the very same trial. In the case of Job, we see in God's light whence proceeds sickness, what is the result which it should have, and how it is possible to be delivered from it.

## *The source of sickness*

Whence comes sickness—from God or from Satan? Opinions on this point vastly differ. Some hold that it is sent of God, others see in it the work of the wicked one. Both are in error as long as they hold their view to the exclusion of that held by the other party, while both are in the right if they admit that there are two sides to this question. Let us say then that sickness comes from Satan, but that it cannot exist without the permission of God. On the one hand, the power of Satan is that of an oppressor, who has not himself any right to pounce upon man and attack him, and on the other hand the claims of Satan on man are legitimate in that the righteousness of God decrees that he who yields himself to Satan places himself under his domination.

Satan is the prince of the kingdom of darkness and of sin; sickness is the consequence of sin. Herein is constituted the right of Satan over the body of sinful man. He is the prince of this world, so recognized by God, until such time as he shall be legally conquered and dethroned. Consequently he has a certain power over all those who remain down here under his jurisdiction. It is he then who torments men with sickness, and seeks thereby to turn them from God, and to work their ruin.

But, we would haste to say, the power of Satan is far from being almighty; it can do nothing without God's authorization. God permits him to do all he does in tempting men, even believers, but it is in order that the trial may bring forth in them the fruit of holiness. It is also said that Satan has the power of death (Hebrews 2:14), that he is everywhere at work where death reigns, and nevertheless he has no power to decide as to the death of God's servants without the express will of God. It is even so with sickness. Because of sin, sickness is the work of Satan, but as the supreme direction of this world belongs to God, it can also be regarded as the work of God. All who are acquainted with the book of Job know how clearly this is brought out there.

## Results of sickness

What ought to be the result of sickness? The result will be good or evil according as God or Satan shall have the victory in us. Under Satan's influence, a sick person sinks always deeper in sin. He does not recognize sin to be the cause of the chastisement, and he occupies himself exclusively with himself and with his sufferings. He desires nothing but to be healed, without dreaming of a desire for deliverance from sin. On the contrary wherever God gains the victory, sickness leads the sufferer to renounce himself, and to abandon himself to God.

The history of Job illustrates this. His friends accuse him, unjustly, of having committed sins of exceptional gravity, and by them to have drawn upon himself his terrible sufferings. It was, however, no such thing, since God Himself had borne him witness that he was "perfect and upright, one that feareth God, and escheweth evil" (Job 2:3). But in defending himself Job went too far. Instead of humbling himself in abasement before the Lord, and recognizing his hidden sins, he fought in all self-righteousness to justify himself. It was not until the Lord appeared to him that he came to say, "I abhor myself and repent in dust and ashes" (42:6). To him sickness became a signal blessing in bringing him to know God in quite a new way, and to humble himself more than ever before Him. This is the blessing which God desires that we also may receive whenever He permits Satan to strike us with sickness, and this end is attained by all sufferers who abandon themselves unreservedly to Him.

## Purpose of chastisement

How are we to be delivered from sickness? A father never prolongs the chastisement of his child beyond the time necessary. God, also, who has his purpose in permitting sickness, will not prolong the chastisement longer than is needful to attain His end. As soon as Job had understood Him, from the time that he condemned himself and repented in dust and ashes, through hearkening to what God had revealed to Him of Himself, the chastisement was at an end. God Himself delivered him from Satan's hand and healed him of his sickness.

Would that the sick in our day understood that God has a distinct purpose in permitting the chastisement, and that as soon as it is attained, as soon as the Holy Spirit shall have led them to confess and forsake their sins and to consecrate themselves entirely to the service of the Lord, the chastisement will no longer be needed—that the Lord could and would deliver them! God makes use of Satan as a wise government makes use of a jailer. He only leaves His children in Satan's power for the given time;

after which His good will is to associate us in the exemption of Him who has conquered Satan, who has withdrawn us from his domination in bearing in our stead our sins and our sickness.

# CHAPTER

## 29

---

# *The Prayer of Faith*

*The prayer of faith shall save the sick, and the Lord shall raise him up. (James 5:15)*

The prayer of faith! Only once does this expression occur in the Bible, and it relates to the healing of the sick. The Church has adopted this expression, but she hardly ever has recourse to the prayer of faith, except for the sake of obtaining other graces; while according to Scripture it is especially intended for the healing of the sick.

Does the apostle expect healing through the prayer of faith alone, or should it be accompanied by the use of remedies? This is generally the question which is raised. It is easily decided, if we take into consideration the power of the Church's spiritual life in the early ages: the gifts of healing bestowed on the apostles by the Lord, augmented by the subsequent pouring out of the Holy Spirit (Acts 4:30; 5:15–16), what Paul says of these gifts of healing by the same Spirit (1 Corinthians 12:9), what James here insists upon when, in order to strengthen the reader in the expectation of faith, he recalls Elijah's prayer and God's wonderful answer (James 5:14–17). Does not all this clearly show that the believer is to look for healing in response to the prayer of faith alone, and without the addition of remedies?

Another question will arise: Does the use of remedies exclude the prayer of faith? To this we believe our reply should be: No, for the experience of a large number of believers testifies that in answer to their prayers God has often blest the use of remedies, and made them a means of healing.

We come here to a third question: Which is then the line to follow, that we may prove with the greatest certainty, and according to the will of God, the efficacy of the prayer of faith? Is it, according to James, in setting aside all remedies or in using remedies as believers do for the most part? In a word, is it with or without remedies that the power of faith best obtains the grace of God? Which of these two methods will be most directly to the glory of God and for blessing to the sick one? Is it not perfectly simple to reply that if the prescription and the promise in James apply to believers of our time, they will find blessing in receiving them just as they were given to believers then, conforming to them on all points, expecting healing only, and without intervention from the Lord Himself, without having any recourse to remedies besides. It is, in fact, in this sense that Scripture always speaks of effectual faith and of the prayer of faith.

Both the laws of nature and the witness of Scripture show us that God often makes use of intermediary agencies to manifest His glory, but whether by experience or by Scripture, we know also that under the power of the Fall, and the empire of our senses, our tendency is to attach more importance to the remedies than to the direct action of God. It often happens that remedies so occupy us as to intercept the presence of our God and turn us away from Him. Thus the laws and the properties of nature, which were destined to bring us back to God, have the contrary effect. This is why the Lord in calling Abraham to be the father of His chosen people had not recourse to the laws of nature (Romans 4:17–21). God would form for Himself a people of faith, living more in the unseen than in the things visible; and in order to lead them into this life, it was necessary to take away their confidence in ordinary means. We see therefore that it was not by the ordinary ways which He has traced in nature that God led Abraham, Jacob, Moses, Joshua, Gideon, the judges, David and many other kings of Israel. His object was to teach them by this to confide only in Him, to know Him as He is: "Thou art a God that doest wonders" (Psalm 77:14).

God wills to act in a similar way with us. It is when we seek to walk according to His prescription in James 5—abandoning the things which are seen (2 Corinthians 5:18) to lay hold of the promise of God, and so receive directly from Him the desired healing—that we discover how much importance we have attached to earthly remedies. Doubtless there are Christians who can make use of remedies without damage to their spiritual life, but the larger number of them are apt to count much more on the remedies than on the power of God. Now the purpose of God is to lead His children into a more intimate communion with Christ, and this is just what does happen, when by faith we commit ourselves to Him as our sovereign Healer, counting solely on His invisible presence. Renouncing remedies strengthens faith in an extraordinary manner. Healing becomes then far more than sickness, a source of numberless spiritual blessings. It makes real to us what faith can accomplish; it establishes a new tie between God and the believer, and commences in him a life of confidence and dependence. The body equally with the soul is placed under the power of the Holy Spirit, and the power of faith, which saves the sick, thus leads us to a life of faith, strengthened by the assurance that God manifests His presence in our earthly life.

# CHAPTER

## 30

---

## *Anointing in the Name of the Lord*

*Is there any sick among you? let him call for the elders of the church; and let them pray over him, anointing him with oil in the name of the Lord. (James 5:14)*

A nointing him with oil in the name of the Lord." These words have given rise to controversy. Some have sought to infer from them that, very far from prescribing recourse to the prayer of faith alone, without the use of remedies, St. James had, on the contrary, mentioned anointing with oil as a remedy to be employed, and that to anoint in the name of the Lord had no other signification than to rub the patient with oil. But as this prescription applies to all kinds of sickness, this would be to attribute to oil a miraculous virtue against all sickness. Let us see what the Scripture tells us about anointing with oil, and what sense it attaches to these two words.

It was the custom of the people in the East to anoint themselves with oil when they came out of the bath; it was most refreshing in a hot climate. We see also that all those who were called to the special service of God were to be anointed with oil, as a token of their consecration to God, and of the grace which they should receive from Him to fulfill their vocation. Thus the oil which was used to anoint the priests and the tabernacle was looked upon as "most holy" (Exodus 30:22–32), and wherever the Bible speaks of anointing with oil, it is an emblem of holiness and consecration.

Nowhere in the Bible do we find any proof that oil was used as a remedy.

Once indeed the anointing with oil is mentioned in connection with sickness, but its place there was evidently as a religious ceremony and not as a remedy. In Mark 6:13, we read that the twelve "cast out many devils, and anointed with oil many that were sick, and healed them." Here the healing of the sick runs parallel with the casting out of devils—both the result of miraculous power. Such was the kind of mission which Jesus commanded His disciples when He sent them two and two: "He gave them power against unclean spirits, to cast them out, and to heal all manner of sickness and all manner of disease" (Matthew 10:1). Thus it was the same power which permitted them either to cast out devils or to heal the sick.

But let us seek to discover what was symbolized by the anointing administered by the twelve. In the Old Testament, oil was the symbol of the gift of the Holy Spirit: "The Spirit of the LORD God is upon me; because the LORD hath anointed me . . . " (Isaiah 61:1). It is said of the Lord Jesus in the New Testament: "God anointed Jesus of Nazareth with the Holy Ghost and with power" (Acts 10:38). And it is said of believers: "ye have an unction [anointing, R.V.] from the Holy One" (1 John 2:20). Sometimes man feels the need of a visible sign, appealing to his senses, which may come to his aid to sustain his faith, and enable him to grasp the spiritual meaning. The anointing, therefore, should symbolize to the sick one the action of the Holy Spirit who gives the healing.

Do we then need the anointing as well as the prayer of faith? It is the Word of God which prescribes it, and it is in order to follow out its teachings that most of those who pray for healing receive the anointing; not that they regard it as indispensable, but to show that they are ready to submit to the Word of God in all things.

In the last promise made by the Lord Jesus, He ordains the laying on of hands, not the anointing, to accompany the communication of healing virtue (Mark 16:18). When Paul circumcised Timothy and took upon himself a special vow, it was to prove that he had no objection to observe the institutions of the Old Covenant so long as the liberty of the gospel did not thereby suffer loss. In the same way, James, the head of the Church of Jerusalem, faithful in preserving as far as possible the institutions of his fathers, continued the system of the Holy Spirit. And we also should regard it, not as a remedy, but as a pledge of the mighty virtue of the Holy Spirit, as a means of strengthening faith, a point of contact and of communion between the sick one and the members of the Church who are called to anoint him with oil.

"I am the LORD that healeth thee" (Exodus 15:26).

# CHAPTER

## 31

---

# Full Salvation Our High Privilege

*Son, thou art ever with me, and all that I have is thine.*
*(Luke 15:31)*

Some time ago, when at Northfield, I was told by Mr. Moody that the best thing that he heard at Keswick two years ago was this verse—given by some parting minister as a closing or parting text—and Mr. Moody said to himself, "Why did I not see that before?"

We may talk a great deal, and write a great deal, about the father's love to the prodigal, but when we think of the way he treated the elder brother, it brings to our hearts a truer sense of the wonderful love of the father; therefore I want to speak on this verse.

I suppose there are not a few Christians who have got "full salvation"; but perhaps more than half of those reading this have not got it, and, if I were to ask you, "Have you got it?" you would probably say, "I don't understand what you mean by it; what is it?" Well, my great object of this book is to bring you to see that full salvation is waiting for you now, that God wants you to experience it, and, if you feel you have not got it, I wish to show you how wrong it is to be without it, and then to show you how to come out of this wrong life into the right one here and now. Oh, may all who have not got the experience pray very humbly, "Oh, my Father, bring me into the full enjoyment of Thy full salvation."

We want to look at:

*First, the high privilege of God's children.*
*Second, the low experience of many of them.*
*Third, the cause of this great discrepancy.*
*Fourth, the way of restoration, or how to get full salvation.*

First, then, the elder son, being ever with the father, had, if he liked, the privilege of two things: unceasing fellowship and unlimited partnership. But he was worse than the prodigal, for, although always at home, yet he had never known, nor enjoyed, nor understood the privileges that were his. All this fullness of fellowship had been waiting for and offered to him, but not received. While the prodigal was away from home in the far country, his elder brother was far from the enjoyment of home, while he was at home.

## Unceasing fellowship

An earthly father loves his child, and delights to make his child happy. "God is love," and He delights to pour out His own nature to His people. So many people talk about God hiding His face; but there are only two things that ever caused God to do so—sin or unbelief. Nothing else can. It is the very nature of the sun to shine, and it can't help shining on and on. "God is love," and, speaking with all reverence, He can't help loving. We see His goodness toward the ungodly, and His compassion on the erring, but His fatherly love is manifested toward all His children. "Ever with me"; but you say, "Is it possible to be always happy and dwelling with God?" Yes, certainly, and there are many Scripture promises as to this. Look at the epistle to the Hebrews, where we read of "boldness to enter within the veil"; how often, too, does David speak of hiding "in the secret of His tabernacle," and "dwelling under the shadow of the Almighty."

My message is that the Lord your God desires to have you living continually in the light of His countenance. Your business, your temper, your circumstances, of which you complain as hindering, are they stronger than God? If you come and ask God to shine in and upon you, you will see and prove that He can do it, and that you as a believer may walk all the day and every day in the light of His love. That is "full salvation." " 'Ever with thee'; I never knew it, Lord, and so I did not enjoy it, but I do now."

## Unlimited partnership

"All I have is thine." The elder son complained of the father's gracious reception of the prodigal, of all the feasting and rejoicing over his return, while to him had never been given a kid that he might make merry with his friends. The father, in tenderness of his love, answers him, "Son, you were always in my house; you had only to ask and you would have got all you desired and required" (Luke 15:31, paraphrased). And that is what our Father says to all His children. But you are saying, "I am so weak, I cannot conquer my sins. I can't manage to keep right. I can't do this and the other thing." No, but God can; and all the time He is saying to you: "All I have is thine; for in Christ I have given it to you. All the Spirit's power and wisdom, all the riches of Christ, all the love of the Father; there is nothing that I have but is thine; I as God am God, that I may love, keep and bless thee." Thus God speaks, but it seems all a dream to some. Why are you so poor? God's Word is sure, and does He not promise all this? See in John, chapters 14 to 16, how He tells us that we may have wonderful answers to prayer if we come in Jesus' name and abide in Him. Do we really believe that it is possible for a Christian to live such a life?

Now, we have looked at this high privilege which is for all, so we pass on to consider our second point: The low experience of many of God's dear children. What is it? Just living in poverty and starvation. The elder son, the child of a rich man, living in utter poverty!—"never had a kid," while all that was his father's was his—just exactly the state of many a child of God. The way He wants us to live is in the fullest fellowship of all His blessings, yet what a contrast!

Ask some if their lives are full of joy; why they don't even believe it is possible to be always happy and holy. "How could we get on thus in business?" they say; and they imagine that the life of fullest blessing possible to them must be one of sighing and sadness and sorrow.

I asked a dear woman at the Cape—a devoted Christian woman—how she was getting on. She answered that in her experience it was sometimes light and sometimes darkness, and argued that, as this was so in nature, the same thing held good in the kingdom of grace. So she just gave herself up to a wretched experience. But I don't read in the Bible that there is to be any night or darkness in the believer's experience; on the contrary, I read, "thy sun shall no more go down"; yet there are many who actually believe that there is nothing so good for them. As I said already, nothing can hide God from us but sin and unbelief. If you are in spiritual poverty, and there is no joy, no experience of victory over sin, temper, wandering, why is it so? "Oh," you say, "I'm too weak; I must fall." But does not the Scripture say that He is "able to keep you from falling [stumbling]"?

A minister once told me that, although God is able, the verse does not say He is willing to do it. God does not mock us, beloved; if He says He is "able," then it is a proof of His willingness to do it. Do let us believe God's Word and examine our own experience in the light of it.

Again, are you working and bearing much fruit for God, and do people by your life see and say, "God is with that man, keeping him humble, pure and heavenly minded"? Or are they forced to confess that you are just a very ordinary Christian, easily provoked, worldy, and not heavenly minded? That is not the life God wants us to live, brethren. We have a rich Father, and as no true earthly father would like to see his child in rags, or without shoes and proper clothing, etc., neither does our God; but He wishes to fill up our life with richest and choicest blessings. How many Sunday school teachers there are who teach, and hope for the conversion of their scholars, but yet they can't say God uses them to the conversion of any of them. They enjoy no close fellowship with God, no victory over sin, no power to convince the world. To which class do you belong? The low-level, or the fully possessed?

Confess it today.

These two sons represent two classes of Christians: the prodigal—away backslidden; the elder son—out of full fellowship with God. They were both alike poor, and the elder son needed as great a change as did the prodigal. He needed to repent and confess and claim his full privileges; and so ought all low-level Christians to repent, confess and claim full salvation. Oh both of you, come today and say, "Father, I have sinned."

Now, we ask, What is the cause of this terrible discrepancy? Why the great difference in the experience, I wonder? Ask yourself, "What is the reason I am not enjoying this full blessing? God's Word speaks of it, others speak of it, and I see some who are living in it." Oh, do ask the reason; come to God and say, "Why is it I never live the life You want me to live?"

You will find the answer in our story. The elder son had an unchildlike spirit, and entertained wrong thoughts about his father; and, if you had known the real character of your Father, your life would have been all right. You have, as it were, said, "I never got a kid to make merry; my Father is rich, but He never gives. I have prayed quite enough, but God does not answer me. I hear other people say that God fills and satisfies them, but He never does that for me."

A dear minister told me once that such a life was not for everybody, that it was of God's sovereignty to give this to whomsoever He pleased. Friends, there is no doubt as to God's sovereignty. He dispenses His gifts as He will; we are not all Pauls or Peters; places at the right and left hand of God are prepared for whomsoever He will. But this is not a matter of divine sovereignty; it is a question of child's heritage. The Father's love offers to give to every child in actual experience His full salvation. Now look at an earthly father. His children are of various ages, but all have equal right to the joy of their father's countenance. True, he gives to his son of 20 years more money than to his son of five, and he has more to speak of to the boy of 15 than to the child of three; but, as regards his love toward them, it is all the same, and in their privileges as children they are all alike. And God's love to His dear children is all the same. Oh, do not try to throw the blame on God, but say, "I have had hard thoughts of Thee, O God, and I have sinned. As a father I have done for my children what I did not believe God was able and willing to do for me, and I have been lacking in childlike faith." Oh, do believe in the love, the willingness and power of God to give you full salvation, and a change must surely come.

## *The way of restoration*

Now let us consider the way of restoration: how to get out of this poor experience. The prodigal repented and so must those children of God who have been living within sight of, but not enjoying His promises. Conversion is generally sudden and a long repentance is usually a long impenitence. Many in the Church of Christ think it must take a long time to get into full salvation. Yes, it will take a long time if you are to do it yourself—indeed, you never will. No, no, friend, if you come and trust God it can be done in a moment. By God's grace, give yourself up to Him. Don't say, "What's the use? It will do no good"; but put yourself, as you are in sin and weakness, into the bosom of your Father. God will deliver you, and you will find that it is only one step out of the darkness into the light. Say, "Father, what a wretch I have been, in being with Thee and yet not believing Thy love to me!"

Yes, I come today with a call to "repent"; addressed, not to the unsaved, but to those who know what it is to be pardoned. For have you not sinned in the hard thoughts you have had of God, and is there not a longing, a thirsting and hungering after something better? Come, then, repent, and just believe that God does blot out the sin of your unbelief. Do you believe it? Oh, do not dishonor God by unbelief, but come today and confidently claim full salvation. Then trust in Him to keep you. This seems difficult to some; but there is no difficulty about it. God will shine His light upon you always, saying, "Son, thou art ever with Me"; and all you have to do is to dwell in and walk in that light.

I began by saying there are two classes of Christians: those who enjoy full salvation, and those who do not understand about it.

Well, if it is not clear to you, ask God to make it clear. But if you do not understand about it, remember it is a definite act. Just let yourself go into the arms of God; hear Him say, "All is thine." Then you say, "Praise God, I believe, I accept, I give up myself to Him, and I believe God gives Himself now to me!"

CHAPTER

32

---

# Ye Are the Branches

*Ye are the branches. (John 15:5)*

W hat a simple thing it is to be a branch, the branch of a tree, or the branch of a vine. The branch grows out of the vine or out of the tree. There it lives and in due time bears fruit. It has no responsibility except just to receive from the root and stem sap and nourishment. And if we only by the Holy Spirit knew of our relationship to Jesus Christ, our work would be changed into the brightest and most heavenly thing upon earth. Instead of there ever being soul-weariness or exhaustion, our work would be like a new experience, linking us to Jesus as nothing else can. For alas! is it not often true that our work comes between us and Jesus? What folly! The very work that He has to do in me, and I for Him, I take up in such a way that it separates me from Christ. Many a laborer in the vineyard has complained that he has too much work, and not time for close communion with Jesus, and that his usual work weakens his inclination for prayer, and that his too much inter-course with men darkens the spiritual life. Sad thought, that the bearing of fruit should separate the branch from the vine! That must be because we have looked upon our work as something else than the branch bearing fruit. May God deliver us from every false thought about the Christian life!

Now just a few thoughts about this blessed branch-life.

In the first place, it is a life of absolute dependence. The branch

*109*

has nothing. It just depends upon the vine for everything. Those words, absolute dependence, are among the most solemn, large and precious of words. A great German theologian wrote two large volumes some years ago, to show that the whole of Calvin's theology is summed up in that one principle of absolute dependence upon God; and he was right. If you can learn every moment of the day to depend upon God, everything will come right. You will get the higher life if you depend absolutely upon God.

Must I understand that when I have got to work, when I have to preach a sermon, or address a Bible class, or go out and visit the poor neglected ones, that all the responsibility of the work is on Christ?

That is exactly what Christ wants you to understand. Christ wants that in all your work the very foundation should be simple, blessed consciousness: Christ must care for all.

And, how does He fulfill the trust of that dependence? He does it by sending down the Holy Spirit—not now and then only as a special gift, for remember the relation between the vine and the branches is such that hourly, daily, unceasingly, there is the living connection maintained. The sap does not flow for a time, and then stop, and then flow again, but from moment to moment the sap flows from the vine to the branches. And just so, my Lord Jesus wants me to take that blessed position as a worker, and, morning by morning and day by day and hour by hour and step by step, in every work I have to go out to, just to abide before Him in the simple, utter helplessness of one who knows nothing, and is nothing, and can do nothing.

Absolute dependence upon God is the secret of all power in work. The branch has nothing but what it gets from the vine, and you and I have nothing but what we get from Jesus.

But secondly, the life of the branch is not only a life of entire dependence, but of deep restfulness. Oh, that little branch, if it could think, and if it could feel, and if it could speak—and if we could have a little branch today to talk to us, and if we could say, "Come, branch of the vine, tell me, I want to learn from thee how I can be a true branch of the living Vine," what would it answer?

The little branch would whisper, "Man, I hear that you are wise, and I know that you can do a great many wonderful things. I know you have much strength and wisdom given to you, but I have one lesson for you. With all your hurry and effort in Christ's work you never prosper. The first thing you need is to come and rest in your Lord Jesus. That is what I do. Since I grew out of that vine I have spent years and years, and all I have done is just to rest in the vine. When the time of spring came I had no anxious thought nor care. The vine began to pour its sap into me, and to give the bud and leaf. And when the time of summer came I had no care, and in the great heat I trusted the vine to bring moisture to keep me fresh. And in the time of harvest, when the owner came to pluck the grapes, I had no care. If there was anything in the grapes not good, the owner never blamed the branch; the blame was always on the vine. And if you would be a true branch of Christ, the living Vine, just rest on Him. Let Christ bear the responsibility."

You say: "Won't that make me slothful?" I tell you it will not. No one who learns to rest upon the living Christ can be slothful, for the closer your contact with Christ the more of the Spirit of His zeal and love will be borne in upon you. But, oh! begin to work in the midst of your entire dependence by adding to that deep restfulness. A man sometimes tries and tries to be dependent upon Christ, but he worries himself about this absolute dependence. He tries and he cannot get it. But let him sink down into the entire restfulness every day.

### Rest in Christ

Rest in Christ, who can give wisdom and strength, and you do not know how that restfulness will often prove to be the very best part of your message. You plead with people and you argue, and they get the idea, *There is a man arguing and striving with me.* They only feel: Here are two men dealing with each other. But if you will let the deep rest of God come over you, the rest in Christ Jesus, the peace and rest and holiness of heaven, that restfulness will bring a blessing to the heart, even more than the words you speak.

But a third thought. The branch teaches a lesson of much

fruitfulness. You know the Lord Jesus repeated that word fruit often in that parable. He spoke first of fruit, and then of more fruit, and then of much fruit. Yes, you are ordained not only to bear fruit, but to bear much fruit. "Herein is my Father glorified, that ye bear much fruit" (John 15:8). In the first place, Christ said: "I am the true vine, and my Father is the husbandman [who has charge of me and you]" (15:1). He who will watch over the connection between Christ and the branches is God; and it is in the power of God, through Christ, we are to bear fruit.

Oh Christians, you know this world is perishing for the want of workers. And it wants not only more workers. The workers are saying, some more earnestly than others, "We need not only more workers, but we need that our workers should have a new power, a different life—that the workers should be able to bring more blessing."

What is wanting? There is wanting the close connection between the worker and the heavenly Vine. Christ, the heavenly Vine, has blessings that He could pour on tens of thousands who are perishing. Christ, the heavenly Vine, has power to provide the heavenly grapes. But "ye are the branches," and you cannot bear heavenly fruit unless you are in close connection with Jesus Christ.

Do not confound work and fruit. There may be a good deal of work for Christ that is not the fruit of the heavenly Vine. Do not seek for work only. Study this question of fruit bearing! It means the very life and the very power and the very Spirit and the very love within the heart of the Son of God—it means the heavenly Vine Himself coming into your heart and mine.

Stand in close connection with the heavenly Vine and say: "Lord Jesus, nothing less than the sap that flows through Thyself, nothing less than the Spirit of Thy divine life is what we ask. Lord Jesus, I pray Thee, let Thy Spirit flow through me in all my work for Thee." I tell you again that the sap of the heavenly Vine is nothing but the Holy Spirit. The Holy Spirit is nothing but the life of the heavenly Vine, and what you must get from Christ is nothing less than a strong inflow of the Holy Spirit. You need it exceedingly, and you want nothing more than that. Remember that. Do not expect Christ to give a bit of strength here, and a bit of blessing yonder, and a bit of help over there. As the vine does its work in giving its own peculiar sap to the branch, so expect Christ to give His own Holy Spirit into your heart, and then you will bear much fruit. And if you have only begun to bear fruit, and are listening to the word of Christ in the parable, "more fruit," "much fruit," remember that in order that you should bear more fruit you just require more of Jesus in your life and heart.

A fourth thought. The life of the branch is a life of close communion. Let us again ask: What has the branch to do? You know that precious inexhaustible word that Christ used: Abide. Your life is to be an abiding life. And how is the abiding to be? It is to be just like the branch in the vine, abiding every minute of the day. There are the branches, in close communion, in unbroken communion, with the vine, from January to December. And cannot I live every day—it is to me an almost terrible thing that we should ask the question—cannot I live in abiding communion with the heavenly Vine? You say, "But I am so much occupied with other things." You may have 10 hours' hard work daily, during which your brain has to be occupied with temporal things; God orders it so. But the abiding work is the work of the heart, not of the brain, the work of the heart clinging to and resting in Jesus, a work in which the Holy Spirit links us to Christ Jesus. Oh, do believe that deeper down than the brain, deep down in the inner life, you can abide in Christ, so that every moment you are free the consciousness will come: "Blessed Jesus, I am still in Thee." If you will learn for a time to put aside other work and to get into this abiding contract with the heavenly Vine, you will find that fruit will come.

What is the application to our life with regard to this abiding communion? What does it mean? It means close fellowship with Christ in secret prayer. I am sure there are Christians who do long for the higher life, and who sometimes have got a great blessing, and have at times found a great inflow of heavenly joy and a great outflow of heavenly gladness; and yet after a time it has passed away. They have not understood that close, personal, actual communion with Christ is an absolute necessity for daily life. Take time to be alone with Christ. Nothing in heaven or earth can free you from the necessity for that, if you are to be happy and holy Christians.

Oh, how many Christians look upon it as a burden, and a tax, and a duty, and a difficulty to get much alone with God! That is the great hindrance to our Christian life everywhere. We want more quiet fellowship with God. I tell you in the name of the heavenly Vine that you cannot be healthy branches, branches into which the heavenly sap can flow, unless you take plenty of time for communion with God. If you are not willing to sacrifice time to get alone with Him, and give Him time every day to work in you, and to keep up the link of connection between you and Himself, He cannot give you that blessing of His unbroken fellowship. Jesus Christ asks you to live in close communion with Him. Let every heart say, "O Christ, it is this I long for; it is this I choose." And He will gladly give it to you.

## A life of entire surrender

And then my last thought. The life of the branch is a life of entire surrender. This word, entire surrender, is a great and solemn word, and I believe we do not understand its meaning. But yet the little branch preaches it. "Have you anything to do, little branch, besides bearing grapes?" "No, nothing." "Are you fit for nothing?" "Fit for nothing!" The Bible says that a bit of vine cannot even be used as a pen; it is fit for nothing but to be burned. "And now, what do you understand, little branch, about your relation to the vine?" "My relation is just this: I am utterly given up to the vine, and the vine can give me as much or as little sap as it chooses. Here I am at its disposal, and the vine can do with me what it likes!"

Oh, we want this entire surrender to the Lord Jesus Christ. This is one of the most difficult points to make clear, and one of the most important and needful points to explain—what this entire surrender is. It is an easy thing for a man or a number of men to offer themselves up to God for entire consecration, and to say, "Lord, it is my desire to give up myself entirely to Thee." That is of great value, and often brings very rich blessing. But the one question I ought to study quietly is: What is meant by entire surrender? It means that just as literally as Christ was given up entirely to God, I am given up entirely to Christ. Is that too strong? Some of you think so. Some think that never can be; that just as entirely and absolutely as Christ gave up His life to do nothing but seek the Father's pleasure, and depend on the Father absolutely and entirely, I am to do nothing but to seek the pleasure of Christ. But that is actually true. Christ Jesus came to breathe His own Spirit into us, to make us find our very highest happiness in living entirely for God, just as He did. O beloved brethren, if that is the case, then I ought to say: "Yes, as true as it is of that little branch of the vine, so true, by God's grace, I would have it be of me. I would live day by day that Christ may be able to do with me what He will."

Ah, here comes the terrible mistake that lies at the bottom of so much of our own religion. A man thinks: I have my business and family duties, and my relations as a citizen, and all this I cannot change. And now alongside of all this I am to take in religion and the service of God as something that will keep me from sin. God help me to perform my duties properly! That is not right. When Christ came, He came and bought the sinner with His blood. If there was a slave market here and I were to buy a slave, I should take the slave away to my own house from his old surroundings, and he would live at my house as my personal property, and I could order him about all the day. And if he were a faithful slave he would live as having no will and no interests of his own, his one care being to promote the well-being and honor of his master. And in like manner, I, who have been bought with the blood of Christ, have been bought to live every day with the one thought—How can I please my Master?

Oh, we find the Christian life so difficult because we seek for God's blessing while we live in our own will. We would be glad to live the Christian life according to our own liking. We make our plans and choose our own work, and then we ask the Lord Jesus to come in and take care that sin shall not conquer us too much, and that we shall not go too far wrong. We ask Him to come in and give us so much of His blessing, but our relation to Jesus ought to be such that we are entirely at His disposal, and every day come to Him humbly and straightforwardly, and say: "Lord, is there anything in me that is not according to Thy will, that has not been ordered by Thee, or that is not entirely given up to Thee?" Oh, if we would wait and wait patiently, there would spring up a relationship between us and Christ so close and so tender, that we should afterwards be amazed how far distant our intercourse with Him had previously been.

I know that there are a great many difficulties about this question of holiness; I know that all do not think exactly the same with regard to it. But that would be to me a matter of comparative indifference if I could see that all are honestly longing to be free from every sin. But I am afraid that unconsciously there are in hearts often compromises with the idea: we cannot be without sin; we must sin a little each day—we cannot help it. Oh, that people would actually cry to God: "Lord, do keep me from sin!" Give yourself utterly to Jesus, and ask Him to do His very utmost for you in keeping you from sin.

## Concluding thoughts

In conclusion, let me gather up all in one word. Christ Jesus said, "I am the vine, ye are the branches" (John 15:5). In other words: "I, the living One who have so completely given Myself to you am the Vine. You cannot trust Me too much. I am the Almighty Worker, full of a divine life and power." Christians, you are the branches of the Lord Jesus Christ. If there is in your heart the consciousness: I am not a strong, healthy, fruit-bearing branch; I am not closely linked with Jesus; I am not living in Him as I should be—then listen to Him saying: "I am the Vine. I will receive you. I will draw you to Myself. I will bless you. I will strengthen you. I will fill you with My Spirit. I, the Vine, have taken you to be My branches; I have given Myself utterly to you. Children, give yourselves utterly to Me. I have surrendered Myself as God ab- solutely to you; I became man and died for you that I might be entirely yours. Come and surrender yourselves entirely to be Mine."

What shall our answer be? Oh, let it be a prayer from the depths of our heart, that the living Christ may take each one of us and link us close to Himself. Let our prayer be that He, the living Vine, shall so link each of us to Himself that we shall go on our way with our hearts singing, "He is my Vine, and I am His branch. I want nothing more—now I have the everlasting Vine." Then, when you get alone with Him, worship and adore Him, praise and trust Him, love Him and wait for His love. Thou art my Vine, and I am Thy branch. It is enough; my soul is satisfied. Glory to His blessed name!

# THE MINISTRY
# OF HEALING

A.J. Gordon

# CHAPTER

## 1

---

## *The Question and Its Bearings*

## Introductory

Have there been any miracles since the days of the apostles? To this question the common answer has been, in our times at least, a decided no. A call recently put forth in one of our religious journals, asking the opinion of ministers, teachers and theological professors on this point was very largely answered; and the respondents were well nigh unanimous in the opinion that the age of miracles passed away with the apostolic period.

The statement contained in several of these replies gave evidence indeed that the question had never been deeply investigated by the witnesses. In some instances there was a perhaps unintentional, evading of the issue by the question, "What is a miracle?" But there were only one or two replies which gave countenance to the view that miracles are possible in all ages and have appeared more or less numerously in every period of the Church's history. If then, the little book which we now send forth shall win any assent for its views, it will not do so in all probability because its sentiments accord with the opinion of the majority of the theologians of the day.

It is therefore no enviable task which we have undertaken. The demand of the times is rather in the contrary direction from that in which our conviction carries us. "The strongest requirement now pressing on the Church is for an adaptation of Christianity to the age,"—so we read not long since. How presumptuous it will look in the face of such an utterance for one to set his face squarely in the opposite direction, and insist that the greatest present demand is for the adaptation of the age to Christianity. And not that exactly; for "this present evil age" can never be made to harmonize with a religion that is entirely heavenly in its origin, in its course and in its consummation. But we trust it will not be presumption to say that the Church in every direction needs to be reshaped to the apostolic model and reinvested with her apostolic powers. For is it not apparent that between the indignant clamor of skeptics against primitive miracles, and the stern frowning of theologians upon any alleged modern miracles, the Lord's people are in danger of being frightened out of their faith in the supernatural?

We speak of what we have often noticed. A simple-hearted believer comes into the assembly of the Church and details some remarkable answer to prayer—prayer for healing or prayer for deliverance, in response to which he alleges that God has wrought marvelously; and then we notice the slowness and shyness with which Christians turn their ears to the story, and the glances of embarrassment amounting almost to shamefacedness which they cast towards the minister, as though appealing for rescue from the perilous neighborhood of fanaticism to which they have been drawn. This we have often observed, and on it we have pondered, and from it we have raised the question again and again, whether the Church has not drifted into an unseemly cautiousness concerning the miraculous. As a religion which is ritual is sure to put vestments on her ministers sooner or later, so a religion which is rational rather than spiritual, will be certain to put vestments on the Lord's providences, insisting on their being draped in the habiliments of decent cause and effect, and attired in the surplice of natural law and order, lest God should "make bare his holy arm in the eyes of all the nations." "The world dislikes the recurrence of miracles." Yes, without question. For the world, which "by *wisdom* knew not God" (1 Corinthians 1:21), is very jealous of everything which it cannot explain or reproduce. "A miracle is something very embarrassing to mock professors." Doubtless; for it brings such, uncomfortably near to God. Accustomed only to such manifestations of the Infinite as have been softened and assuaged by passing through the medium of the natural, they cannot bear this close proximity to the Cause of causes. "He that is near to me is near to the fire;" is one of the sayings which apocrypha puts into the mouth of Christ. How shall they whose feet have never put off their shoes of rationalism and worldliness come near the burning bush, and into open vision of the "I AM."

But it is not worldlings and false professors alone that dislike miracles. Real, true hearted and sincere disciples are afraid of them and inclined to push away with quick impatience, any mention of their possible occurrence in our time. In most cases probably this aversion comes from a wholesome fear of fanaticism.

## Fanaticism

On which point permit us to observe that fanaticism is in most instances simply the eccentric action of doctrines that have been loosened from their connection with the Christian system. Every truth needs the steadiness and equipoise which come from its being bound into harmony with all other truths. If the Church by her neglect or denial of any real doctrine of the faith thrusts that doctrine out into isolation and contempt, thus compelling it to become the property of some special sect, she need not be surprised if it loses its balance. She has deprived it of the conserving influence which comes from contact and communion with other and central doctrines and so doomed it inevitably to irregular manifestations. If the whole body of Christians had been faithful to such truths as that of the second coming of Christ, and scriptural holiness, for example, we probably should never have heard of the fanaticism of adventism and perfectionism. Let a fragment be thrown off from the most orderly planet and it will whirl and rush through space till it is heated hot by its own momentum. It is nothing against a doctrine in our minds therefore that it has engendered fanaticism. One who studies the history of important religious revivals indeed must take quite an opposite view, and suspect that it is a proof of the vitality of the truth around which it has gathered.

Who that is acquainted with the religious movements led by Luther and Wesley and with the endless extravagances that followed in their wake does not see that in these instances the stir produced came from the birth of falsehood, from the contortions of the strangled serpents around the cradle of a new Hercules come for reformation. So let us be less disturbed by the unaccustomed stir of truth than by the propriety of dead and decent error.

But we are offering no apology for fanaticism and providing no place for it in connection with the doctrine which we are defending. It need have no place. We believe in regeneration, the work in which God comes into immediate contact with the soul for its renewal. That is no less a miracle than healing in which God comes into immediate contact with the body for its recovery. In the one case, there is a direct communication of the divine life to the spirit, which Neander calls "the standing miracle of the ages"; in the other there is a direct communication of the divine health to the body which in the beginning was called "a miracle of healing."

An able writer has said, we believe with exact truth: "You ask God to perform as real a miracle when you ask him to cure your soul of sin as you do when you ask him to cure your body of a fever."[1] Yet who of us thinks of encouraging fanaticism by preaching and praying for man's regeneration? Enthusiasm has often kindled about this truth indeed, when it has had to be revived after long neglect and denial, but not when it has been held in orderly and recognized relation to other cardinal doctrines.

Very beautifully did one say of the sister of the poet Wordsworth, that "it was she who couched his eye to the beauties of nature." More than anything else is it needed today that someone couch the eyes of Christians to the realities of the supernatural. Holden of unbelief, filmed with suspicion and distrust, how many of the Lord's truest servants would be unable to discern His hand if He were to put it forth in miracles? It is not easy for those whose daily bread has always been forthcoming, with no occasion for the raven's ministration to believe in miraculous feeding. The eyes that "stand out with fatness" would be the last ones to catch sight of the angels if they should chance to be sent with bread to some starving disciple. To whom saith the Lord "anoint thine eyes with eyesalve, that thou mayest see" (Revelation 3:18)? Is it not to those that say "I am rich, and increased with goods, and have need of nothing" (3:17)? If then we protest that we do not see what others claim to have witnessed of the Lord's outstretched hand, it may be because of a Laodicean self-satisfaction into which we have fallen. When shall we learn that "the secret of the LORD is with them that fear him" (Psalm 25:14) most deeply, and not of necessity with those who have studied the doctrines most deeply? And so, if the eyes long unused to any sight of the Lord's wonder-working are to be couched to the realities of the supernatural, it may be some very humble agent that shall perform the work, some saintly Dorothea of Mannedorf at whose feet theologians sit to learn things which their utmost wisdom had failed to grasp, or some Catharine of Siena who speaks to learned ecclesiastics with such depth of insight that they exclaim with astonishment "never man spoke like this woman." In other words let us not be too reluctant to admit that some of God's children in sore poverty and trial and distress, and with the keener faith which such conditions have developed may have had dealings with God of which we know nothing. At all events be not angry, oh ye wise and prudent, at those Christians of simple faith, who believe with strong confidence that they have had the Savior's healing touch laid upon them.

Nor should we unwittingly limit the Lord by our too confident theories about the cessation of miracles. The rationalist, jealous of any suggestion that God in these days may cross the boundary line that divides the natural from the supernatural, cries out against "the dogma of divine interference" as he names it. The traditionalist viewing with equal jealousy any notion that the Lord may pass the line that separates the apostolic from the post-apostolic age and still act in His office of miracle working, sounds the cry of fanaticism. But what if some meantime should begin to talk about "the crown rights of Immanuel" as the old Covenanters did, insisting on His prerogative to work what He will, and when He will and how He will, without our compelling it to be said of us and of our century that He could not do many mighty works among them because of their unbelief (Matthew 13:58)? Certainly the time has come for us to make use of all the divine assistance that is within our reach. If there are any residuary legacies of power and privilege accruing to us since the fathers fell asleep, and yet remaining unclaimed, every consideration is pressing us to come forward and take possession of them. For observe what confessions of weakness our Protestant churches are unconsciously putting forth on every hand. Note the dependence which is placed on artistic music, on expensive edifices, on culture and eloquence in the pulpit; on literary and social entertainments for drawing in the people, and on fairs and festivals for paying expenses. Hear the reports that come in at any annual convention of churches, of the new organs and frescoings and furnishings, and of the—not saints' festivals—but strawberry festivals and the large results therefrom accruing. And all this from churches that count themselves to be the body of Christ and the habitation of God through the Spirit! Is not this an infinite descent from the primitive records of power and success—the Lord "confirming the word with signs following" (Mark 16:20), and the preaching which was "not with enticing words of man's wisdom but in demonstration of the Spirit and of power" (1 Corinthians 2:4)?

How deeply we need the demonstration of the Spirit in these days! We have not utterly lost it indeed. When men are renewed by the Holy Ghost, and give the world the exhibition of a life utterly and instantly transformed, that is a master stroke for our divine religion. "And that is all we want," most will say. But did such ever witness an instance of a drunkard cured in a moment of an enslaving appetite by the prayer of faith; the opium habit which had baffled for years every device of the physicians broken and utterly eradicated by the direct energy of God's Spirit; the consumptive brought back from the edge of the grave, or the blind made to see by the same power, after long years of darkness—and the glowing love, the exultant thankfulness, the fervid consecration which almost invariably follow such gracious deliverances? If they have not, they have not witnessed a sight that has within our own time and knowledge extorted conviction from the most reluctant witnesses.

These are some of the practical bearings of the question before us. It is not our purpose in this volume to define a miracle any further than we have already done so. For the definitions generally given are widely variant; and it is easy for a disputant to evade facts by entrenching himself behind a definition. We prefer rather to appeal to specimens of acknowledged miracles and then to press the question whether there have been any like them in modern days. It is written in the Acts of the Apostles as follows. "And it came to pass, that the father of Publius lay sick of a fever and of a bloody flux; to whom Paul entered in, and prayed, and laid his hands on him and healed him" (28:8). This is conceded, we suppose, to be a miracle of healing. Has anything of the same sort occurred in the Church since the days of the apostles?

Again it is written in the same book:

> And a certain man lame from his mother's womb was carried, whom they laid daily at the gate of the temple which is called Beautiful, to ask alms of them that entered into the temple; Who, seeing Peter and John about to go into the temple, asked an alms. And Peter, fastening his eyes upon him with John, said, Look on us. And he gave heed unto them, expecting to receive something of them. Then Peter said, Silver and gold have I none; but such as I have give I thee: In the name of Jesus Christ of Nazareth rise up and walk. And he took him by the right hand, and lifted him up: and immediately his feet and ankle bones received strength. And he leaping up stood, and walked, and entered with them into the temple, walking, and leaping, and praising God. (3:2–8)

This transaction is expressly called a "miracle of healing" in the same Scripture. Has there been any recurrence of such a miracle since the time of Christ's immediate disciples? It has been our purpose in preparing the present volume to let the history of the

Church of all ages answer to the teaching of Scripture on this question without presuming to dogmatize upon it ourselves. One who has not committed himself on this subject, as it was the fortune of the writer to do a year ago in a little tract called "The Ministry of Healing" has several things to learn. First, that there is a sensitiveness, amounting often to extreme irritability, towards any who venture to disturb the traditional view of this question. Credulity is sure to get more censure than honest doubt; and while one may with impunity fall behind the accepted standard of faith concerning the supernatural, provided he does it in a regretfully necessitous spirit, it is hardly safe for one to go beyond that standard. Thus a little experience has made us aware of the peril to which we have exposed ourselves of being sorely shot at by the theological archers. But being defamed we still entreat our critics to deal kindly and candidly with us since we desire naught but the furtherance of the truth. But in another way one has a real advantage who has published his views on such a question. His communication puts him *en rapport* with those like-minded, and opens to him sources of information which he could not otherwise have had. It has been an occasion of no little surprise to us to learn how widely the minds of Christians of all names and countries are exercised upon this subject. Information to this effect has come to us not only in the constant testimonies from humble Christians who bear witness to what God has wrought in their own bodies; but also from pastors and evangelists and Bible readers and foreign missionaries and in one instance from a theological professor expressing their strong assent to the view which is herein set forth.

We are well aware indeed that it is not a question of human opinion, but of scriptural testimony. On the word of God therefore we wish our argument to lean its heaviest weight. The witnesses which we have brought forward from the Church of all the ages, have been summoned only that they may corroborate this word. May the Lord graciously use whatever of truth there may be in this volume for the comfort and blessing of His children; may He mercifully pardon whatever of error or forwardness of opinion it may contain. And if by His blessing and furtherance our words should bring a ray of hope to any who are sick, let not those who are "whole" and who "need not a physician," unreasonably grudge their suffering and afflicted brethren this boon of comfort.

# ENDNOTES

[1]Jellett, *Efficacy of Prayer*, Donnellan Lectures, 1877, p. 43.

# CHAPTER

## 2

---

# *The Testimony of Scripture*

In the atonement of Christ there seems to be a foundation laid for faith in bodily healing. Seems, we say, for the passage to which we refer is so profound and unsearchable in its meaning that one would be very careful not to speak dogmatically in regard to it. But it is at least a deep and suggestive truth that we have Christ set before us as the sickness-bearer as well as the sin-bearer of His people. In the gospel it is written, "And he cast out [devils] and healed all that were sick: that it might be fulfilled which was spoken by Esaias the prophet saying, Himself took our infirmities and *bare our sicknesses*" (Matthew 8:16b–17). Something more than sympathetic fellowship with our sufferings is evidently referred to here. The yoke of His cross by which He lifted our iniquities took hold also of our diseases; so that it is in some sense true that as God "made him to be sin for us, who knew no sin" (2 Corinthians 5:21), so He made Him to be sick for us, who knew no sickness. He who entered into mysterious sympathy with our pain which is the fruit of sin, also put Himself underneath our pain which is the penalty of sin. In other words the passage seems to teach that Christ endured vicariously our diseases as well as our iniquities.[1]

If now it is true that our Redeemer and substitute bore our sicknesses, it would be natural to reason at once that He bore them that we might not bear them. And this inference is especially strengthened from the fact, that when the Lord Jesus removed the burden of disease from "all that were sick," we are told that it was done "*that the [Scripture] might be fulfilled, . . .* Himself took our infirmities and bare our sicknesses." Let us remember what our theology is in regard to atonement for sin. "Christ bore your sins, that you might be delivered from them," we say to the penitent. Not sympathy—a suffering with, but substitution—a suffering for, is our doctrine of the Cross; and therefore we urge the transgressor to accept the Lord Jesus as his sin-bearer, that he may himself no longer have to bear the pains and penalties of his disobedience. But should we shrink utterly from reasoning thus concerning Christ as our pain-bearer? We do so argue to some extent at least. For we hold that *in its ultimate consequences* the atonement affects the body as well as the soul of man. Sanctification is the consummation of Christ's redemptive work for the soul; and resurrection is the consummation of His redemptive work for the body. And these meet and are fulfilled at the coming and kingdom of Christ.

But there is a vast intermediate work of cleansing and renewal effected for the soul. Is there none of healing and recovery for the body? Here, to make it plain, is the Cross of Christ; yonder is the coming of Christ. These are the two piers of redemption, spanned by the entire dispensation of the Spirit and by all the ordinances and offices of the gospel. At the cross we read this two-fold declaration:

*Who his own self bare our sins.*
*Himself bare our sicknesses.*

At the coming we find this twofold work promised:

*The sanctification of the Spirit.*
*The redemption of the body.*

The work of sanctification for the spirit stretches on from the cross to the crown, progressive and increasing till it is completed. Does the work of the body's redemption touch only at these two remote points? Has the gospel no office of healing and blessing to proclaim meantime for the physical part of man's nature? In answering this question we only make the following suggestions, which point significantly in one direction.

Christ's ministry was a twofold ministry, affecting constantly the souls and the bodies of men. "Thy sins are forgiven thee," and "Be whole of thy plague," are parallel announcements of the Savior's work which are found constantly running on side by side.

The ministry of the apostles, under the guidance of the Comforter, is the exact facsimile of the Master's. Preaching the kingdom and healing the sick; redemption for the soul and deliverance for the body—these are its great offices and announcements. Certain great promises of the gospel have this double reference to pardon and cure. The commission for the world's evangelization bids its messengers stretch out their hands to the sinner with the message, "He that believeth shall be saved," and to "lay hands on the sick and they shall recover" (Mark 16:16, 18). The promise by James, concerning the prayer of faith, is that it "shall save the sick, . . . and if he have committed sins, they shall be forgiven him" (5:15). Thus this twofold ministry of remission of sins and remission of sickness extends through the days of Christ and that of the apostles.

We only suggest these facts, leaving the example and acts and promises of the Lord and His apostles to stretch out their silent index in the direction which our argument will obediently pursue throughout this discussion.

Only one other fact need be alluded to—the subtle, mysterious, and clearly recognized condition of sin and disease. The ghastly flag of leprosy, flung out in the face of Miriam, told instantly that the pirate sin had captured her heart. Not less truly did the crimson glow of health announce her forgiveness when afterwards the Lord had pardoned her and restored her to His fellowship. And it is obvious at once that our Redeemer cannot forgive and eradicate sin without in the same act disentangling the roots which that sin has struck into our mortal bodies.

He is the second Adam come to repair the ruin of the first. And in order to accomplish this He will follow the lines of man's transgression back to their origin, and forward to their remotest issue. He will pursue the serpent trail of sin, dispensing His forgiveness and compassion as He goes, till at last He finds the wages of sin, and dies its death on the cross; and He will follow the wretched track of disease with His healing and recovery, till in His resurrection He shall exhibit to the world the first fruits of these redeemed bodies, in which "this corruptible shall have put on incorruption, and this mortal shall have put on immortality" (1 Corinthians 15:54).

## The Promises

From this mysterious and solemn doctrine of the gospel, let us turn now to some of its clear and explicit promises.

We will take first the words of the gospel according to Mark:

> *These signs shall follow them that believe; In my name shall they cast out devils; they shall speak with other tongues; they shall take up serpents; and if they drink any deadly thing, it shall not hurt them; they shall lay their hands on the sick, and they shall recover. (16:17–18)*

It is important to observe that this rich cluster of miraculous promises all hangs by a single stem, faith. And this is not some exclusive, or esoteric faith. The same believing to which is attached the promise of salvation, has joined to it also the promise of miraculous working. Nor is there any ground for limiting this promise to apostolic times and apostolic men, as has been so violently attempted. The links of the covenant are very securely forged, "*He that believeth* and is baptized shall be saved," in any and every age of the Christian dispensation. So with one consent the Church has interpreted the words, "And these signs shall follow *them that believe,*" in every generation and period of the Church's history—so the language compels us to conclude.

And let us not unbraid this two-fold cord of promise, holding fast to the first strand because we know how to use it, and flinging the other back to the apostles because we know not how to use it. When our Lord gives command *to the twelve,* as He sends them forth, "to heal all manner of sickness and all manner of diseases"

(Matthew 10:1), we might conclude that this was an apostolic commission, and one which we could not be warranted in applying to ourselves. But here the promise is not only to the apostles, but to those who should believe on Christ through the word of these apostles; or as Bullinger the Reformer very neatly puts it in his comment on the passage, to "both the Lord's disciples and the disciples of the Lord's disciples."[2]

Whatever practical difficulties we may have in regard to the fulfillment of this word, these ought not to lead us to limit it where the Lord has not limited it. For if reason or tradition throws one half of this illustrious promise into eclipse, the danger is that the other half may become involved. Indeed we shall not soon forget the cogency with which we heard a skillful skeptic use this text against one who held the common opinion concerning it. Urged to "believe on the Lord Jesus Christ," that he might be saved, he answered: "How can I be sure that this part of the promise will be kept with the Church of today?" And certainly, standing on the traditional ground, one must be dumb before such reasoning.

The only safe position is to assert emphatically the perpetuity of the promise, and with the same emphasis to admit the general weakness and failure of the Church's faith in appropriating it.[3] For who does not see that a confession of human inability is a far safer and more rational refuge for the Christian than an implication of the divine changeableness and limitation?

There is a phrase of the Apostle Paul which has always struck us as containing marvelous keenness and wisdom, if not covert irony—"What the law could not do, in that it was weak through the flesh" (Romans 8:3). The law must not be impugned by even a suspicion; "the law of the LORD is perfect" (Psalm 19:7). But there has been utter failure under its working—the perfection which it requires has not appeared. Rashly and dangerously, it would seem, the apostle has arraigned the law, telling us what it "*could not do*" and wherein it was "*weak*"—and then, having brought us to the perilous edge of disloyalty, he suddenly turns and puts the whole fault on us where it belongs—"What the law could not do, in that it was *weak through the flesh*."

The one weak spot in the law is human nature; there is where the break is sure to come; there is where the fault is sure to lie. In like manner this great promise, with which Christ's commission is enriched and authenticated, has failed only through our unbelief. It was weak through the weakness of our faith, and inoperative through lack of our cooperating obedience.[4] We believe, therefore, that whatever difficulties there may be in us, there is but one attitude for us to take as expounders of the Scripture, that of unqualified assent.

The treatment which the commentator Stier gives to this passage is truly refreshing. It is a brawny Saxon exegesis laying hold of a text, to cling to it, not to cull from it; to crown it with an amen! not to condition it with a date. For he puts the two sayings side by side and bids us look at them: [pisteusas], "He that believeth; shall be saved"; [pisteusasi], "Them that believe; these signs shall follow." And then he gives us these strong words:

> *Both the one and the other apply to ourselves down to the present day and indeed for all future time. Every one applies the first part of the saying to ourselves: teaching everywhere that faith and baptism are necessary in all ages to salvation, and that unbelief in all ages excludes from it. But what right has any to separate the words that Jesus immediately added from His former words? Where is it said that these former words have reference to all men and all Christians, but that the promised signs which should follow those who believe referred solely to the Christians of the first age? What God hath joined together, let not man put asunder.*

It should be observed however, that while the same word is employed in both clauses of this text, there is a change in number from the singular to the plural form. "*He* that believeth and is baptized shall be saved." The promise of eternal life is to personal faith, and to every individual on the ground of his faith. "*Them that believe*, these signs shall follow." The promise of miracles is to the faithful as a body. The Church has come into existence so soon as any have believed and been baptized; and thus this guarantee of miraculous signs seems to be to the Church in its corporate capacity. "Are all workers of miracles? have all the gifts of healing? do all speak with tongues?" (1 Corinthians 12:29–30) asks the apostle. Nay, but some employ these offices, so that the gifts are found in the Church as a whole. For the Church is "the body of Christ," and to vindicate its oneness with the Head it shall do the things which He did, as well as speak the words which He spake. How significant the place where this promise is found! It was given just as the Lord was to be received up into heaven to become "Head over all things to his church." It is Elijah's mantle let fall upon Elisha; so that having this, the disciple can repeat the miracles of the Master. Oh timid Church, praying for a "double portion of the Spirit" of the ascending prophet, and having His promise *"greater works* than these shall he do, because I go to my Father" (John 14:2), and yet afraid to claim even a fragment of His miracle-working power! We conclude, therefore, that this text teaches that the miraculous gifts were bestowed to abide *in the Church* to the end, though not that every believer should be endowed with them.

This promise given in Mark emerges in performance in the Acts of the Apostles. But it is significant and to be carefully observed, that the miraculous gifts are not found exclusively in the hands of the apostles. Stephen and Philip and Barnabas exercised them. These did not belong to the twelve, to that special and separated body of disciples with whom it has been said that the gifts were intended to remain. It was not Stephen an apostle, but "Stephen a man *full of faith and of the Holy Ghost,*" "Stephen *full of faith and power*" that "did great wonders and miracles among the people" (Acts 6:5, 8). We in these days cannot be apostles; but we are commanded to be "filled with the Spirit," and, therefore, are at least required and enjoined to have Stephen's qualifications. According to the teaching in Corinthians it is as members of Christ's body and partakers of His Spirit, that we receive these truths.[5]

We come now to consider the promise in James 5:14–15:

> *Is any sick among you? let him call for the elders of the*

*church; and let them pray over him, anointing him with oil in the name of the Lord: And the prayer of faith shall save the sick, and the Lord shall raise him up; and if he have committed sins they shall be forgiven him.*

Now let us note the presumption there is that this passage refers to an established and perpetual usage in the Church.

That command in the Great Commission—"Baptizing them in the name of the Father, and of the Son, and of the Holy Ghost" (Matthew 28:19)—appears in the Acts of the Apostles in constant exercise; and in the letters of the apostles as explained unfolded and enforced (Romans 6:3–4; Colossians 2:12; 1 Peter 3:21).

The injunction given at the institution of the supper, "This do in remembrance of me," appears in the Acts of the Apostles as explained and unfolded, and enforced (Acts 2:46; 1 Corinthians 10:11).

The promise given also in the Great Commission, "They shall lay their hands on the sick and they shall recover," appears in the Acts of the Apostles in constant exercise, and in the letters of the apostles as explained, unfolded and enforced (1 Corinthians 12:29; James 5:14–15). Thus, this office, like the great ordinances of Christianity, rests on the threefold support of promise and practice and precept. And we cannot too strongly emphasize this fact that what was given by our Lord in promise before His ascension should appear as an established usage in the Church after His ascension. For we all insist that the church of the apostles was the model for all time. When we are called "followers of the Lord," we might rightly protest that though His followers, we surely could not be expected to walk in His steps as He enters the field of the miraculous. When we hear Paul saying, "Be ye followers of me, even as I also am of Christ" (1 Corinthians 11:1) we might well insist that we could not imitate him in working wonders since he is an apostle and we only humble disciples. But when we read "For ye, brethren, became *followers of the churches of God* which in Judea are in Christ Jesus" (1 Thessalonians 2:14) we say "Yes! in every point and punctilio. For these are the pattern for all churches in all time." So we all hold and teach. We believe that there is nothing in all the ordering and furniture of the Church which was present in the beginning which should be absent now. And if we rejoice in having the laver and the bread of the ordinances, the ministry of the Word and prayer, none the less should we willingly be without the primitive miraculous gifts which were like the Shekinah glory, the outward visible signs of God's presence among His people.

To return now to the text which we are considering. Here is the calling for the elders of the church—a voluntary appeal to the ministry and intercessions of the servants of God. Oil is applied as a symbol of the communication of the Spirit, by whose power healing is effected. It does not seem reasonable to suppose that it is used for its medicinal properties. Because observe, it is the elders of the church, not the doctors of physic, who are called to apply it; and it is accompanied by prayer, not by manipulations and medications. As in baptism, the disciple confesses his faith in the cleansing power of Christ's atonement by the use of water; or, as in the Communion, he declares his dependence on Christ for spiritual sustenance by the use of bread; so here he avows his faith in the saving health of the Spirit by the use of oil.[6] In other words, this whole ceremony is a kind of sacramental profession of faith in Jesus Christ as the Divine Physician acting through the Holy Ghost. Such public profession of faith in Christ as the Healer, the Lord seems rigidly to require, just as He demands baptism as a confession of faith in Him as the Redeemer. Neither in the forgiveness of sin nor in the remission of sickness will He permit a clandestine blessing.

There are many who would gladly secure His healing virtue by stealth, laying hold of it secretly, but avoiding the publicity and possible reproach of having applied to such a Physician. But this cannot be. The Lord will have an open acknowledgment of our faith. It will be remembered that from the woman whom He healed of an issue of blood, He drew forth a public confession before He pronounced that full and authoritative absolution from sickness,[7] "go in peace, and be whole of thy plague" (Mark 5:34).

The promise of recovery is explicit and unconditional—"And *the prayer of faith shall save the sick and the Lord shall raise him up;* and if he have committed sins they shall be forgiven him" (James 5:15). Doubtless the words "*prayer of faith*" should be strongly emphasized. It is the intercession accompanied by the special miraculous faith alluded to in the Scriptures as "the gift of faith," and "the gift of healing"—a faith which we believe to be not wanting in this age, though comparatively so rare. And the words which Bengel italicizes in his Commentary ought to be strongly marked—"Let them use oil who are able by their prayers to obtain recovery for the sick; let those who cannot do this abstain from the empty sign." If the peculiar miraculous faith of which we speak had utterly disappeared from the Church, then it would certainly be best that the usage of anointing should be wanting also, rather than continue as a hollow sign, or as in the extreme unction of the church of Rome, a standing sacramental confession of inability to render any help to the diseased.

But we are persuaded better things than this. We believe that there are those in our own time who have humbly sought, and manifestly obtained this gift of prevailing faith. If the larger majority of Christians, either through wrong teaching or indifference have willingly consented to surrender this primitive birthright of the Church, and have learned to say without emotion to the sick that lie at their doors, "thy bruise is incurable, and thy wound is grievous. There is none to plead thy cause that thou mayest be bound up" (Jeremiah 30:12–13); there are some who are more jealous for the Lord's honor in this matter. Because they believe that the miraculous gifts are for all ages, they have thought it not covetous to seek them for themselves—and yet not for themselves, but that through them the Lord might still show forth His glory. And why should it be thought a thing incredible that they may have obtained what they sought? In the old dispensation were miracles of healing shut up within some narrow and special age? Run through the list and see:—Abraham healing Abimelech and his household by his prayers to God; Moses crying unto God for Miriam, "Heal her now, O God I beseech thee" (Numbers

12:13), and the Lord, answering with the promise that after seven days her leprosy should depart; God's cure of the bitten Israelites in answer to Moses' prayer, and through a look of faith at the brazen serpent; Naaman the Syrian recovered of his leprosy by the faith of Elisha; Hezekiah raised up from his death bed in answer to prayer and his life lengthened out 15 years, and other instances to which we have not space to refer.

These miracles of healing were not confined to the opening of a dispensation, but belonged to its entire history. Indeed intercession for healing was a part of the very ritual of Jewish worship and its answer a part of God's explicit covenant with His people. Hear Solomon's prayer at the dedication of the Temple. "Whatsoever sore or whatsoever sickness there be: then what prayer or what supplication soever shall be made of any man, or of all thy people Israel, . . . then hear thou from heaven thy dwelling place and forgive" (2 Chronicles 6:28–30). And hear God's promise in reference to this same matter. "I have heard thy prayer and thy supplication, that thou hast made before me: I have hallowed this house, . . . to put my name there forever" (1 Kings 9:3). "If I shut up heaven, . . . *or if I send pestilence among my people; If my people, . . . humble themselves, and pray,* and seek my face, and turn from their wicked ways; then will I hear from heaven, and will *forgive their sin, and will heal their land*" (2 Chronicles 7:13–14).

Here is a broad promise, conditioned indeed by the repentance and faith of the people of Israel, but fenced by no statute of limitations, shutting up God's mercies within a certain miraculous era. And we know from the history of prophets and saints how constantly this promise opened to the key of faith and poured forth its treasures. This under the old covenant! How much greater things might we expect under the new, after that the Lord had ascended up on high and given gifts to men—the Comforter the greatest and supreme gift to abide perpetually in the Church; and with Him and through Him, "miracles, then gifts of healings, helps, governments, diversities of tongues" (1 Corinthians 12:28).

It is comparatively easy indeed to credit miracles in these olden times of patriarchs and prophets, because of the enchantment of distance and the halo of superior sanctity through which the men of these times are seen. But antiquity has no monopoly of God's gifts, and ancient men as such had no *entrée* into God's treasure house which is denied to us. How very significantly James enforces the doctrine, "the effectual fervent prayer of a righteous man availeth much." After the exhortation, "pray one for another *that ye may be healed*" (James 5:16)—as though reading the thoughts which might come into our minds, of the superior faith of prophets and the higher privilege of apostles the Spirit adds, "Elias was a man subject to like passions as we are . . ." (5:17). Not some privileged courtier of the King of kings, not some high and titled chancellor of the exchequer of heaven having rights of access and intercourse with God of which we know nothing—"and he prayed earnestly that it might not rain: and it rained not on the earth by the space of three years and six months. And he prayed again and the heaven gave rain, and the earth brought forth her fruit" (5:17–18). If he could shut and open heaven, not the less can you the children of today, since he is a brother and kinsman in the same bonds of frailty, and fear, and also a son and disciple of "the same Lord over all [who] is rich unto all that call upon him" (Romans 10:12).

Such is the Spirit's practical enforcement of this great promise of healing. How much we need to ponder it! How much we need to relearn the truth, that, though Christ who heard the cry of the suffering and touched them with healing, has gone far off "above all heavens," and ages have been added to His eternal years "whose goings forth have been of old, from everlasting" (Micah 5:2), still His "hand is not shortened, that it cannot save; neither is his ear heavy, that it cannot hear" (Isaiah 59:1).

## ENDNOTES

[1]Dr. Hovey, commenting on this passage, says: "The words quoted by the evangelist are descriptive in the original passage of *vicarious suffering*. It is next to impossible to understand them otherwise. Hence in the miraculous healing of disease, a fruit if not a penalty of sin, Jesus appears to have had a full sense of the

evil and pain which He removed. His anguish in the garden and on the cross was but the culmination of that which he felt almost daily while healing the sick, cleansing the leprous or forgiving the penitent. By the holy sharpness of his vision he pierced quite through the veil of sense and natural cause, and saw the *moral evil,* the black root of all disorder, the source of all bodily suffering. *He could therefore heal neither bodily nor spiritual disease without a deep consciousness of his special relation to man as the substitute, the Redeemer, the Lamb of God who was to bear the penalty of the world's guilt."* The Miracles of Christ, p. 120.

[2] "Et discipuli Domini, et discipulorum Domini discipuli." And to show his belief in the fulfillment of the promise, Bullinger adds, "To this the Acts of the Apostles bear witness. Ecclesiastical history bears witness to the same. *Lastly, the present times bear witness; wherein through confidence in the name of Christ numbers greatly afflicted and shattered with disease are restored afresh to health."*

[3] "The reason why *many* miracles are not now wrought is not so much because faith is established, as that *unbelief reigns."*— Bengel.

[4] "It is the want of faith in our age which is the greatest hindrance to the stronger and more marked appearance of that miraculous power which is working here and there in quiet concealment. *Unbelief is the final and most important reason for the retrogression of miracles."*—Christlieb, *Modern Doubt,* p. 336.

[5] "You say that *Christ Jesus and his Apostles and Messengers* were endued with power from on high not only to preach the word for conversion but also with power of casting out Devils and healing bodily diseases. I answer, as an holy witness of Jesus Christ once answered a Bishop. 'I am a member of Christ Jesus as well as Peter himself.' The least Believer and Follower of Jesus partakes of the nature and spirit of him their holy head and husband as well as the strongest and holiest that ever died or suffered for his holy name." Roger Williams *Experiments of Spiritual Life and Health,* 1652.

[6]Lange commenting on Mark 5:13: "And they *anointed with oil many that were sick and healed them*," says that oil here is "simply a symbolic medium of the miraculous work;" and that "the anointing was a symbol of the bestowment of the Spirit as a preliminary condition of healing."

[7]"Therefore when she held her peace trustyng that she might still be undescryed, he looked round about upon the people. This looking about was a gesture of him that *courteously required a confession of the benefit receyved.* He would not utter her by name, lest he should have seemed to hit her in the teeth with the good turn he dyd her. It was a pricke or provocation given to make her to put away that unprofitable shamefasteness and to *wryng out of her a holesome confession.*"—Thomas Key.

# CHAPTER

## 3

---

# *The Testimony of Reason*

N owise contrary to Scripture and very agreeable to reason" is the opinion with which Archbishop Tillotson closes his observations on the recurrence of Christian miracles in modern times.

It may be asked, what reason has to do with such a question. Nothing, except as corroborating the testimony of faith. Miracles have not been generally defended on the ground of their intrinsic reasonableness, but on that of their scriptural authority; and that in us which first assents to their reality is not so much the logical mind as the docile heart—"the heart proffering itself by humiliation to inspiration" as Pascal expresses it. And yet we hold that to believe in miracles is reasonable, *after* it is faithful. That supreme miracle, the resurrection of our Lord, was first credited and published by loving and devoted believers; but it has since been defended again and again by Christian philosophers. So then, reason is not forbidden to look into the empty tomb and see the folded grave clothes and therefrom to conclude that Christ is risen, only she must be accompanied by faith and not be surprised if faith like that "other disciple" shall outrun her and come first to the sepulcher (John 20:4).

Believing miracles to have existed in the days of Christ and the apostles, is it reasonable to conclude that they may have continued to exist until our own time? It seems to us that it is.

For in the first place if they should cease they would form quite a distinct exception to everything else which the Lord introduced by His ministry. The doctrines which He promulgated and which His apostles preached—atonement, justification, sanctification and redemption—have never been abrogated or modified. The ordinances which He enjoined—baptism and the Lord's Supper—have never been repealed. The divine operations in the soul, which He ordained for man's recovery from the fall—"the washing of regeneration, and the renewing of the Holy Ghost" (Titus 3:5)—have never been suspended. These belong to the dispensation of grace which Jesus Christ introduced and which is to span the whole period between His first and His second advents. All orthodox Christians hold them to be perpetual and unchangeable.

And not only so, there was to be a development of these doctrines and operations of Christianity under the administration of the Spirit, so that the stream which started with Christ's ministry was to widen and deepen under the ministry of those who should come after him. "I have yet many things to say unto you, but ye cannot bear them now. Howbeit when he, the Spirit of truth, is come, *he will guide you into all truth*" (John 16:12–13)—an enlargement of knowledge and a development of doctrine under the ministry of the Comforter rather than a decrease!

"Verily, verily, I say unto you, He that believeth on me, the works that I do shall he do also; *and greater works than these shall he do; because I go unto my Father*" (John 14:12). A reinforcement of power for service rather than an abatement! And all intelligent Christians admit that these promises were fulfilled in the wider unfolding of truth and the more extensive work of regeneration which have occurred under the administration of the Spirit.

The law of Christianity is from less to greater and not from greater to less. "Of all that Jesus *began both to do and teach,* until the day in which he was taken up" (Acts 1:1–2) are the significant words with which the Acts of the Apostles opens; and as the beginnings are less than the unfoldings, we may conclude that the Lord was to do more through the Spirit's ministry than through His own. And so far as works of regeneration and salvation are concerned this undoubtedly proved true and is proving just as true today. The conversion of 3,000 souls in a single day under Peter's

preaching surpasses anything which occurred in the earthly ministry of Christ; and the conversion of 10,000 in a year on a single
mission field in India, also surpasses the results of any single year
in the Savior's ministry.

## Healing stood side by side

Now as the "*works*" of Christ are among the things which He
"*began to do*," miracles of healing stood side by side with miracles
of regeneration and therefore we say that the theory of the "gradual
cessation" of miracles contradicts all analogy. We have read of
certain South African rivers which instead of beginning as tiny
brooks and flowing on deepening and widening as they go, burst
out from prolific springs and then become shallower and shallower
as they flow on until they are lost in the wastes of sand without
ever reaching the sea. Two streams of blessings started from the
personal ministry of our Lord, a stream of healing and a stream of
regeneration. The one for the recovery of the body and the other
for the recovery of the soul, these two flowed on side by side
through the apostolic age. Is it quite reasonable to suppose that the
purpose of God was that one should run on through the whole
dispensation of the Spirit and that the other should fade away and
utterly disappear within a single generation? We cannot think so.

If miracles were abnormal manifestations of divine power,
against nature as well as above nature they might indeed be
expected to cease, for the abnormal is not as a rule perpetual. The
earthquakes and volcanoes, nature's agues and fever fits are soon
over; but the sunshine and the rain, the breezes and the blossoms,
nature's tokens of health are perennial. And miracles of healing are
manifestations of nature's perfect health and wholeness, lucid
intervals granted to our deranged and suffering humanity. They
are not catastrophes, but exhibitions of that divine order which
shall be brought in when our redemption is completed. We cannot
for a moment admit the complaint of skeptics that miracles are an
infraction of the laws of nature. Alas! for them that they have so
lost their ear for harmony that they cannot distinguish earth's wail
from Heaven's Alleluia; and know not the difference between the

groans of suffering creation and the music of the spheres, as it was on that day when "the morning stars sung together and all the sons of God shouted for joy." Miracles of healing and dispossession are reminiscences of an unfallen Paradise and prophecies of a Paradise regained. Though we call them supernatural, they are not contranatural. "For surely" as one has said,

> *It is plainly contrary to nature and indeed most unnatural that one should have eyes and not see, ears and not hear, organs of speech and not speak, and limbs without the power to use them; but not that a Saviour should come and loose his fetters. It was contrary to nature that ruthless death should sever the bands of love which God Himself has knit between mother and son, between brother and sister but not that a young man of Nain or a Lazarus should be released from the fetters of death through a mighty word! And that was the climax of the unnatural that the world should nail the only righteous one to the cross; but not that the holy bearer of that cross should conquer undeserved death, should rise and victoriously enter into his glory.*[1]

If then miracles of healing are exhibitions of divine recovery and order in nature and not rude irruptions of disorder, why having been once begun should they entirely cease? We are under the dispensation of the Spirit which we hold to be an unchangeable dispensation so long as it shall continue. On the day of Pentecost the Holy Spirit was installed in office to abide in the Church perpetually. Exactly as the first disciples were under the personal ministry of Christ, we are under the personal ministry of the Comforter. Having begun His miracles at Cana of Galilee, Jesus never permanently suspended them. His last gracious act before He was delivered into the hands of wicked men was to stretch forth His hand and heal the ear of the high priest's servant. And having wrought the first notable miracle after Pentecost by the hand of Peter at "the Beautiful Gate," why should the Holy Ghost in a little while cease from His miraculous works? We know that the Lord "*did not* many mighty works" in a certain place "because of their unbelief" (Matthew 13:58). And that the place where He was thus hindered was "in his own country, and in his own house" (13:57). But we know not that He *would not* do mighty works in any place if faith were present; and were it not a simpler solution of this whole question to say that possibly Christ through the Holy Ghost *will not* do many miracles today on account of man's unbelief, than to say that He wills not to do them?

## Healing as a sign

Then again the use which was made of miracles of healing as signs seems to argue strongly for their permanency.

If the substance remains unchanged why should the sign which was originally chosen to exhibit it be superseded?

It is said, indeed, with some show of reasonableness, that Christianity being a spiritual system, physical miracles were but the staging employed for the erection of that system, destined to fall away and disappear so soon as it should be completed. That certainly might be so. But how do we regard the argument of those who have reasoned precisely thus about the ordinances of Christianity? The Friends and other bodies of religionists have said that the rites of Baptism and the Lord's Supper are too physical to be perpetuated in connection with a spiritual religion; that whatever place they may have had in the founding of Christianity they are not demanded for its continuance. To which we reply at once— first, that they constitute a vivid sign and picture-writing of the great foundation facts of Christianity, the death and resurrection of our Lord; that they are a pledge and earnest of those great things to come at the resurrection of the just and the marriage supper of the Lamb, and that by the constant and glowing appeal which they make to the senses, they tend to keep these facts in perpetual remembrance; and, secondly, that however we may reason about it, these are *ordinances*, established for continual observance by the Lord until He come, and therefore we are forbidden to terminate them. This reasoning would be accepted, doubtless, as sound by all orthodox believers. But we can argue in precisely the same way about the "signs" which attested the first preaching of the gospel. In the great commission we have them solemnly established as the accompaniments of preaching and believing the gospel. In James' epistle we find healing recognized as an ordinance, just as in Paul's epistles to the Romans and to the Corinthians we find Baptism and the Supper recognized as ordinances. As signs, they could never lose their significance till the Lord comes again. They pointed upward and told the world that Christ who had been crucified was alive and on the throne. They pointed forward and declared that He would come again and subdue all things unto Himself. This last we believe to be the chief testimony of miracles as signs: They were given to be witnesses to the "restitution of all things" which Christ shall accomplish at His coming and kingdom. For notice how invariably our Lord joins the commandment to heal the sick and to cast out devils with the commission to preach the kingdom. Thus: "Jesus went about . . . preaching the gospel of the kingdom, and healing all manner of sickness and all manner of disease among the people" (Matthew 4:23). "And as ye go, preach, saying, The kingdom of heaven is at hand. Heal the sick, cleanse the lepers, raise the dead, cast out devils" (10:7–8; see also Luke 9:1 and 10:9). Healing and resurrection and the casting out of demons were a kind of firstfruits of the kingdom, to be presented along with its announcement. As, to use a familiar illustration, the commercial traveler carries samples of his goods as he goes forth soliciting trade, the Lord would have His ministers carry specimens and tokens of the kingdom in their hands as they went forth to preach that kingdom.[2]

This seems to be what is referred to in that picture of the groaning creation which we find in the eighth chapter of Romans: "But ourselves also, *which have the firstfruits of the Spirit,* even we ourselves groan within ourselves, waiting for the adoption, to wit, the redemption of the body" (8:23). As though it were said: "We have witnessed the works of the Spirit in healing the body of its sicknesses, in dispossessing it of the evil spirit, in quickening it from the power of death; and this makes us long only the more for that crowning and consummated work of the Spirit, of which these things are but an earnest;" when "he that raised up Christ from the dead shall also quicken your mortal bodies by his Spirit that dwelleth in you" (8:11). These signs were the foretokens of the body's redemption which the Lord at the first bade His messengers carry with them as they went forth preaching Jesus and the resurrection. Even dumb, suffering nature would be made glad by the sight of them. Goethe beautifully says, "Often have I had the sensation as if nature in wailing sadness entreated something of me, so that not to understand what she longed for cut me to the heart." But we understand what she longs for, "For we know that the whole creation groaneth and travaileth in pain together until now. . . . *waiting for the adoption, to wit, the redemption of the body*" (8:22–23). And they who "have tasted the powers of the world to come" were bidden to go forth and preach the kingdom, bearing in their hands the grapes of Eschol, which they have brought from that kingdom, that they may show what a goodly land that is where "The inhabitant shall not say, I am sick" (Isaiah 33:24). Thus, not only our wounded and pain-stricken humanity shall be cheered with the hope of better things, but even dumb nature shall be comforted by these foregleams of that millennium wherein "the creature itself also shall be delivered from the bondage of corruption into the glorious liberty of the children of God."[3]

Now why, if these credentials were so rigidly attached to the first preaching of the kingdom, should they utterly disappear from its later proclamation? There is the same groaning of creation to be answered; the same coming of the King to be announced; the same unrepealed commission of the Master to be carried out. The answer given by the majority to this question is: "Signs are no longer needed." If reason can be satisfied with this answer, faith cannot. For "faith has its reasons, which reason cannot understand." Among these is this: "Jesus Christ the same yesterday, today, and forever" (Hebrews 13:8). Miracles we hold to be a shadow of good things to come. The good thing to come for the soul is its full and perfect sanctification at the appearing of the Lord. The work of regeneration and daily renewal by the Holy Ghost is the constant reminder and pledge and preparation for

*THE TESTIMONY OF REASON*     *151*

that event; and regeneration is a "perpetual miracle." The good thing to come for the body is "glorified corporeity," resurrection and transformation into Christ's perfect likeness when He shall appear. Healing by the power of the Holy Ghost is the pledge and foretoken of this consummation. Was it in God's purpose that we should never again witness this after the apostolic age was past?

Here let us answer three or four objections which have been urged against our position. "If you insist that miracles of healing are possible in this age, then," it is said, "you must logically admit that such miracles as raising the dead, turning water into wine, and speaking in unknown tongues are still possible." But it requires only a casual glance to see that healing through the prayer of faith stands on an entirely different basis from any of these other miracles.

Raising the dead is nowhere promised as a privilege or possibility for the believers of today. There is, indeed, in one instance, Matthew 10:8, a command to raise the dead; but this was given specifically *to the twelve* and in a temporary commission. It therefore differs very materially from the promise in Mark 16, which was to *all believers,* and is contained in a commission which was for the entire dispensation of the Spirit. That the Lord did this miracle, and that His apostles did it, in one or two instances is not enough. Unless we can show some specific promise given to the Church as a whole we are bound to concede that such works are not for us or for our age. Healing the sick, on the contrary, rests on a distinct and specific promise to believers.

Miracles of external nature, like the turning of water into wine, and the multiplying of the loaves, belong exclusively to the Lord; we do not find them perpetuated beyond His own ministry either in fact or in promise. Miracles of cure, on the contrary, being in the direct line of the Lord's redemptive work, abound in the ministry of the disciples as they do in that of the Lord, and have the clear pledge of Scripture for their performance. The discrimination which Godet makes between miracles of healing and those performed on the outward world we believe to be strictly accurate. He says: "One consequence of the close connection of soul and body is that when the spirit of man is in this way vivified by the power of God it can sometimes exert upon the body, and through it upon other bodies, an influence which is marvelous. *This kind of miracle is therefore possible in every age of the Church's history; it was possible in the middle ages, and is possible still.* That which would seem to be no longer possible is the miraculous action of the divine power upon external nature. The age of such miracles seems to have closed with the work of revelation, of which they were but the auxiliaries."[4]

As to miracles of prophecy, we see no reason to believe that they were strictly limited to apostolic times. We recall, indeed the one important text on this question, "But whether there be prophecies, they shall fail; whether there be tongues, they shall cease; whether there be knowledge, it shall vanish away. For we know in part, and we prophesy in part. But *when that which is perfect is come,* then that which is in part shall be done away" (1 Corinthians 13:8–10). Thus speaks the Spirit in the Epistle to the Corinthians.

By this Scripture some have attempted to shut up all miracles within the apostolic era as belonging to the things which were "in part," and therefore destined to pass away. But, in the first place, let it be noted that it is only prophecies, tongues and knowledge that are specified, not healings. And we are to put no more within this limitation than the Word of God has put there. And, in the second place, the bounds set to the exercise of these gifts is "*when that which is perfect is come,*" which scholarship has generally held to mean, when the Lord Himself shall return to earth.[5] The gifts of tongues and of prophecy therefore do not seem to be confined within the first age of the church. We cannot forget, indeed that the utterances of prophecy and knowledge culminated and found their highest expression when the Canon of the New Testament Scriptures was completed; so that some thoughtful expositors have conjectured that this may have been the coming of that which is perfect so far as prophecy and knowledge are concerned. But in either event this does not touch the gifts of healing. These cannot have culminated so long as sickness and demoniacal possession are unchecked in the world; nor until the great Healer and Restorer shall return from above.

To sum up these observations then: Is it reasonable to conclude that the office of healing through faith, resting on the same apostolic example, and held by the same tenure of divine promise and precept as the other functions of the Christian ministry, was alone destined to pass away and disappear within a single generation? With the advance in power and knowledge which was to take place under the administration of the Holy Spirit after Pentecost, is it reasonable to believe that in this one particular instance there was designed to be a signal retarding of supernatural energy? Is the Lord less likely to heal those who extend to Him the touch of faith now that He is on the right hand of God,[6] having all power in heaven and earth given to Him, than He was while on earth? Is it reasonable to believe that the administration of the Comforter has changed since its first inauguration, so that, while his mission and his offices were to continue till the end of this age, it is found that one of His ministries has entirely disappeared since the days of the apostles? With sin and sickness still holding sway in the world, is it reasonable to consider the latter as entirely beyond the redemptive work of Christ, while the former is so entirely met by that work, which was not the case in the beginning? And, finally, until the harvest shall come, is it reasonable to suppose that we are to be left entirely without the firstfruits of our redemption? Until we can answer these questions perhaps caution is becoming us, at least, in denying that miracles of healing are still wrought.

## ENDNOTES

[1]Christlieb.

[2]"The devil is said to be he who has the power of death: he is the author of death; he introduced sin into the world, and through sin death; and as he is the author of death, so he is the author of disease, which is just a form of death, and which, as well as death, is the work of the devil. And, therefore, Jesus while he was upon the earth healed the sick and raised the dead, not merely to typify a spiritual healing and quickening, but to prove that he was indeed the promised Deliverer by destroying the

works of the devil, and also to give a fore-taste and a shadow of the ultimate effect of his redemption upon the whole man, body and soul. And thus we find in the New Testament that the healing of the sick and the preaching of the Gospel of the Kingdom are almost always co-joined, and are so spoken of as though they meant the same thing." Thos Erskine, *Brazen Serpent*, p. 272.

[3] "Sickness is sin apparent in the body, the presentiment of death, the forerunner of corruption. Disease of every kind is mortality begun. Now as Christ came to destroy death, and will yet redeem the body from the bondage of corruption, if the Church is to have a first-fruits or earnest of this power it must be by receiving power over diseases which are the first-fruits and earnest of death." Edward Irving, *Works. V.*, p. 464.

[4] *Defence of the Christian Faith*, p. 208.

[5] First Corinthians 13:10. "This verse shows by the emphatic *then* that the time when the gifts shall cease is the end of this dispensation. The imperfect shall not cease till the perfect is brought in."—Ellicott.

[6] "Is the truce broke? or cause we have
   A Mediatour now with thee,
Dosst thou therefore old treatyes wave,
   And by appeales from him decree?

Or is 't so, as some green heads say,
   That now all miracles must cease?
Though thou hast promised they should stay
   The tokens of the Church, and peace."
—Henry Vaughan, 1654.

# CHAPTER

## 4

---

# *The Testimony of the Church*

Witnesses who are above suspicion leave no room for doubt that the miraculous powers of the apostolic age continued to operate at least into the third century." Such is the conclusion of Dr. Gerhard Uhlhorn; and one who has read the work from which this opinion is taken will not doubt his eminent fitness to judge of such a question.[1] This concession is a very important one in its bearing on this whole subject. Prove that miracles were wrought, for example, in the second century after Christ, and no reason can thereafter be urged why they might not be wrought in the 19th century. The apostolic age, it must be admitted, was a peculiarly favored one. So long as the men were still living who had seen the Lord, and had companied with Him during His earthly ministry, there were possible secrets of power in their possession that a later generation might not have. It is easy to see, therefore, that this period might be especially distinguished by the gifts of the Spirit.

And yet the Savior seems to be careful to teach that there would be an augmenting rather than a diminishing of supernatural energy after His departure. "But ye shall receive power, after that the Holy Ghost is come upon you" (Acts 1:8). "Verily, verily, I say unto you, He that believeth on me, the works that I do shall he do also; and greater works than these shall he do; *because I go to my Father*" (John 14:12). He made no provision for the arrest of the stream of divine manifestations which He had started, either in the next age or in a subsequent age. But, conceding certain marked advantages possessed by the immediate followers of Christ, if we find in history that there is no abrupt termination of miracles with the expiration of the apostolic age, then we must begin to raise the question why there should be any termination at all, so long as the Church remains and the ministry of the Spirit is perpetuated?

Now, when we turn to the writings of the Christian Fathers, as they are called, we find the testimonies abundant to the continuance of the miraculous powers. We will quote only a few as specimens from a large number, which may be readily collated by anyone who will take the pains. Justin Martyr says:

> *For numberless demoniacs throughout the whole world and in your city, many of our Christian men, exorcising them in the name of Jesus Christ, who was crucified under Pontias Pilate, have healed, and do heal, rendering helpless and driving the possessing devils out of the men, though they could not be cured by all the other exorcists and those who used incantations and drugs.*[2]

Irenaeus says:

> *Wherefore also those who are in truth the disciples receiving grace from him do in his name perform miracles so as to promote the welfare of others, according to the gift which each has received from him.*

Then after enumerating the various gifts he continues:

> *Others still heal the sick by laying their hands upon them, and they are made whole.*[3]

Tertullian says:

> *For the clerk of one of them who was liable to be thrown upon the ground by an evil spirit was set free from his affliction, as was also the relative of another, and the little*

*boy of a third. And how many men of rank, to say nothing of the common people, have been delivered from devils and healed of disease.*[4]

Origen says:

*And some give evidence of their having received through their faith a marvellous power by the cures which they perform, invoking no other name over those who need their help than that of the God of all things and of Jesus, along with a mention of his history. For by these means we too have seen many persons freed from grievous calamities and from distractions of mind and madness, and countless other ills which could be cured neither by men or devils.*[5]

Clement says, in giving directions for visiting the sick and afflicted:

*Let them, therefore, with fasting and prayer, make their intercessions, and not with the well arranged and fitly ordered words of learning, but as men who have received the gift of healing confidently, to the glory of God.*[6]

The weight of these and like testimonies is so generally acknowledged by Church historians that it seems little less than hardihood for scholars to go on repeating that well-worn phrase "the age of miracles ended with the apostles." Mosheim, speaking of the fourth century says:

*But I cannot on the other hand assent to the opinion of those who maintain that in this century miracles had entirely ceased.*[7]

Dr. Waterland says: "The miraculous gifts continued through the third century, at least."[8]

Dodwell declares that "though they generally ceased with the third century, there are several strongly attested cases in the fourth."

Dr. Marshall, the translator of Cyprian, says "there are successive evidences of them down to the age of Constantine."

"*The age of Constantine*"[9] is a significant date at which to fix the termination of miracles. For almost all Church historians hold that there was a period when the simpler and purer forms of supernatural manifestation ceased to be generally recognized, or were supplanted by the gross and spurious type which characterize the Church of the middle ages. And the era of Constantine's conversion confessedly marks a decided transition from a purer to a more degenerate and worldly Christianity. From this period on, we find the Church ceasing to depend wholly on the Lord in heaven, and to rest in the patronage and support of earthly rulers; and ceasing to look ever for the coming and Kingdom of Christ as the consummation of her hopes and to exult in her present triumph and worldly splendor. Many of her preachers made bold to declare that the kingdom had come, and that the prophetic word, "He shall have dominion from sea to sea, and from the river to the ends of the earth" had been fulfilled.[10]

If now, as we have indicated elsewhere, the miracles were signs of the sole kingship of the living and exalted Christ and pledges of His coming again to subdue all things to Himself, it is not strange that as the substance of these truths faded from men's minds, their sign should have gradually disappeared also. At all events, it is very significant that precisely the same period, the first three centuries, is that generally named by historians as the era in which that apostolic hope "the glorious appearing of the great God and our Saviour, Jesus Christ" (Titus 2:13), and that apostolic faith, "they shall lay hands on the sick, and they shall recover" (Mark 16:18), remained in general exercise. It is not altogether strange, therefore, that when the Church forgot that "her citizenship is in heaven," and began to establish herself in luxury and splendor on earth, she should cease to exhibit the supernatural gifts of heaven. And there is a grim irony in the fact, that after death and the grave had gradually become the goal of the Christian's hope, instead of the personal coming of Christ, then we should begin to find miracles of healing alleged by means of contact with the bones of dead saints and martyrs, instead of miracles of healing through the prayer of faith offered to the living Christ. Such is the change introduced by the age of Constantine.[11]

## A revival of faith

But now comes a most suggestive fact: that whenever we find a revival of primitive faith and apostolic simplicity, there we find a profession of the chaste and evangelical miracles which characterized the apostolic age. These attend the cradle of every spiritual reformation, as they did the birth of the Church herself. Waldenses, Moravians, Huguenots, Covenanters, Friends, Baptists and Methodists all have their record of them.

Hear the following frank and simple confession of the Waldenses, that people who for so many ages kept the virgin's lamp trimmed and burning amid the gross darkness with which the Papal harlot had overspread the people:

> *Therefore, concerning this anointing of the sick, we hold it as an article of faith, and profess sincerely from the heart that sick persons, when they ask it, may lawfully be anointed with the anointing oil by one who joins with them in praying that it may be efficacious to the healing of the body according to the design and end and effect mentioned by the apostles; and we profess that such an anointing performed according to the apostolic design and practice will be healing and profitable.*[12]

Then after condemning extreme unction, that sacrament of the Papists wherein an ordinance for life is perverted into an ordinance for death, they say further:

> *Albeit we confess that the anointing of the sick performed according to the design, end and purpose of the apostles, and according to their practice and power of which St.*

> *Mark and James make mention, is lawful; and if any priest*
> *possessing the grace of healings had so anointed the sick and*
> *they have recovered we would exhort all that when they are*
> *really ill they omit not to receive that ordinance at their*
> *hands, and in no way despise it, because despisers of that*
> *or of other ordinances, so far as they are ordained by Christ,*
> *are to be punished and corrected, according to the rules of*
> *the evangelical law.*

The Moravians, or United Brethren as they are otherwise called, have obtained a good report among all Christians for their simple piety, and especially for their fervent missionary zeal. They have not only been earnest reformers, but reformers of reformers; so that such men as Wesley, catching their light and getting kindled by it, have brought a new revival to the backslidden children of the Reformation. On principles already referred to, we might expect to find their missionary zeal signalized by supernatural tokens. And so it has been, if we may believe what seems to be trustworthy records. In what is regarded as a very faithful history of the United Brethren, that of Rev. A. Bost, the author gives his own view of the continuance of the apostolic gifts in a very clear manner, and records for us with equal clearness the sentiments of the Moravians. He says:

> *We are, indeed, well aware that, so far from its being*
> *possible to prove by scripture, or by experience, that visions*
> *and dreams, the gift of miracles, healings and other extraor-*
> *dinary gifts, have absolutely ceased in Christendom since*
> *the apostolic times, it is on the contrary proved, both by facts*
> *and by scripture, that there may always be these gifts where*
> *there is faith, and that they will never be entirely detached*
> *from it. We need only take care to discern the true from the*
> *false, and to distinguish from miracles proceeding from the*
> *Holy Ghost, lying miracles, or those which without being*
> *so decidedly of the devil do not so decidedly indicate the*
> *presence of the Lord.*[13]

In this book are several statements of the Brethren concerning the character and discipline of their churches. The famous Zinzendorf writes as follows:

> *To believe against hope is the root of the gift of miracles; and I owe this testimony to our beloved Church, that apostolic powers are there manifested. We have had undeniable proofs thereof in the unequivocal discovery of things, persons, and circumstances, which could not humanly have been discovered, in the healing of maladies in themselves incurable, such as cancers, consumptions, when the patient was in the agonies of death, etc., all by means of prayer, or of a single word.*[14]

Speaking of the year 1730, he says:

> *At this juncture various supernatural gifts were manifested in the Church, and miraculous cures were wrought. The brethren and sisters believed what the Saviour had said respecting the efficacy of prayer; and when any object strongly interested them they used to speak to him about it, and to trust in him as capable of all good; then it was done unto them according to their faith. The count (Zinzendorf) rejoiced at it with all his heart, and silently praised the Saviour who thus willingly condescended to what is poor and little. In this freedom of the brethren towards our Saviour, Jesus Christ, he recognized a fruit of the Spirit, concerning which they ought on no account to make themselves uneasy, whoever it might be, but rather to respect him. At the same time he did not wish the brethren and sisters to make too much noise about these matters, and regard them as extraordinary but when, for example, a brother was cured of disease, even of the worst kind, by a single word or by some prayer, he viewed this as a very simple matter, calling to mind, ever that saying of scripture, that signs were not for those who believed, but for those who*

*believed not.*[15]

Thus we have the sentiment of the Moravians on the subject of miracles very distinctly indicated. And the statements quite accord with their simple faith and filial confidence in the Lord, as indicated in other things.

The following furnishes a very beautiful glimpse into the actual miraculous experiences above referred to:

> *Jean de Watteville had a childlike confidence in our Saviour's promise to hear his children's prayers. Of this he often had experience. One example we will here offer:—A married sister became extremely ill at Hernnhut. The physician had given up all hopes, and her husband was plunged in grief. Watteville visited the patient, found her joyfully expecting her removal, and took his leave, after having encouraged her in this happy frame. It was at that time still the custom of unmarried brethren, on Sunday evening, to go about singing hymns before the brethren's houses, with an instrumental accompaniment. Watteville made them sing some appropriate hymns under the window of the sick sister, at the same time praying in his heart to the Lord that he would be pleased, if he thought good, to restore her to health. He conceived a hope of this so full of sweetness and faith that he sang with confidence these lines:*

> > *'Sacred Cross, oh sacred Cross!*
> > *Where my Saviour died for me,*
> > *From my soul, redeemed from loss,*
> > *Bursts a flame of love to thee.*

> > *When I reach my dying hour*
> > *Only let them speak thy name;*
> > *By its all prevailing power*
> > *Back my voice returns again.'*

*What was the astonishment of those who surrounded the bed of this dying sister when they saw her sit up, and join with a tone of animation in singing the last line:*
  *'Back my voice returns again.'*

*To his great amazement and delight he found her, on ascending to her chamber, quite well. She recovered perfectly, and not till thirty-five years after did he attend her earthly tabernacle to its final resting place.*

And now we come to the testimony of that most illustrious band of Christian worthies, the Scotch Covenanters. Illustrious, we said, and yet with a light altogether ancient, apostolic and strange to our modern age. Let one read that book of thrilling religious adventure and heroic faith, *The Scots Worthies*, and he will almost seem to be perusing the acts of the apostles reacted. Such sterling fortitude; such mighty prayers; such conquests of preaching and intercession! Howie, its author, seems to have had in mind especially, in writing it, the rebuke it would bring to a later, faithless and degenerate age, by showing, as he says in his preface, "how at the peril of their lives they brought Christ into our hands," and "how quickly their offspring are gone out of the way piping and dancing after a golden calf." Nor did he think such a luxurious and unbelieving generation would be able to credit these mighty deeds of their fathers. For he continues:

*Some may be ready to object that many things related in this collection smell too much of enthusiasm; and that other things are beyond all credit. But these we must suppose to be either quite ignorant of what the Lord did for our forefathers in former times, or else, in a great measure, destitute of the like gracious influences of the Spirit by which they were actuated and sustained.*

If we are inclined to discredit the marvels of divine interposition recorded in this book, we have to remember that the men who

relate them, and of whom they are related, are the historic charac-
ters of the Scottish Kirk: Knox, Wishart, Livingston, Welch,
Baillie, Peden and Craig. We never tire of repeating the great and
holy things which these men did in other fields of spiritual service.
Who has not heard how John Livingston preached with such
extraordinary demonstration of the Spirit that 500 souls were
quickened or converted under a single sermon? And what Christian has not had his spiritual indolence rebuked by reading of John
Welch, rising many times in the night to plead for his flock, and
spending seven and eight hours a day in Gethsemane intercessions
for the Church and for lost souls. These things we have read and
repeated without incredulity. But how few have read or dared to
repeat the story of the same John Welch praying over the body of
a young man, who, after a long wasting sickness, "has closed his
eyes and expired to the apprehension of all spectators"; how, in
spite of the remonstrance of friends, he held on for three hours,
12 hours, 25, 36, 48 hours, and when at last it was insisted that
the "cold dead" body should be borne out to burial, how he begged
for an hour more, and how, at the end of that time, he "called
upon his friends and showed them the dead young man restored
to life again, to their great astonishment." All this is told with the
utmost detail in the book of *Scots Worthies.*

If we are startled to ask in amazement—as who will not be—"Are
such things possible in modern times?" we might better begin with
the question, has such praying and resistless importunity with God
ever been heard of in modern times? If we can get a miraculous
faith the miraculous works will be easy enough to credit. Yet this
is a specimen of the men who compose this extraordinary group
of Christian heroes. The wonders recorded of them are of every
kind—marvels of courage, marvels of faith, marvels of martyrdom,
and marvels of prophetic foresight. Theirs was a faith born and
nourished of the bitterest persecution. But if, according to the
saying of their biographer, they were "followed by the prophet's
shadow, the hatred of wicked men," it is equally true that they were
crowned with the apostle's halo, the power of the Holy Spirit.

Here we read of the holy Robert Bruce, of whom the beautiful incident is told, that once being late in appearing in his pulpit a messenger was sent for him who reported: "I think he will not come today, for I overheard him say to another: 'I protest I will not go unless thou goest with me.' Howbeit, in a little time he came, accompanied by no man but full of the blessing of Christ; for his speech was with much evidence and demonstration of the Spirit." Of this man, mighty in pulpit prayers, it is affirmed that "persons distracted, and those who were past recovery with falling sickness, were brought to him and were, after prayer by him on their behalf, fully restored from their malady."[16] Also we read of Patrick Simpson, whose insane wife, from raving and blaspheming as with demoniacal possession, was so wonderfully healed by his importunate prayers that the event was found gratefully recorded upon some of the books of his library: "Remember, O my soul, and never forget the 16th of August, 1601, what consolation the Lord gave thee, and how he performed what he spoke according to Zechariah, 'is not this a brand plucked out of the fire.' "[17]

We give verbatim one incident of healing as recorded in this book, admonishing the reader that this story, as well as several others, has been somewhat softened in later editions of the work, with the avowed purpose of making it accord more exactly with modern religious sentiments. It is from the life of John Scrimgeour, minister of Kinghornin Fife, and "an eminent wrestler with God:"

*Mr. Scrimgeour had several friends and children taken away by death: and his only daughter who at that time survived, and whom he dearly loved, being seized with the King's evil, by which she was reduced to the point of death, so that he was called up to see her die; and finding her in this condition he went out into the fields, (as he himself told) in the nighttime in great grief and anxiety, and began to expostulate with the Lord, with such expressions as for all the world, he durst not again utter. In a fit of displeasure he said—"thou O Lord knowest that I have been serving thee in the uprightness of my heart according to my power and measure: nor have I stood in awe to declare thy mind*

> *even unto the greatest in the time; and thou seest that I take pleasure in this child. O that I could obtain such a thing at thy hand as to spare her!" and being in great agony of spirit at last it was said to him from the Lord—"I have heard thee at this time, but use not the like boldness in time coming for such particulars." When he came home the child was recovered, and sitting up in the bed took some meat: and when he looked on her arm it was perfectly whole.*[18]

Now when we reflect that these things are recorded by the pen of some of the holiest men the Church of God has ever seen: and recorded too as the experiences of their own ministry of faith and prayer, the fact must at least furnish food for reflection to those who continue to assert with such confident assurance that the age of miracles is past. Past it may be indeed, if the age of faith is past. For that we conceive, to be the real question. It is not geography or chronology that determines the boundary lines of the supernatural. It is apostolic men that make an apostolic age, not a certain date of *Anno Domini.* We are forever thinking to turn back the shadow certain degrees upon the dial, to bring again the age of miracles, forgetting that He who is "without variableness or the shadow of turning" has said, "if thou canst believe"—not if thou wast born in Palestine and within the early limits of the first Christian century—"all things are possible to him that believeth" (Mark 9:23). When by the stress of violent persecution or by the sore discipline of reproach and rejection by the world the old faith is revived, then we catch glimpses once more of the apostolic age. And such perhaps beyond all others in modern times was the age of the Covenanters.

No one can read this stirring narrative of their sufferings and triumphs, their martyrdoms and miracles, without a profound spiritual quickening. There is little danger withal of the book ministering to fanaticism, for if anyone should be inspired by it with an ambition to be a miracle worker he will meet the challenge on every page—"Can ye drink of the cup that I drink of? and to be baptized with the baptism that I am baptized with" (10:38).

If we come to the Huguenots, those faithful followers of the Lamb, among generations that were so greedily and wantonly following the Dragon, we get glimpses of the same wonderful things. In the story of their sufferings and obedience to the faith in the mountains of Cevennes where they had fled from their pursuers upon the revocation of the Edict of Nantz, we hear constant mention of the exercise of miraculous gifts. There were divine healings and extraordinary actings of the Spirit in quickening and inspiration. They who in their exile carried their mechanical arts and inventions into England to the great blessing of the nation, carried here and there the lost arts of supernatural healing to the wonder of the Church of Christ.[19]

Among the early Friends, as is well known the same manifestations were constantly reported. Whatever we may think of the general teaching of this sect, no one can read the Journal of George Fox without feeling that he was a devoted man of God, doing a wholesome work of quickening and rebuke in a time of great spiritual deadness and conformity to the world. His quaint prayer that he "*might be baptized into a sense of all conditions*" seems to have been literally fulfilled. Like a latter day apostle he went among all ranks, rebuking the gay and worldly, turning away the wrath of those at enmity, visiting the sick and ministering to the prisoner. A worthy model is he for any minister, in any age who would learn how to labor "in season out of season" for the Lord.

Not only in his teaching but especially in his active service does he recognize the continuous operation of the Spirit in miraculous ministries. He records these manifestations without comment as though they were as much a matter of course as conversion or regeneration.

In a record of evangelizing in Twy-cross in Lincolnshire, England, he says:

> *Now there was in that town a great man that had long lain sick and was given over by the physicians: and some friends in that town desired me to go and see him, and I went up to him in his chamber and spoke the word of life*

*to him and was moved to pray for him, and the Lord was
entreated and restored him to health.*[20]

While preaching in Hertfordshire, they told him of a sick woman
and requested him to go to her help. He says:

> *John Rush of Bedfordshire went along with me to visit
> her, and when we came in, there were many people in the
> house that were tender about her: and they told me she was
> not a woman for this world, but if I had anything to
> comfort her concerning the world to come I might speak to
> her. So I was moved of the Lord to speak to her, and the
> Lord raised her up again to the astonishment of the town
> and country.*[21]

This book abounds in such instances, told without ostentation
or enlargement, but almost always alluded to as "miracles."

In the earlier days of the Baptists, days of simplicity and purity,
we meet with similar illustrations of miraculous faith and manifestation. As usual it was in times of great straits, when the prison
doors were shut upon the persecuted flock, that the windows of
heaven were opened in miraculous blessing.

Vavasor Powell, "the morning star of the Welch Baptists" as he
has been named, has left a clear affidavit to his faith and practice
on the subject we are considering. He was a man of the same fiber
as the Covenanters; endued with such power of the Spirit that
extraordinary revivals followed his life lain in 13 different prisons
for his testimony for Christ.

Besides the uncommon blessing which attended his preaching,
it is recorded that "many persons were recovered from dangerous
sickness through the prayer of faith which he offered." He took
the promise in James 5, literally, as shown in the story of his own
recovery, and especially as declared in the following article of his
creed—"Visiting the sick and for the elders to anoint them in the
name of the Lord is a gospel ordinance and not repealed."[22] That
his creed was to some extent adopted by the English Baptists

appears from the account given in the same book, of the ceremony of anointing and prayer as performed for a blind woman at Aldgate in London. Rev. Hansard Knollys, and Rev. Henry Jessey, eminent names in the early ministry of the body, united with others in the service, prayer being offered and the words pronounced, "the Lord Jesus restore thee thy sight."[23]

Among the Methodists, we find references here and there to the appearance of miraculous manifestations in the churches. There is one very striking instance which is recorded of Ann Mather, daughter of Joseph Benson the Methodist commentator, the story being given in full by the father in his journal. She had been afflicted with lameness in the feet, for some years having no use of her limbs, and not for a long time having walked a step. We give the narrative in the words of Mr. Benson's journal abridging in unimportant details:

> *Oct. 4th. This evening the Lord has shown us an extraordinary instance of his love and power. My dear Ann yet remained without any use of either her limbs and indeed without the least feeling of them, or ability to walk a step, or lay the least weight upon them, nor had she any use of them for upward of twelve months. I was very much afraid that the sinews would be contracted, and that she would lose the use of them forever. We prayed however, incessantly, that this might not be the case; but that it would please the Lord, for the sake of her three little children, to restore her.*
>
> *This day a part of my family and some of my pious friends went to take tea at her house; Mr. Mather bringing her down in his arms into the dining-room. After tea I spoke of the certainty of God's hearing the prayer of his faithful people, and repeated many of his promises to that purpose. I also enlarged on Christ's being the same yesterday, to-day, and forever, and still both able and willing to give relief to his afflicted people: that though he had doubtless done many of his miracles of healing chiefly to prove himself to be the Messiah, yet that he did not do them for that end only, but*

*also to grant relief to human misery, out of his great compassion for suffering mankind; and that not a few of his other miracles of mercy he had wrought principally or only for this latter purpose, and that he was still full of compassion for the miserable. I then said, "Ann, before we go to prayer, we will sing the Hymn which was full of consolation to your mother," and I gave out the words of the hymn beginning:—*

> *Thy arm, Lord, is not shortened now,*
> *It wants not now the power to save;*
> *Still present with thy people, thou, etc.*

*After singing, we then kneeled down to pray, and Ann took her infant child to give it the breast that it might not disturb us with crying while we were engaged in prayer. I prayed first, and then Mr. McDonald; all the company joining fervently in our supplications. We pleaded in prayer the Lord's promises, and especially that he has said that whatever two or three of his people should agree to ask, it should be done for them. Matt. xvii: 19. Immediately on our rising from our knees, Ann beckoned to the nurse to take the child, and then instantly rose up, and said, "I can walk, I feel I can"; and proceeded half over the room: when her husband, afraid she should fall, stepped to her, saying, "my dear Ann, what are you about?"*

*She put him off with her hands, saying, "I don't need you: I can walk alone," and then walked three times over the floor; after which, going to a corner, she knelt down and said, "Oh let us give God thanks!" we kneeled down, and gave thanks; Ann continuing on her knees all the time, at least twenty minutes; she then came to me, and with a flood of tears threw her arms about my neck, and then did the same first to one of her sisters, and to the other, and afterwards to Mrs. Dickenson; every one in the room shedding tears of gratitude and joy. She then desired her husband's brother to come up stairs; and when he entered the room, she cried out, "Adam, I can walk;" and to show him that she could, immediately walked over the floor, and back again.*

*It was, indeed, the most affecting scene I ever witnessed in my life. She afterward, without any help, walked up stairs into her lodging room, and with her husband kneeling down, joined in prayer and praise.*

*In conversation with her afterward, I learned from her the following particulars:—that when she was brought into the dining-room a little stool was put under her feet, but which she felt no more than if her feet had been dead. While we were singing the hymn, she conceived faith that the Lord would heal her; began to feel the stool, and pushed it away; then set her feet on the floor, and felt that; while we prayed she felt a persuasion she could walk, and felt inclined to rise up with the child in her arms; but thinking to do that would be thought rash, she delayed till we had done praying, and then immediately rose up, and walked as above related.*

Among the persons present who witnessed this remarkable scene was Rev. James McDonald, who followed Mr. Benson in prayer and was afterwards his biographer. In making reference to this wonderful healing he says: "All believed that the power to walk, which she received in an instant was communicated by an immediate act of omnipotence." The account was also published in the London Methodist Magazine, from which this is quoted.

We have thus set before us as a mass of evidence for the continuance of miraculous interventions which few, we imagine, would wish to condemn as utterly false. Whatever deduction or allowance any may wish to make, there remains too solid a substratum of well-proven fact to be easily set aside. Untimely—born out of due season, is the objection which will at once be urged indeed. That is to say, put the same facts and the same witnesses back into the age of the apostles and they can be easily enough credited, but not as speaking for modern times. But some believe that the Church like the tree of life "whose leaves are for the healing of the nations," not only bears 12 manner of fruits but *"yields her fruit every month."* "All supernatural manifestations determined with apostolic times and apostolic men"—so I read from a learned author, as I glanced for a moment from the page which I was writing. Then casting another glance through my window I saw a tree just before me crowned with a fresh coat of green leaves and white blossoms. Strange sight to witness *in the month of October!* Yet such was the season in which it came to pass. For it had happened that the canker worms had stripped the tree of all its foliage and left it bare and naked; but because there was life in its veins and the sap had not yet returned downward, it must find expression, and so even in autumn it had leaved and blossomed.

Alas that the Church should ever have been shorn of her primitive beauty! But so it was: apostacy succeeding to purity, and papacy to apostacy, and corruption to papacy, and infidelity to corruption, till it was literally as the prophet has written: "That which the palmerworm hath left hath the locust eaten; and that which the locust hath left hath the cankerworm eaten, and that which the cankerworm hath left hath the caterpillar eaten" (Joel 1:4).

But because there is life still remaining in the Church, because the sap has not utterly departed from the tree of God, fresh shoots are constantly putting out bearing the leaves and blossoms of primitive piety, and not less certainly the rich fruits of miraculous blessing. And so we are persuaded it shall be until the end. For it belongs to the Church as the body of Christ to do the works of Christ and it belongs to believers as the habitation of the Spirit to manifest the gifts and fruits of the Spirit.

## ENDNOTES

[1] *Conflict of Christianity with Heathenism*, p. 169.
[2] *Apol. II*, Chapter 6.
[3] *Adv. Haer Book II*, 4.
[4] *Ad. Scap. IV*, 4.
[5] *Contra Celsum B. III*, Chapter 24.

[6]*Epis, C,* XII.

[7]Cent. IV.

[8]See list of citations in *Creation and Redemption*, (London, 1877), p. 50.

[9]"With regard to the continuance of miracles after the apostolic age, we have testimonies, not only from Tertullian and Origen, who tell us that many in their time were convinced, against their will, of the truths of Christianity by miraculous visions, but, also, much later from Theodore of Mopsueste (429). The latter says: Many heathen amongst us are being healed by Christians from whatever sickness they have, so abundant are miracles in our midst." Cristlieb, *Modern Doubt,* p. 321.

[10]Eusebius L.X., pp. 3–4.

[11]"Ah, Constantine! of how much ill was cause,
Not thy conversion, but those rich domains
That the first wealthy Pope received of thee."
—Dante

[12]Johannis Lukawitz Waldensis, *Confession,* 1431. (See also Waldensia, p. 25).

[13]Bost I, p. 17.

[14]Idem, p. 111.

[15]Idem, pp. 405–406.

[16]p. 118.

[17]p. 116.

[18]Edinburgh Ed., 1812, pp. 89–90.

[19]*Morning Watch, B.,* IV, p. 383.

[20]*Journal B,* I, p. 111.

[21]Id. Vol.I, p. 281.

[22]*Ivimy's History of the Baptists,* p. 333.

[23]Idem, p. 332.

# CHAPTER

## 5

---

# *The Testimony of Theologians*

Admitting, with the historians, that miracles ceased to be recognized in the Church as a whole, after the third century, there have still continued to be witnesses here and there to their occurrence through all the ages. We call to the stand several theologians, who have not only defended the doctrine of the continuance of miracles, but have cited illustrations of what they regarded as credible instances in support of their theory.

Augustine, it has been claimed, denied the existence of miraculous interpositions in his day; and he certainly said some things that give occasion for that opinion. But, on the other hand, he has left on record what cannot but be regarded as the strongest testimony to their continuance in his generation. Archbishop Trench considers that the true solution of this seeming contradiction is, that he held to their cessation in his earlier writings, and changing his opinion, maintained their continuance in his later.[1] If this be so, we must take the last opinion as his true conviction, not that which he had retracted. How decidedly, indeed, he commits himself to the doctrine of the perpetuity of miracles will appear if we read the heading of one of the chapters of the *De Civitate Dei:* "Concerning the miracles which were wrought in order that the world might believe in Christ and *which cease not to be wrought now that the world does believe.*" He lived in a time, indeed, when the shadows of superstition had already begun to creep over the Church, and the records of miracles which he makes are occasionally marred by some trace of such superstition:

*For even now miracles are wrought in his name whether by the sacraments, or by prayers, or at the tombs of the saints. But they are not proclaimed with the same renown, so as to be spread abroad with the former. For the sacred volume which was to be made known on all sides caused the former to be told everywhere and to hold their place in all men's memories; but the latter are known of scarcely beyond the whole city or neighborhood where they may happen to be wrought.*[2]

In the same chapter he goes on to give instances to corroborate this assertion. We reproduce one, abridging the narrative, which is very extended, but retaining the essential points. The story is exceedingly natural and affecting. It is concerning Innocentius, a devout Christian, and a man of high rank in Carthage.

He was suffering from a painful malady, and had submitted to several surgical operations for its removal, but without effect. An eminent surgeon, Alexandrinus by name, being summoned, declared that there was no hope except possibly in another operation. This was decided on, and several officers of the Church were with him the evening before his trial, of whom he begged that they would be present the next day at what he feared would be his death.

"Among those present," says Augustine, "was Aurelius, now the only survivor and a bishop: a man ever to be mentioned with the greatest regard and honor, with whom, in calling to mind the wonderful works of God, I have often conversed on the occurrence, and I find that he retains the fullest recollection of what I now relate." The rest we give in the words of Augustine:

*We then went to pray; and, while we were kneeling and prostrating ourselves, as on other occasions, he also prostrated himself, as if some one had forcibly thrust him down, and began to pray: in what manner, with what earnestness, with what emotion, with what a flood of tears, with what agitation of his whole body, I might almost say with what suspension of his respiration, by his groans and sobs, who shall attempt to describe? Whether the rest of the party were so little affected as to be able to pray I knew not. For my part I could not. This, alone, inwardly and briefly, I said: "Lord, what prayers of thine own children wilt thou ever grant if thou grant not these?" For nothing seemed more possible but that he should die praying. We arose, and, after the benediction by the bishop, left him, but not till he had besought them to be with him in the morning, nor till they had exhorted him to calmness. The dreaded day arrived, and the servants of God attended as they had promised. The medical men made their appearance; all things required for such an occasion are got ready, and, amidst the terror and suspense of all present, the dreadful instruments are brought out. In the meantime, while those of the bystanders whose authority was the greatest, endeavored to support the courage of the patient by words of comfort, he is placed in a convenient position for the operation, the dressings are opened, the seat of the disease is exposed, the surgeon inspects it, and tries to find the part to be operated upon with his instrument in his hand. He first looks for it, then examines by the touch; in a word, he makes every possible trial, and finds the place perfectly healed. The gladness, the praise, the thanksgiving to a compassionate and all powerful God, which, with mingled joy and tears, now burst from the lips of all present, cannot be told by me. The scene may more easily be imagined than described.*

It will be seen, on careful reading, that aside from the testimony of the writer himself, there is everything in this story to indicate the genuineness and authenticity of the miracle. Its detailed narration shows how unquestionably the writer believes in healing through the prayer of faith.

Martin Luther, "whose prose is a half battle," would be likely to speak strongly on this subject if he spoke at all. Martin Luther, whose prayers were victorious battles, so that they who knew him were wont to speak of him as "*the man who can have whatever he wishes of God,*" would be likely to plead efficaciously in this field if he entered it at all. And so he did.

The testimony of Luther's prayers for the healing of the body are among the strongest of any on record in modern times. He has been quoted, indeed, as disparaging miracles. And the explanation of this fact is perfectly easy for those who have investigated his real opinions. Like the other reformers, like Huss and Latimer, for example, he revolted violently from the impudent Romish miracles which in his day put forth their claims on every side. This frequently led him to speak in very contemptuous terms of modern signs and wonder-working. And it is not strange that some, lighting on these utterances, should have concluded that he denied all supernatural interventions in modern times.

But if we turn from Luther the controversialist to Luther the pastor, we find a man who believed and spoke with all the vehemence of his Saxon heart on the side of present miracles. "How often has it happened and still does," he says, "that devils have been driven out in the name of Christ, also by calling on his name and prayer that the sick have been healed?" And he suited his action to his words on this point; for when they brought him a girl saying that she was possessed with a devil, Luther laid his hand on her head, appealed to the Lord's promise: "He that believeth on me, the works I do shall he do also; and greater works than these shall he do" (John 14:12), and then prayed to God, with the rest of the ministers of the Church, that, for Christ's sake, he would cast the devil out of this girl.[3] Perfect recovery is recorded in this instance, as well as in several others where he prayed for the sick.

The most notable instance is that of Philip Melancthon. An account of this recovery, which seems to be trustworthy, is given by the historian to whom we have just referred. Melancthon had fallen ill on a journey, and a messenger had been despatched to Luther. The story continues:

*Luther arrived and found Philip about to give up the*

*ghost. His eyes were set; his consciousness was almost gone; his speech had failed, and also his hearing; his face had fallen; he knew no one, and had ceased to take either solids or liquids. At this spectacle Luther is filled with the utmost consternation, and turning to his fellow travellers says: "Blessed Lord, how has the devil spoiled me of this instrument!" Then turning away towards the window he called most devoutly on God.*

Then follows the substance of Luther's prayer:

*He beseeches God to forbear, saying that he has struck work in order to urge upon him in supplication, with all the promises he can repeat from scripture: that he must hear and answer now if he would ever have the petitioner trust in him again.*

The narrative goes on:

*After this, taking the hand of Philip, and well knowing what was the anxiety of his heart and conscience, he said "Be of good courage, Philip, thou shalt not die. Though God wanted not good reason to slay thee, yet he willeth not the death of a sinner, but that he may be converted and live. Wherefore, give not place to the spirit of grief, nor become the slayer of thyself, but trust in the Lord who is able to kill and to make alive." While he uttered these things Philip began, as it were, to revive and to breathe, and gradually recovering his strength, is at last restored to health.*

If the reader should conclude hastily that this recovery may be accounted for on entirely natural principles, we have to remind him that the conviction of both parties to the transaction was quite otherwise.

Melancthon writing to a friend says:

> *I should have been a dead man had I not been recalled*
> *from death itself by the coming of Luther.*

Luther speaks in the same manner writing to friends:

> *Philip is very well after such an illness, for it was greater*
> *than I had supposed. I found him dead, but, by an evident*
> *miracle of God, he lives.*

Again, referring to his attendance at the diet, he says:

> *Toil and labor have been lost, and money spent to no*
> *purpose; nevertheless, though I have succeeded in nothing,*
> *yet I fetched back Philip out of Hades, and intend to bring*
> *him now, rescued from the grave, home again with joy, etc.*

Such is the witness of the great reformer, and, if needful, it might
be strengthened by reference to other remarkable instances of his
power in prayer for the sick.

That of Myconius is well known, who wrote of himself: "Raised
up in the year 1541 by the mandates, prayers and letter of the
reverend Father, Luther, from death."

Luthardt furnishes this version of the event:

> *Myconius, the venerated superintendent of Gotha, was*
> *in the last stage of consumption, and already speechless.*
> *Luther wrote to him that he must not die: "May God not*
> *let me hear so long as I live that you are dead, but cause*
> *you to survive me. I pray this earnestly, and will have it*
> *granted, and my will will be granted herein, Amen." "I*
> *was so horrified," said Myconius, afterwards, "when I read*
> *what the good man had written, that it seemed to me as*
> *though I had heard Christ say, 'Lazarus come forth.'" And*
> *from that time Myconius was, as it were, kept from the*
> *grave by the power of Luther's prayers, and did not die till*
> *after Luther's death.*[4]

The stout lion heart of the Reformer revolted against the grotesque miracles of Antichrist; but the believing heart of the Christian took the promises of God, and pleaded them and proved them; and he gained what he regarded as the greatest of conquests: that of having demonstrated Scripture, so as to be able to say of one text in the Bible: "This I know for certain to be true."

Richard Baxter will be listened to with special deference on the question before us. He was so bold in uttering his convictions that Boyle said of him that "he feared no man's displeasure, nor hoped for any man's preferment;" and he was also so devout that Joseph Alleine was accustomed to preface his quotations from him with the words "As most divinely saith that man of God, holy Mr. Baxter." He wrote very decidedly in defense of present miraculous interpositions for God's faithful. Speaking of what he calls "eminent providences," he says:

> *I am persuaded that there is scarcely a godly experienced Christian that carefully observes and faithfully recordeth God's providence toward him but is able to bring forth some such experiment, and to shew you some strange and unusual mercies which may plainly discover an Almighty disposer, making good the promises of this scripture to his servants; some in desperate diseases of body; some in other apparent dangers delivered so suddenly or so much against the common course of nature when all the best remedies have failed, that no second cause could have any hand in their deliverance.*[5]

After referring to some remarkable instances in the lives of the reformers he says:

> *But why need I fetch examples so far off? or to recite the multitude of them which Church history doth afford us? Is there ever a praying Christian here who knoweth what it is importunately to strive with God, and to plead his promises with him believingly, that cannot give in his*

*experiences of most remarkable answers? I know men's atheism and infidelity will never want somewhat to say against the most eminent providences, though they were miracles themselves. That nature which is so ignorant of God, and at enmity with him, will not acknowledge him in his clear discoveries to the world, but will ascribe all to fortune or nature, or some such idol, which, indeed, is nothing. But when mercies are granted in the very time of prayer, and that when to reason there is no hope, and that without the use or help of any other means or creature, yea, and perhaps many times over and over; is not this as plain as if God from heaven should say to us, I am fulfilling to thee the true word of my promise in Christ my Sonne? How many times have I known the prayer of faith to save the sick when all physicians have given them up as dead. [Here Baxter subjoins a note to be given presently.] It has been my own case more than once or twice or ten times, when means have all failed, and the highest art of reason has sentenced me hopeless, yet have I been relieved by the prevalency of fervent prayer, and that (as the physician saith "tuto, cito, et jucunde," my flesh and my heart failed, but God is the strength of my heart and my portion for ever.) And though he yet keep me under necessary weakness, and wholesome sickness, and certain expectation of further necessities, and assaults, yet am I constrained by most convincing experiences, to set up this stone of remembrance, and publickly to the praise of the Almighty, to acknowledge that certainly God is true of his promises, and that they are indeed his own infallible word, and that it is a most excellent privilege to have interest in God, and a Spirit of supplication to be importunate with him. I doubt not but most Christians that observe the Spirit and providences are able to attest this prevalency of prayer by their own experiences.[6]*

He then gives a detailed account of his own remarkable healing which we quote in full.

> *Among abundance of instances that I could give, my conscience commandeth me here to give you this one, as belonging to the very words here written. I had a tumor rise on one of the tonsils or almonds of my throat, round like a pease, and at first no bigger; and at last no bigger than a small button, and hard like a bone. The fear lest it should prove a cancer troubled me more than the thing itself. I used first dissolving medicines, and after lenient for palliation, and all in vain for about a quarter of a year. At last my conscience smote me for silencing so many former deliverances, that I had had in answer of prayers; merely in pride, lest I should be derided as making ostentation of God's special mercies to myself, as if I were a special favorite of heaven, I had made no public mention of them: I was that morning to preach just what is here written, and in obedience to my conscience, I spoke these words which are now in this page, viz: "how many times have I known the prayer of faith to save the sick when all physicians have given them up as dead"—with some enlargements not here written. When I went to church I had my tumor as before, (for I frequently saw it in the glasse, and felt it constantly.) As soon as I had done preaching, I felt it was gone, and hasting to the glasse, I saw that there was not the least vestigium or cicatrix, or mark wherever it had been: nor did I at all discern what became of it. I am sure I neither swallowed it nor spit it out, and it was unlikely to dissolve by any natural cause, that had been hard like a bone a quarter of a year, notwithstanding all dissolving gargarismes. I thought fit to mention this, because it was done just as I spoke the words here written in this page. Many such marvellous mercies I have received, and known that others have received in answer to prayers.[7]*

At once we imagine the explanations which will be given to this artlessly narrated incident. We do not vouch for its supernatural character. We have introduced it simply to show that Richard Baxter believed in modern miracles of healing, and there we leave it. It is not the authenticity of the wonder but the opinion of the man which we wish now to establish. That must be considered unquestionable.

John Albert Bengel is not only greatly esteemed but held in real affection by lovers of God's Word who have studied his commentary. He expounds pithily, but what is far better he believes intensely. "His works," says Dorner, "were the first cockcrowing of that new kind of exegesis which the Church so much needed." His is pre-eminently the exegesis of faith in distinction from the exegesis of reason. If he finds things in the Bible too hard for his critical faculty he finds nothing too hard for his believing faculty. Hence, his interpretations are not a sizing and sorting of Scripture to the dimensions of human experience, but a frank acceptance of it as God's truth. The word never appears shrunken as it comes forth from his hand; it does not present a scant weight as though it had paid toll to modern doubt. "Faith takes up all she can get and marches bravely onward," is a saying of his that describes better than any other his conduct in handling scripture. Now by faith Bengel staggered not at the promise of miraculous healing, which he found in the New Testament, but believed it, and confessed it, and rejoiced in it. In speaking of the gift of healing he says: "It seems to have been given by God *that it might always remain in the Church* as a specimen of the other gifts: Just as the portion of manna betokened the ancient miracles" (comment on James 5:17). "O happy simplicity! interrupted or lost through unbelief," he exclaims. And yet he declares, "even in our day faith has in every believer *a hidden miraculous power.* Every result of prayer is really miraculous even though this be not apparent; although in many, because of their own weakness and the world's unworthiness,— not merely because the Church once planted needs not miracles (though no doubt the early New Testament miracles have made for the Lord an everlasting name)—that power does not exert itself in our day. Signs were in the beginning the props of faith: now they are the object of faith" (comment on Mark 16:14).

And then, for confirming his assertions of his belief in the possibility of modern miracles, he introduces the following instance:

> *"At Leonberg a town of Wirtembergh, A.D. 1644, thirteenth Sunday after Trinity, a girl of twenty-three years of age, was so disabled in her limbs as hardly to be able to creep along by the help of crutches. But whilst the Dean, Raumier was his name, was from the pulpit dwelling on the miraculous power of Jesu's name she suddenly was raised up and restored to the use of her limbs."* This story the American editor omits as though solicitous for the critics reputation; but Faucett the English translator retains it in its place, and adds from information gathered from other sources that *"this, happened in the presence of the Duke of Eberhard, and his courtiers and was committed to the public records which are above all suspicion."*

Edward Irving is another illustrious confessor bearing witness to the doctrine we are defending. A man of wonderful endowments,[8] his highest gift seems to have been that of faith. He believed, with the whole strength and intensity of his nature, everything which he found written in the Scriptures. Cast upon times of great spiritual deadness, he longed to see Christendom mightily revived, and he conceived that this could only be effected by stirring up the Church to recover her forfeited endowments. "To restore is to revive," was emphatically his motto. He gave great offence by his utterances and had his name cast out as evil. He was accused of offering strange fire upon the altar of his Church, because he thought to relight the fire of Pentecost. Need enough was there of restoration, when teachers had so far made void the Word of God by their traditions that in their discussion with him they openly appealed from the Bible to the standards. Have you never read what Jehoiakim the son of Judah did with his penknife upon the prophet's roll?—How "it came to pass, that when Jehudi had read three or four leaves, he cut it with the penknife, and cast it into the fire" (Jeremiah 36:23). Alas! that modern theology should have given occasion to be accused of doing likewise with the 12th chapter of First Corinthians and sundry other parts of Scripture that tell about "*to another the gift of healing by the same Spirit*; to another the working of miracles; to another prophecy" (12:9–10) etc.

Irving, with a zeal for the Lord not always temperate, accused the Church of having clipped out these portions from the Scripture with her exegetical penknife, because she had said "these things do not pertain to the Church of today." And he went farther: "the Lord commanded Jeremiah to take another roll and to write in it all the former words that were in the first roll which Jehoiakim the son of Judah had burned." Irving conceived that he had a similar commission or at least permission,—not to make any new revelation, as he was accused,—but to retrace the faded lines of the old, wherein it spoke of "spiritual gifts": and so he encouraged his flock to seek for, and if the Lord should permit, to exercise the gifts of prophecy and of healing. This was his chief affront, and that which brought his splendid career under an eclipse—a result inevitable indeed considering that he was to be judged by those who knew no distinction between innovation and renovation.

But bating any extravagances into which he may have fallen, we confess that our heart has always gone out to him in reverence for his heroic fidelity to the Word of God, and his willingness, in allegiance to that Word, to follow Christ "without the camp, bearing his reproach" (Hebrews 13:13). And we believe that when the Master shall come to recompense His servants, this one will attain a high reward and receive of the Lord double for the broken heart with which he went down to his grave.

Irving wrote upon this subject with his usual masterly ability. Considering the Church to be "the Body of Christ," and the endowment of the Church to be "the fullness of him that filleth all in all," he held that the Church ought to exhibit in every age something of that miraculous power which belongs to the Head. That as she endures hardness and humiliation as united to Him

who was on the cross, so she should exhibit something of supernatural energy as united with Him who is on the throne. This he
conceived to be essential for the Church's full witness to Christ—
to him "who is now creation's sceptre-bearer as he was heretofore
creation's burden-bearer."

He lamented that the Church in her working has descended so
much to the plane of the merely natural, that in preaching, the arts
of the logician and the rhetorician have so far supplanted the gifts
of the Spirit. "The power of miracles must either be speedily
revived in the Church," he says, "or there will be a universal
dominion of the mechanical philosophy, and faith will be fairly
expelled to give place to the law of cause and effect acting and
ruling in the world of mind as it doth in the world of sense."[9]

He considered miracles to be intended not only for a perpetual
demonstration of Christ's power as now living and glorified, but
also as a visible foretoken of His coming kingdom. He has pointed
out with marked clearness the significance of the various signs
promised in the great commission, showing how these were given
as firstfruits of the kingdom of God as it shall appear in its full
consummation. As that kingdom was always to be preached, he
held that these signs were promised as the perpetual accompaniment of that preaching. He concluded that their withdrawal is due
to the Church's unfaithfulness, and not to any revocation on the
part of God.

> *These gifts have ceased, I would say, just as the verdure
> and leaves and flowers and fruits of the spring and summer
> and autumn cease in winter. Because by the chill and
> wintry blasts which have blown over the Church, her power
> to put forth her glorious beauty hath been prevented. But
> because the winter is without a green leaf or beautiful
> flower do men thereof argue that there shall be flowers and
> fruits no more?*
>
> *Trusting in the word of God, who hath created everything
> to produce and bring forth its kind, man puts out his hand
> in winter and makes preparations for the coming year: so*

*if the Church be still in existence, and that no one denies:
and if it be the law and end of her being to embody a first
fruit and earnest of the power which Christ is to put forth
in the redemption of all nature; then, what though she hath
been brought so low, her life is still in her, and that life will
under a more genial day put forth its native powers.*

It was from such convictions as these that he reasoned so
powerfully and prayed so earnestly for the recovery by the Church
of her primitive gifts. If the effort brought pain and persecution
to him, we believe it has brought forth some very sweet and genial
fruits in others. He was no mere theorist. He not only exhorted
his flock "to live by faith continually on Jesus for the body as well
as the soul," but he has told us the story of his casting himself on
the Lord when mighty disease laid hold of him; and how his faith
was tried to the last extremity till with swimming brain and deathly
sweat he stood holding on to the sides of the pulpit, waiting for
God to fulfill in the eyes of the people His word "the prayer of
faith shall save the sick" (James 5:15); and how his Redeemer at
last appeared for his help and loosed for him the bands of sickness
enabling him to preach on that morning with such demonstration
and power of the Spirit as he had rarely known.

Thomas Erskine has written on this subject with rare insight and
depth of conviction. Those who have read his writings know what
a subtle and intuitive spiritual apprehension he has. A barrister by
profession he is far more widely known as a theologian, while he
is most deeply revered as a Christian, "who" to use Dr. Hanna's
words in his preface to his letters, "moved so lovingly and attrac-
tively among his fellow-men and who walked so closely and
constantly with God."

Speaking of miraculous healing and the other gifts he says:

*But I still continue to think, that to any one whose
expectations are formed by and founded on the New Testament, the disappearance of these gifts from the Church must
be a far greater difficulty than their re-appearance could*

*possibly be.*[11]

In his correspondence with Dr. Chalmers, when the latter argued that we ought not to desire signs from the Lord, but to be satisfied with the ordinary manifestations of the Spirit, he replied that we ought to desire them, if God has ordained them:

> *If the Lord gives these things as means, surely it is not genuine humility which says I am satisfied without them. When the Lord desired Ahaz to ask a sign he answered, "I will not ask neither will I tempt the Lord:" but he is severely rebuked for this apparent humility. (Isaiah 7:12–13)*

His strong conviction was that the miraculous gifts were designed to be a permanent endowment of the Church:

> *The great and common mistake with regard to the gifts is that they were intended merely to authenticate or to witness to the inspiration of the Canon of Scripture, and that therefore when the Canon was completed they should cease: whereas they were intended to witness to the exaltation of Christ as the head of the body, the Church. Had the faith of the Church, continued pure and full these gifts of the Spirit would never have disappeared. There is no revocation by Christ of that word.*[12] *(Mark 16:17–18)*

With such views, he watched with great interest any indications of a revival of these gifts, and in the movement in that direction going on in his day, he believed he witnessed some genuine instances of miraculous healing, as well as of speaking with tongues. We refer to one case mentioned in his letters:

> *In March, 1830, in the town of Port Glasgow, on the Clyde, lived a family of MacDonalds, twin brothers, James and George, with their sisters. One of the sisters, Margaret, of saintly life, lay very ill, and apparently nigh to death.*

*She had received a remarkable baptism of the Spirit on her sick bed, and had been praying for her brothers that they might be anointed in like manner. One day when James was standing by, and she was interceding that he might at that time be endowed with the power of the Holy Ghost, the Spirit came upon him with marvellous manifestations. His whole countenance was lighted up, and with a step and manner of most indescribable majesty he walked up to Margaret's bedside and addressed her in these words, "Arise and stand upright." He repeated the words, took her by the hand, and she arose. Her recovery was instantaneous and complete, and the report of it produced a profound sensation, and many came from great distances to see her. Mr. Erskine visited the house and made careful and prolonged inquiry into the facts, and put on record his conviction of the genuiness of the miracle.*[13]

His whole discussion of the subject in the work referred to, *The Brazen Serpent,* is deeply instructive, and especially his exposition of the intention and significance of miracles of healing as signs.

Dr. Horace Bushnell, in his well-known work *Nature and the Supernatural,* not only admits the existence of present-day miracles, but considers that a denial of their possibility would imperil his whole argument for the supernatural. Conceding that the Church as a whole has lost her miraculous faith, and would be inclined to repel it were it offered to her, and admitting that thinking men are not open to conviction on this point, because "the human mind, as educated mind is just now at the point of religious apogee, where it is occupied or preoccupied by nature and cannot think it rational to suppose that God does anything longer which exceeds the causalities of nature," he yet holds that among humble and simple-hearted believers "sporadic cases" of miracles have constantly appeared, and continue to appear. And not only this; he considers that in our time there are signs of a revival of the primitive apostolic gifts; that Christians "feeling after some way out of the dullness of second-hand faith, and the dryness of merely reasoned gospel, are longing for a kind of faith that shows God in living commerce with men such as he vouchsafed them in former times." "Probably, therefore," he continues, "there may just now be coming forth a more distinct and widely attested dispensation of gifts and miracles than has been witnessed for centuries."

Dr. Bushnell's testimony as a whole is quite remarkable, because it is that of a cultivated reasoner, looking at the question through the eyes of logic as well as through the eyes of faith. His well-argued discussion and wide array of facts ought at least to arrest the attention of the *savans* who toss off this subject with a derisive sneer. That unripe skepticism, which denies before it has even doubted, has nowhere been more arrogant than on this field. Presumptuous enough it is to attempt to pick a miracle to pieces with the steel fingers of logic, but to leave it coolly alone is worse. And yet this is the method which reason has too often taken with anything professedly supernatural in these days. Scientific reason and Christian reason have passed by modern miracles as poor relations, to be looked at askance but not to be admitted into the best circles of faith and credence. And it is, therefore, quite gratifying to note the frank and cordial recognition which a thinker like Dr. Bushnell extends to them. Healing, prophecy and gifts of tongues he admits as possible, and to some extent operative today as in the beginning. From a large array of instances adduced in his work we give place to but one, referring the reader for further information to the 14th chapter of the work named, in which he discusses the proposition: "*Miracles and supernatural gifts not discontinued.*"

The case cited is from the experience of a friend of his, who had been healed by prayer himself, and had, as he believed, received the gift of healing. He gives the instance to Dr. Bushnell in writing, and the doctor considers his character and veracity to be such as to put his story beyond question:

> *At length one of his children, whom he had with him away from home, was taken ill with scarlet fever. And now the question was, I give his own words, "what was to be*

done? The Lord had healed my own sickness, but would he heal my son? I conferred with a brother in the Lord, who, having no faith in Christ's healing power, urged me to send instantly for the doctor, and I dispatched his groom on horseback to fetch him. Before the Doctor arrived my mind was filled with revelation on the subject. I saw that I had fallen into a snare by turning away from the Lord's healing hand to lean on medical skill. I felt greviously condemned in my conscience; a fear also fell on me that if I persevered in my unbelieving course my son would die, as his oldest brother had. The symptoms in both were precisely similar. The doctor arrived. My son, he said, was suffering from a scarlet fever, and medicine should be sent immediately. While he stood, prescribing, I resolved to withdraw the child and cast him on the Lord. And when he was gone I called the nurse and told her to take the child into the nursery, and lay him on the bed. I then fell on my knees, confessing the sin I had committed against the Lord's healing power. I also prayed most earnestly that it would please my heavenly Father to forgive my sin, and to show that he forgave it by causing the fever to be rebuked. I received a mighty conviction that my prayer was heard, and I arose and went to the nursery, at the end of a long passage, to see what the Lord had done, and on opening the door, to my astonishment, the boy was sitting up in his bed, and on seeing me cried out, 'I am quite well and want to have my dinner.' In an hour he was dressed, and well, and eating his dinner, and when the physic arrived it was cast out of the window.

"Next morning the doctor returned, and on meeting me at the garden gate he said, 'I hope your son is no worse?' 'He is very well, I thank you,' said I in reply. 'What can you mean?' rejoined the doctor. 'I will tell you; come in and sit down.' I then told him all that had occurred, at which he fairly gasped with surprise. 'May I see your son,' he asked. 'Certainly, doctor; but I see that you do not believe me.' We *proceded up stairs, and my son was playing with his brother on the floor. The doctor felt his pulse and said, 'Yes, the fever is gone.' Finding also a fine, healthy surface on his tongue, he added, 'Yes, he is quite well; I suppose it was the crisis of his disease.'* [14]

These testimonies might be increased by the addition of such names as those of Hugh Grotius, the Dutch theologian, and Lavater, the "Fenelon of Switzerland," as he has been called, and Hugh McNeil, the eminent English evangelical minister of the last generation, and Thomas Boys, M.A., of Trinity College, Cambridge, England, and others.[15]

But we have not space to refer to more. These are a goodly array of witnesses; yet not because of their eminence have we summoned them. We care little for the testimony of a deep thinker except he has thought deeply and devoutly upon the subject in hand. The shorter sounding line, if it has dropped its lead to the utmost limit, has told us more of the depth than the longer one that remained coiled and dry. And so the very mediocre theologian who has studied this question to the extent of his capacity is a better witness than the most profound who has never investigated it, but has rested in unreasoning assent to what Dr. Bushnell calls "the clumsy assumption" that all miracles closed with the apostolic age.

## ENDNOTES

[1] "In an early work, *De Vera Religione XXV.* 47, he denies their continuance, while in his *Retractions* he withdraws this statement, or limits it to such miracles as those that accompanied baptism at the first. In *De Civ. Dei. XXII.* 8, he enumerates at great length miracles, chiefly those of healing, which he believed to have been wrought in his own time, and coming more or less within his own knowledge." Trench, *Notes on Miracles*, p. 59.

[2] *Works V.,* p. 299.

[3] Seckendorf's *History of Lutheranism*, B. III., p. 133.

[4] Luthardt, *Moral Truths of Christianity*, p. 298.

[5] *Saint's Rest*, Part II. chap. VI. Sec. V.

[6] Ibid.

[7] Ibid.

[8] "But I hold, withal and not the less firmly for these discrepancies in our moods and judgments, that Edward Irving possesses more of the spirit and purpose of the first Reformers, that he has more of the head and heart, the life and unction and the genial power of Martin Luther, than any man now alive: yea, than any man of this or the last century. I see in Edward Irving a minister of Christ after the order of Paul." Coleridge, *Works V., VI.*, p. 115.

[9] *Works V.*, p. 479.

[10] The Church with her Endowment of Holiness and Power, *Works, V.*, p. 61.

[11] *Letters*, p. 198.

[12] *Brazen Serpent*, p. 203, Id. p. 198.

[13] *Letters*, pp. 176, 182, 183.

[14] *Nature and the Supernatural*, p. 480.

[15] The works of Thomas Boys, *The Christian Dispensation Miraculous*, and *Proofs of Miraculous Faith and Experience of the Church in all Ages*, are full of learning and information on this whole subject, and this book gratefully acknowledges its indebtedness to them for several quotations and translations from rare and inaccessible works.

# CHAPTER

## 6

---

# *The Testimony of Missions*

There is a special and weighty reason why we should lay emphasis on any testimonies on this subject coming from those who are preaching the gospel among the pagans. The rigid logic which is supposed to fence out miracles from modern Christendom, does not seem to have been careful to include heathendom in its prohibition. For when it is said that "miracles belong to the planting of Christianity not to its progress and development," it will at once strike us that missions are practically the planting of Christianity.

There is really little if any difference between Paul at Melita, and Judson in India. In each instance it is the herald of the gospel set down among a superstitious and idolatrous people. And admitting the proposition just quoted to be true, it would be very difficult to say why if Paul went into the house of Publius in the one place and laid his hands on his sick father and healed him, it might not be permitted for Judson to go into some home in Burma and do the same. And if it be said that signs are not needed while we have the history of the Christian Church, and the influence of powerful Christian nations for the authentication and enforcement of the gospel,[1] it must still be remembered that these forces are practically powerless until by the planting of Christianity the heathen have been made acquanted with ecclesiastical history and brought in contact with Christian civilization; so that the argument comes back again to this conclusion: that if miracles belong to the planting of Christianity, there would be no inherent improbability of their appearing on missionary fields and among those who are engaged in introducing the gospel into new countries. The justness of this conclusion has been recognized by several writers. We are glad to find, for example so devout and eminent a theologian as Professor Christlieb of Bonn accepting most candidly and frankly this position. For after admitting the force of the argument against miracles in Christianized countries he says:

> Our age however is still characterized by the establishment of new Churches. The work of missions is outwardly at least more extended than it ever was before. In this region therefore, according to our former rule, miracles should not be entirely wanting.[2] Nor are they. We cannot therefore fully admit the proposition that no more miracles are performed in our day. In the history of modern missions we find many wonderful occurrences which unmistakably remind us of the apostolic age. In both periods there are similar hindrances to be overcome in the heathen world and similar confirmations of the word are needed to convince the dull sense of men: we may therefore expect miracles in this case.[3]

And then as though less afraid of the imputation of credulity than of skepticism, he gives several instances, in the genuineness of which he expresses entire confidence. These we believe are but samples of hundreds that might be produced were it not for the exceeding timidity, the shyness amounting almost to shame-facedness, with which so many Christians approach this subject. Of course with this sentiment of distrust generally prevailing on the subject, we could hardly expect that witnesses would be very forward in reporting things indiscreetly supernatural, though quite confident of having seen them.

We venture however to give several instances of what seems to be divine healing, as they have been reported from missionary fields—the first three being those cited by Dr. Christlieb in the work just referred to:

*And now read the history of Hans Egede, the first Evangelical missionary in Greenland. He had given the Eskimos a pictorial representation of the miracles of Christ before he had mastered their language. His hearers, who, like many in the time of Christ, had a perception only for bodily relief, urge him to prove the power of this Redeemer of the world upon their sick people. With many sighs and prayers he ventures to lay his hands upon several, prays over them, and lo, he makes them whole in the name of Jesus Christ! The Lord could not reveal himself plainly enough to this mentally blunted and degraded race by merely spiritual means, and therefore bodily signs were needed.*

*At a Rhenish mission station in South Africa in 1858, an earnest native Christian saw an old friend who had become lame in both legs. Impressed with a peculiar sense of believing confidence, he went into the bushes to pray, and then came straight up to the cripple, and said, "the same Jesus who made the lame to walk, can do so still: I say to thee, in the name of Jesus, rise and walk!" The lame man, with kindred faith, raised himself on his staff and walked, to the astonishment of all who knew him. (Vide the Memoire of Kleinschmidt, Barmen 1866, p. 58ff)*

Another most remarkable instance occurred in the case of a missionary of the Rhenish society, named Nommensen, working in Sumatra.

*On one occasion a heathen who had designs on his life managed secretly to mix a deadly poison in the rice which Nommensen was preparing for his dinner. Without suspicion, the missionary ate the rice, and the heathen watched for him to fall down dead. Instead of this, however, the promise contained in Mark xvi: 18, was fulfilled, and he did not experience the slightest inconvenience. The heathen, by this palpable miraculous proof of the Christian God's power, became convinced of the truth, and was*

*eventually converted; but not until his conscience had*
*impelled him to confess his guilt to Nommensen, did the*
*latter know from what danger he had been preserved. This*
*incident is well attested, and the missionary still lives.*
*1873, (vd v, Rohden Geschichte der rhein, Mis-*
*sionsgesellsschaft, p. 324.)*

It will be seen that these instances cover several specifications in
Mark 16:17–18. Their miraculous character cannot of course be
vouched for with certainty. For we have not witnesses supernaturally inspired to accredit works supernaturally wrought, if
there are such still. But one would hardly wish to charge deception
on those who have reported them. For us, however, their probability rests more strongly on the words of the Great Commission[4]
under which these missionaries were acting, than on the trustwor-
thiness of human testimony.

Doctrines which have been almost universally denied are certain
to force themselves into acceptance again if they are in the Bible,
and that Bible is studied. And a promise in the missionary's
commission which says: "These signs shall follow" is liable now
and then to break through custom and prejudice and get itself
fulfilled. Besides that commission is certain to fall into the hands
of native preachers, who are unskilled in the arts of refining and
spiritualizing Scripture, and who know no better than to take God
literally at His word. And who can tell what may not happen when
a Christian who has not learned to doubt comes to God to claim
the fulfillment of one of His promises? In such a case we may hear
of miracles quite artless and rude in their form.

A missionary of the Presbyterian Board who has been laboring
for many years in China, declares that with the New Testament in
their hands the native Christians are constantly finding and putting in practice the promises for miraculous healing. This fact has
led him to a careful revision of his opinions on the subject. He
writes:

*Fully believing that the gifts of the Spirit were not to be taken from the Church, I feel assured that our faith ought to exercise and claim their use now. The salvation aimed for by all, should be present release from sin and the power of Satan. If this is attained then the whole advantage of Christ's life, death and resurrection will be secured. Healing is as much a part of this as any verbal proclamation of the good news. The ministry of healing, therefore, can not be divorced from the duty of the missionary.*

An honored missionary among the Karens gives the following experience:

*While travelling in the Pegu district I was strongly urged to visit an out of the way village, in which were only a few Christians. Entering the house of one of them, I had been seated but a little while when there came in a Karen, an entire stranger, but whose salutation proved him a Christian. He at once said that hearing that the teacher had come to visit the village, he came to beg that I would go and pray for his son who was very ill, he feared dying. He quoted James v., 14–15 as his excuse. Of course Mrs.____ and myself went at once, accompanied by the three or four Christians of the house in which we were. The patient was found to be a child of about fifteen years of age, possibly not over fourteen, but through scrofula, he was distorted and crippled so that he could not walk, indeed had never walked upright but crept painfully on knees and hands. He was greatly wasted, and had been much worse for some weeks, and at the time was perfectly helpless through extreme weakness. He had every appearance of one near death. We prayed, each in turn, the lad mingling short requests with ours. I think in all seven brethren offered petitions. A little bottle of medicine was left from our scanty supplies and we took leave of the poor little fellow. Six months afterwards the father came to the city, and on inquiring of him he said that his son was well,—well as he had never been in his life, and was actually walking on his feet, that the heathen families living in the village were deeply impressed, and said unhesitatingly that our prayers had saved him. I asked him his own opinion. He, most emphatically, in his strong Karen way, said: "God has done it; God has healed him." He then said, "Teacher this is no new thing; I was with your father-in-law many times when God, in answer to prayers, healed the sick, and that is why I asked you to pray with my boy, and now he is healed."*

Many testimonies have been recently published by missionaries of their own recovery from hopeless sickness through the prayers of faith. We can give place to but one, and that quite abridged in form. It is from Rev. Albert Norton, and is written to Dr. Stanton of Cincinnati, formerly moderator of the General Assembly. After describing his terrible sickness in Elichpoor, India, June, 1879— an abscess in the liver which had worked itself through the pleura and was discharging itself into the right lung—the most intense pain ever endured, and withal malarious remittent fever, he continues:

*I was thinking only of how I might die as easy as possible, when I was aroused by strong desire to live for my family, and to preach the unsearchable riches of the Gospel, and the thought came "why cannot God heal you?" My dear wife was the only Christian believer, except an ignorant Kerkoo lad, within eighteen miles. At my request she anointed me with oil, and united her prayers with mine that God might at once heal me. While I was praying vocally, before I felt any change in my body, I felt perfectly certain that God had heard and answered our prayers. When we were through praying we commenced praising; for the acute pain in my right side, and the fever, had left me. I was able at once to read some from the Bible, and to look out some passages from the Greek Testament. Neither the fever nor the acute pain returned, and from that hour*

*I began rapidly to grow stronger. In a few days I was able
to walk half a mile without fatigue. In this sickness I took
no medicine, and had the help of no physician but Jesus.
To him be all the praise and glory. Why should it be thought
a strange thing that he can heal our bodies? It is written of
him, "Himself took our infirmities and bare our sicknesses."
Is it not said of our Lord "Who healeth all thy diseases," as
well as "Who forgiveth all their iniquities?"*[5]

We must believe, however, that if God really stretched forth his
hand to heal in these instances, it was for the furtherance of the
gospel as the chief purpose. Miracles are the signs and not the
substance of Christianity. They are for the confirmation of the
Word, and not merely for the comfort of the body. And this fact
especially enhances the probability that they might not be entirely
wanting in heathen lands.

The blind man must read his Bible by means of raised letters and
through the coarser sense of touch, since he is lacking in eyesight.
And what if to the blind pagans, God should be pleased now and
then to present the gospel embossed in signs and wonders, if
"haply they might feel after him and find him" in this way, when
they could not at first discern him with the spiritual understanding? No more serious objection could be made against this
method than that it is a revival of the primitive.—"And they went
forth, and preached everywhere, the Lord working with them, and
confirming the word with signs following" (Mark 16:20). Not for
the satisfaction of the flesh, but for the glory of God and the
vindication of His truth, does our Lord stretch out His healing
hand and make "bare his holy arm in the eyes of all the nations"
(Isaiah 52:10). If it should be His good pleasure to make use of
those other miracles, the miracles of martyrdom,[6] and to show the
power of His grace in the supernatural endurance of His servants
under suffering, the same end has been reached. Perpetua and
Felicitas, going to a terrible death with a serenity rising into
absolute joy—the declaration of utter insensibility to pain made
before a multitude of witnesses—who has not read of the thrilling

impression thus produced upon the heathen, and of the irresistible impulse thereby given to the truth? These are but miracles of healing seen on their reverse side; the Lord's hand stretched out to rob death of its pain, instead of robbing death of its victim. "That the word of the Lord may have free course, and be glorified" (2 Thessalonians 3:1); whether by my cure or by my patience under suffering—this must be our prayer always. But God be praised that He willeth the health of His people and not their hurt. The priests of Baal seek to prove their god by cutting themselves with knives and lancets. Elijah has just proved his God by calling the widow's dead son to life and delivering him to his mother. How greatly do the idolaters, with their endless worship of self-torture need to be taught this truth: that our God is one that makes alive and not one that killeth.

Would, then, that the heathen could know Christ as the Healer! Who has not said it as he has read of the awful loathsomeness of their sicknesses and the cruel impositions of their doctors. Next to the intolerable tyranny of evil priests is that of the forgers of lies, the physicians of no value (Job 13:4), with which every pagan nation is afflicted. Can we describe or imagine the joy of the heathen's deliverance from the hopeless search for peace of con-science, as he finds Christ, the sin pardoner? "Great Spirit untie the load of our sins. If this load were bound round our shoulders we could untie it for ourselves; but it is bound round our hearts, and we cannot untie it, but thou canst. Lord untie it now." So prayed a poor Fiji Islander.[7] Was not the revelation beyond all price that made known to him the fact that Christ "bare our sins in his own body on the tree" (1 Peter 2:24), and so could instantly lift the load which he had toiled in vain to lift? And what if added to this he could hear and appropriate that other revelation, that Himself "bare our sicknesses" (Matthew 8:17)? If when "the whole head is sick, and the whole heart faint. From the sole of the foot even unto the head there is no soundness in it; but wounds, and bruises, and putrefying sores" (Isaiah 1:5–6); and if, after spending all his living on false physicians, his wounds "have not been closed, neither bound up, neither mollified with ointment" (1:6), he could then know the Savior's healing touch laid upon him, and hear the word "thou art made whole," what glory would he give to our Lord and Redeemer!

Is it unbecoming or presumptuous for us to conjecture what effects would ensue if the gospel were thus to be preached on heathen fields "with signs following"? Sickness is the dark shadow of sin, and nowhere does it lie so heavily as on the pagan nations. If now and then that shadow were seen to be lifted by the Lord's hand, the event could hardly fail to open a wide and effectual door of entrance for the gospel.

God forbid that we should desire or grasp for anything which it is not His pleasure to give. But what if it should seem to us that the Great Commission demands these signs instead of forbidding them? Baptism, that sign of Christ's death and resurrection and of our justification thereby, is in the commission; and what bitter battles have been fought in the Church for its maintenance! And healing the sick, that sign of Christ glorified and alive forevermore, is in the commission just as unequivocally. And yet we are so weak and perplexed and impotent before it. Yes! it is there; but who is sufficient for these things? Who of us would quite dare to repeat on behalf of our missionary brethren, some of whom are laboring among hostile rulers and bloodthirsty tribes, the apostles prayer: "And now, Lord, behold their threatenings: and grant unto thy servants, that with all boldness they may speak thy word, *by stretching forth thine hand to heal*, and that signs and wonders may be done by the name of thy holy child Jesus" (Acts 4:29–30)? If we cannot utter this prayer we may at least join in the petition which a devout commentator breathes over the closing words of Mark's Gospel:

> *Let us cry to the Lord: strengthen and bless thou the hands of thine authenticated messengers: that they may rightly lay them upon men; and that before thy coming again thy promise may be abundantly fulfilled: they shall be healed: it shall be well with them.*[8]

# ENDNOTES

[1] See Alford on Mark 16.

[2] Abp. Tillotson puts forth a similar view. *Works, X.,* p. 230.

[3] *Modern Doubt and Christian Belief,* p. 332.

[4] "But, inasmuch as far later times are full of testimonies to this point, I know not from what motive some persons restrain the gift to the first ages. While I readily grant to such persons that there was a richer abundance of miracles in order that the foundation of so great a structure might, in spite of the world's power, be laid, I cannot with them perceive why we should believe that this promise of Christ has ceased to be in force. Wherefore, if any one preach Christ, as he would have himself preached, to the nations that know him not (for miracles are peculiarly intended for such, I Cor. XIV. 22), I doubt not that the promise will still be found to stand good; for the gifts of God are without repentance (Rom. XI. 29). But we, whenever the fault lies in our own sloth or unbelief, throw the blame on him."—Hugo Grotius. 1583–1645.

[5] Rev. W.E. Boardman, *The Great Physician,* p. 73.

[6] "Martyrdoms I reckon amongst miracles, because they exceed the strength of human nature."—Bacon.

[7] *Journal of Wesleyan Missions.*

[8] Stier's *Words of Jesus.*

# CHAPTER

## 7

---

# *The Testimony of the Adversary*

His testimony ought not to be cited, it will be said, since he is "a liar and the father of it" (John 8:44). But if we bear in mind always who and what he is, his witness may serve a very excellent end. For we must know, unless we are utterly "ignorant of his devices" (2 Corinthians 2:11), that his deceptions are generally counterfeits of divine realities. His business is to resist the Almighty by mimicking His words and His works. Hence his lies are often very serviceable as the negatives from which to reproduce photographs of God's truths. And if we will notice what the adversary is especially busy in bringing forward at any period, we may by contrast infer what vital doctrine or important truth of God is struggling into recognition.

We regard this principle as so unquestionable and so distinctly scriptural, that we are always surprised to see Christian writers betrayed by overlooking it. "If you credit any modern miracles in God's true Church, you must logically concede the genuineness of the alleged miracles of the Romish Church," it is often confidently said. Nay! but have you never read of him "whose coming is after the working of Satan with all power and signs and *lying wonders*" (2 Thessalonians 2:9, 12; also Revelation 16:14, "spirits of devils working miracles"). The working of Antichrist is the counterpart of the working of Christ. Not feeble, transparently false, and contemptible are the miracles of the adversary. "Signs and wonders"" are predicted of him—the same terms as those applied to the works of Christ. And not only that, but "*all*power," is ascribed to him—the same words employed which Christ used at His ascension, when laying claim to universal authority. Without stopping to consider what limitations the language may have in such connection, its use is certainly startling and indicates that the miracles of Antichrist are likely to be powerful and impressive, and fitted to "deceive the very elect" (Matthew 24:24). But it is most illogical to conclude that we must believe in lying wonders, because we believe in real wonders; and that we must credit the miracles of the Apostate Church because we find those which we credit in the true Church. We say "miracles of the Apostate Church." The fathers and the reformers attributed actual miracles to Antichrist,—wonders of a superhuman character, only demoniacal instead of divine, wrought through the agency of evil spirits to simulate the works of the Spirit of God.[1] And this view seems scriptural. In describing the perils of the last days, Paul declares concerning false teachers that "as Jannes and Jambres withstood Moses, so do these also resist the truth" (2 Timothy 3:8). The method of resistance which these magicians offered, it will be remembered, was to reproduce the miracles of God's servants. When Aaron wrought wonders with his rod "they also did in like manner with their enchantments." Miracle was matched by miracle, and wonder by wonder, up to the point where God triumphed by confounding the deceivers.

## Imitation rather than denial

So has it been with the Church of Christ all through her history. Satan has ever been seeking to thwart God by imitation rather than by denial. And we imagine that he has done more for building up his kingdom through the Papal miraclemongers who have claimed divine power than through the infidel miracle-deniers who have disputed it. But there have been nevertheless certain evident tokens of spuriousness attaching to Romish miracles, that have indicated their true character to believers. There is a kind of Egyptian crudeness about them which suggests the art of the sorcerer rather than the touch of God's finger. Alleged healing by contact with the bones of dead saints; pains assuaged by making the sign of the

Cross over the sufferer; recoveries effected by pilgrimages to the shrines of martyrs, and evil spirits exorcised by the crucifix or the image of the virgin! Who does not see the vast contrast in these methods, from the dignified and simple methods of Christ and His apostles?

"God never puts a man upon the stage that Satan does not immediately bring forward an ape," says Godet. He will approach as near the truth as possible, and still keep to his lie. He will give us miracles through his false prophets that seem divine in their end and purpose, but will always be careful to link them to some deadly superstition or fatal heresy.

We emphasize the assertion, therefore, that false miracles are a testimony to the existence somewhere of the true, and that we ought to be very careful lest in our revolt from the caricature, we swing over to a denial of the genuine.[2]

In our own time we have witnessed an extraordinary forth-putting of satanic energy in the works of modern spiritualism. This is a system more versatile in uncleanness, more fertile in blasphemy, and more prolific of adulteries, fleshly and spiritual than any probably that has appeared for many generations. In all its acts and exhibitions, it is so redolent of the foul smoke of Gehenna, that it would seem impossible that any Christian could be deceived by it; yet it has taken thousands of professed disciples of Christ captive, so that they have "gone in the way of Cain, and run greedily after the error of Balaam for reward, and perished in the gainsaying of Core" (Jude 11). Its manifestations are characterized by just those impish, grotesque and fantastic exhibitions, which always distinguish the devil's work from that of Christ. Its rappings and table-tippings and materializations, and communions with the dead,—what evident tokens of perdition these should be to one who has been at all accustomed to discriminate between divine and satanic traits! And yet as a competent writer declares "these things are unblushingly and openly professed and practiced by Christian men in all lands: those who believe them to be really spiritual, affirming that they are wrought by good spirits; and those who disbelieve them to be the work of spirits at all, playing with them in their unbelief." Alas! that such a system should be able to boast of its millions of adherents, and that in those millions, thousands should be found who have borne or still bear the name of Christ. Looking at the matter in the light of Scripture, we know of no more conspicuous sign of the last days and of the "perilous times" therein predicted than this.[3] Now it is well known that one of the loudest pretensions of spiritualism is the claim to effect miraculous healing. It declares that Christ wrought His cures through the agency of spirits and that it can do the same. Hence, the legion of "healing mediums," and the innumerable "lying wonders" by which their assumptions are enforced.

It is very natural that decent Christians in their recoil from such revolting wonderworking, should take the position of stout denial of all miraculous interventions in modern times, and of any supernatural healing. But we believe this to be an unworthy and unfaithful attitude. It is as though Moses and Aaron had retreated in disgust before Jannes and Jambres, instead of pressing on with miracle upon miracle till they had compelled them to surrender to the Lord of Hosts. It is as though Paul had been ashamed of the power of the Spirit that was in him when he met the "damsel possessed with a spirit of divination" (Acts 16:16), and had renounced his miraculous gifts for fear of being identified with soothsayers and necromancers, instead of asserting his power as he did the more mightily, and saying to the evil spirit that possessed her, "I command thee in the name of Jesus Christ to come out of her" (16:18).

To us this outbreak of satanic empiricism[4] would be a strong presumptive proof that somewhere the Lord is reviving among His people the gifts of divine healing. And this constant presentation of the devil's coin would lead us to search diligently for the genuine coin bearing Christ's own image and superscription.

A thoughtful writer on this subject has called attention to the fact that the era of modern spiritualism covers almost exactly the era of the alleged revival of the gifts of healing. The most striking instances of professed miraculous cure in modern times happened, as we have shown elsewhere, about 50 years ago in Scotland and in England. The instances have increased and multiplied since, until today the number of devout, prayerful, evangelical Christians who claim to have been miraculously recovered is very large, and their names are sent up from every nation where the gospel has been preached.

It may be that "the prince of the power of the air, the spirit that now worketh in the children of disobedience" (Ephesians 2:2), seeing God about to put forth His hand again in signs and wonders, and miracles of healing, has determined, as he is wont, to thwart the Lord by caricaturing His work, and bringing it into contempt in the eyes of His own true people. Thus, perhaps, he has thrown himself into the very path which the Almighty is about to enter, so that he may frighten His church from treading it. Or, to state the matter as it seems to us most probable, it may be that the adversary has seized as his most opportune occasion a time when a belief in the supernatural is at its lowest ebb[5] in the church, and when a denial of modern miracles is well nigh universal among the learned, and that in such a period he is putting forth the most signal displays of superhuman power in order to set his evil impress upon those who may be impressed by these things. Thus he is copying the Lord's own method in using miracles as an evidential testimony, only with this end, to establish "the doctrines of devils," and to convert people to the creed of the prince of darkness. But are we to turn against the witness of miracles, because of this attempt to make it perjure itself in the interest of the evil one? Or, to reverse the hypothesis, and suppose that the evil one is the first to enter this field, then comes the question with equal force, whether because of his preoccupancy we should refuse to go into it, if God's Spirit leads the way. If Antichrist is about to make his mightiest and most malignant demonstration, ought not the Church, if the Lord will give her power, to confront him with sweet and gracious and humble displays of the Spirit's saving health? Here we believe Professor Christlieb speaks again with true scriptural wisdom when he says:

*In the last epoch of the consummation of the Church she*

*will again require for the final decisive struggle with the powers of darkness the miraculous interference of her risen Lord; and hence the scriptures lead us to expect miracles once more for this period.*[6]

Meanwhile, let us be careful that the adversary does not cheat us out of our birthright. If he has set his trademark on miracles, and is using them mightily in his traffic with simple souls, let us not make haste therefore to forfeit whatever right and title in them the Lord has bequeathed to us. Let us not abandon our wheat field because the devil has sowed tares in it. The fact that he sows tares, is his testimony to the genuineness of the wheat.

Of course we should expect in the event of the Church's recovery to any extent of her supernatural gifts that the enemy would put forth redoubled energy to baffle and confound her. Before a sleeping church the adversary walks very softly, and modulates his roar to the finest tones, lest he wake her from her slumber. But let her once rise up and take to herself some long disused power and he will quickly manifest himself in his old character of "a roaring lion [walking] about, seeking whom he may devour" (1 Peter 5:8).

Erskine, speaking concerning those texts which so clearly confer miraculous gifts upon the Church, says:

> *I may here remark it, as a striking fact illustrative of the cunning of the prince of darkness, that he has not permitted his instruments to press these texts much, nor to argue from them so triumphantly as they might have done, that the absence of miracles from the Church was a refutation of the Bible. The Bible says, "These signs shall follow them that believe." And yet here is a Church holding this faith and unfollowed by these signs. The ready conclusion from this fact certainly is that the Bible is not true; and we might have expected that this argument would be much used by those who deny the Bible to be a divine revelation. But it has not been much urged; and why? The subtle enemy of man saw that there was more danger to his own kingdom*

*from the use of this weapon than advantage. It might have
led to a result very different from that of disproving the
divine authority of the Bible. There is another conclusion
to which it might have led, and that is a lack of faith in
the Church. And thus the pressing of this argument might
have awakened the Church to a sense of her true condition;
and this Satan fears more than the Bible, knowing that a
church asleep is the most powerful weapon against the
world, much more powerful than any infidel arguments.*[7]

Awake, then, oh Church! Put on thy strength! Awake indeed to
evil surmisings and contempt and opprobrium. For none ever yet
escaped these things in attempting to revive a forgotten truth. But
these may be tokens of the Lord's favor. Certainly they are not the
credentials of a slumbering and world-pleasing church. At all
events, let us fear them less than that other alternative, that the
heathen shall cry "Where is thy God?" and none shall be able to
answer "*Jehovah Rapha is with us.*"

## ENDNOTES

[1] Augustine declares that miracles may emanate "*either from seduc-
ing spirits or from God himself.*" Huss says, "the disciples of
Anti-christ are more distinguished by miracles than those of
Christ, and will be so in days to come."—*Defence of Wickliffe*,
p. 115. Calvin says, "Satan perverts the things which otherwise
are truly works of God and *misemploys miracles to obscure God's
glory.*" Comment on Second Thessalonians 11:9.

[2] "According to all evidence of Scripture there never were spurious
miracles without genuine: there never were those from beneath,
without those from above at the same time. And prophecy
agrees with fact. As tokens of the last day our Lord foretells the
signs and wonders of false Christs and prophets, and Joel
foretells true ones. Thus every counterfeit implies something
counterfeited; and if you prove counterfeit miracles, you only
tell *us to open our eyes the wider and look for the originals.*" Rev.
Thomas Boys, *Proofs of Miraculous Faith and Experience of the*

*Church*, p. 11–12.

[3]"Whenever these things have appeared it was a sign approaching doom. When the Canaanites practised them the measure of their iniquity was full. When Saul applied to the Witch of Endor, his end was near. When these things prevailed among the Jews, their day was closing. Let us not permit such among us lest it should become the sign to us of declension and doom"—Tract, "What Is Mesmerism," London: Bosworth and Harrison.

[4]It is a curious fact that in the New Testament Greek, the term for sorcery is the same as that for drugs. For example, Revelation 22:15: "Without are dogs and sorcerers," [pharmakoi] pharmacists, and Galatians 5:19: "The works of the flesh are adultery, uncleanness, lasciviousness, idolatry, witchcraft," [pharmakeia] pharmacy. And when we think of the legion of medicinemen and medicinewomen who prey upon the sick; the spiritualists and trance-doctors with their prescriptions dictated by the dead, who swarm into the sickrooms of our afflicted humanity, as thick as the frogs of Egypt in the bedchambers of Pharaoh, there seems to be a grim significance in the use of these words.

[5]"When men no longer believe in God they begin to believe in ghosts. In truth there has scarcely ever been an age when men have snatched more greedily after the extravagant than our own which derides the supernatural."—Schenkel. Hear also Carlyle's powerful ridicule of Paris, casting off God and running after mesmerism, "O women! O men! great is our infidel faith!"—*French Revolution*, p. 50.

[6]*Modern Doubt and Christian Belief*, p. 332.

[7]*Brazen Serpent*, p.204.

# CHAPTER

## 8

---

## *The Testimony of Experience*

"Prove me now herewith" is the challenge which the Lord has given in His Word; and there are many in the present generation who have accepted and tested His challenge on the promises of bodily recovery.

We wish in this chapter to consider the experiences and testimony of certain ones, who within our own times have exercised a ministry of healing. Let us not be misunderstood. We do not attribute to any man the power of curing sickness, though we think many are called to be instruments to that end. A physician is a mediator between nature and our suffering humanity. And his skill depends solely upon his ability to interpret and apply the laws of health to the sick, and to bring the sufferer into contact with the recuperative forces of the natural world. In like manner, if the primitive "gifts of healing" are still bestowed in the Church, as we believe, those endowed with them have power only through the mediation of their faith and prayers. We are told that Paul entered into the house of Publius, and, finding his father sick, "prayed, and laid his hands on him, and *healed* him" (Acts 28:8). But we do not understand from this that the apostle had any inherent personal power to heal disease; else why did he pray?

Prayer is touching the hem of Christ's garment by the human intercessor, while in the laying on of hands he at the same moment touches the body of the sufferer. It is simply, in a word, the repetition of what was done again and again during the earthly ministry of our Lord, the bringing of the sick to Jesus for healing and cleansing. "Why look ye so earnestly on us, *as though by our own power or holiness* we had made this man to walk?" (3:12) asks Peter of those who were wondering at the miracle at the Beautiful Gate. If it were a question of human power or holiness we might be quite ready to relegate the gifts of healing to the apostolic age, confessing our utter lack of these qualifications. But since it is a question of the power and holiness of "Jesus Christ, the same yesterday, today, and forever," it is quite another matter. "*If thou canst believe*" is the question now. "A year famous for believing," is the language in which Romaine designated a certain unusual year of his ministry. If such a year should be graciously injected into the calendar of any Christian life, it would be a year of success. For believing is knowing God and finding the depths of power and privilege that are hidden for us in Him: and "the people that do know their God shall be strong, and do exploits" (Daniel 11:32) says the Scripture.

Now, there have been some in our day who have had faith to take the Lord at His Word in connection with the promises of healing. And having, as they believed, proved Him and found Him faithful, their testimony will be deeply instructive to our readers.

## Dorothea Trudel

Dorothea Trudel is a name especially honored in this relation. The story of her life and labors in connection with the home for invalids in the Swiss village of Mannedorf on Lake Zurich has been very widely read, and has caused great searchings of heart in many who have pondered it.[1] The Lord provides deep roots when there are to be wide-spreading branches. And this life, whose boughs so ran over the wall and stretched beyond the bounds of ordinary service, was unusually rooted and established.

The mother from whom she received her birth and early training was so remarkable for her faith and consecration that, though living in the utmost obscurity and poverty, her biography has been placed among those of the illustrious Christian women of the ages.[2] The wife of a brutal and godless husband, and so cut off from human sympathy that there was none but God to whom she could appeal in her need, she was schooled by this bitter tuition into a life of faith and absolute dependence on God. She looked to Him for food for her family when they must otherwise have starved; for deliverance when they must otherwise have perished; for healing when they must otherwise have died. Dorothea grew up with perpetual exhibitions before her eyes of the Lord's restoring of the sick for the poor household which could employ no other physician. The faith which it is so difficult for us to recover was her native inheritance. Hence, what we doubt so painfully whether we may do, she bitterly condemned herself for not doing when she had subsequently neglected it.

After her parents had died, we find her engaged in labors of love among the working people; teaching them the gospel, and seeking to lead them to the Savior. How her personal use of the prayer of faith, begun in connection with these labors, she tells in the following words:

> Four of them fell ill, and, as each could do as he pleased, all four summoned a doctor. It was remarked, however, that they got worse after taking the medicine, until, at last, the necessity became so pressing that I went as a worm to the Lord, and laid our distress before him. I told him how willingly I would send for an elder, as is commanded in James v., but, as there was not one, I must go to my sick ones in the faith of the Canaanitish woman, and, without trusting to any virtue in my hand, I would lay it upon them. I did so, and, by the Lord's blessing, all four recovered. Most powerfully then did the sin of disobeying God's word strike me, and most vividly did the simple life of faith, the carrying out just what God orders, stand before me.

Soon after she gave herself wholly to the Master's work; and as the effects of her evangelistic efforts, and the answers to her earnest prayers were noticed, she was importuned to receive patients into her house. Consenting reluctantly, the life-work thus began, from which was to flow such a blessing to the souls and bodies of men.

Her methods were very simple: the Bible and prayer were her medicines. She dealt with the soul first, using every effort to bring it to faith and obedience to the gospel; she prayed for the body, laying hands on the sick and anointing them with oil in the name of the Lord. In all this she recognized the necessity of the most absolute consecration on her part and that of her helpers, and of the most surrendering faith on the part of the sick. Very beautifully does she thus speak of the believer's privilege:

> *In the New Testament we are called kings, and priests. Power accompanied the anointing of the kings, and if we really belong to the kingly priesthood shall not strength to heal the sick by prayer come on us also through the anointing of the Spirit? If we only wear our Levite dress, and are consecrated in soul and body—if we are only prepared to be vessels of his grace—it is his part to bless. Oh, that we were willing not to do more than God would have us do, then would this day be one of great reviving to us!*

Thus, her work was inaugurated, and thus was she inducted by unseen hands into her remarkable ministry.

Rarely have we traced the story of a life whose consecration was so even and unreserved. Among the sayings which she left on record is this: "The heart ought not to be an inn where the Lord sometimes comes, but a home where he always abides." It was her calling for many years to keep an inn where the sick could lodge, a hospice into which the suffering and distracted wanderer could turn for solace. These came and went with the recurring months, but so constantly was the Lord abiding with her, that it might be said, according to Luther's beautiful simile, that the wayfarer coming and knocking at her heart and asking "who lives here?" would hear the instant answer from within, "Jesus Christ." Not that she ever claimed as much, for none was ever more humble and self depreciatory, but her life declared it. It comes out in her biography that her prayers were sometimes prolonged into midnight: that her soul so wrought with intense desire that often the sweat would stand in beads upon her forehead. Once in busy labors among the sick, she passed the whole day without food, utterly forgetting the claims of nature in her absorbing devotion to her work; and then finding it impossible to get food on account of the lateness of the hour she fell at Jesus' feet, and begged for that meat that the world knows not of, and was so refreshed and filled that she went all night in the strength of it.

Such rare and Christlike consecration has always proved an apt soil for the manifestation of the miraculous; especially when chastened and fertilized by bitter persecutions. And this token which the Scripture promises to "all who will live godly in Christ Jesus" was not wanting to her, as the spirit to endure it with unresenting meekness was not wanting. "I have had enemies," she writes, "both known and unknown in crowds; and thickly scattered falsehoods and slanders were no pleasant portion. I write this with the feeling that whoever cannot bear, without emotion, even the blackest falsehoods and slanders has yet to experience something of the peace of God which is like an ocean without bounds." Medical men and others conceived great hostility to her, and sought to convict her of malpractice in the courts; though it was shown in testimony that most of her patients were such as had spent all their living upon physicians only to be made worse; and that the only medicine she employed was prayer. Speaking of this adversity she says:

> But a storm was now to burst over the work; for in 1856 when the second house was filled with invalids, and the Lord was working mightily we were fined sixty francs, and were ordered to send away all the patients by a certain time. Though it was the most grievous day of my life I obeyed the command; but the houses so hastily emptied, filled as fast as ever with the blind, the lame, and the deaf, for whom the Lord did great things. Evil spirits were cast out of some of the invalids by prayer, and the sufferer became instantly free. Many were delivered from the power of darkness which had been exercised over their minds, though less visibly and

*outwardly and received what we consider the highest and best blessing, that of being changed from wolves into lambs.*

In 1861 a second persecution was raised against this most saintly and inoffensive woman. At the instigation of a physician, the magistrates imposed a heavy fine upon her, and ordered her patients to be sent away. Then, through appeal to a higher tribunal, her case was brought into court, and the world was made acquainted through the testimony of scores of living witnesses, with the wonderful work which God had wrought through her prayers.

Mr. Spondlin an eminent advocate of Zurich volunteered to conduct her case; Prelate Von Kopff, Prof. Tholuck and many others were witnesses on her behalf and the result was that she was fully acquitted and left undisturbed in her gracious work. Henceforth, her house which had too often through the malice of enemies been a *Bethaven* "house of affliction," became only a *Bethesda* "house of mercy." If her own simple record, confirmed by the word of scores who bore testimony at her trial, could prove that miracles of healing were wrought in her house, the fact must be considered as established.

With a deep conviction that sin is often the hidden root of sickness, she dealt most earnestly with the souls of her patients. "Confess your faults one to another, and pray one for another, *that ye may be healed*" (James 5:16), was an injunction that had a deeply practical meaning to her, and often conviction and conversion were the first symptoms of physical convalescence.

*On one occasion a young artisan arrived, in whom cancer had made such progress as to render any approach to him almost unbearable. At the Bible lessons this once frivolous man, now an earnest inquirer, learned where the improvement must begin; and from the day that he confessed his sins against God and man, the disease abated. Some time afterwards he acknowledged one sin he had hitherto concealed, and then he speedily recovered his bodily health and returned to his home cured in spirit also.*

In some instances her prayers and her eager seeking for the will of God were long continued before any sign of recovery was manifested, in others, healing was vouchsafed at once.

> *A lady in S. had so injured her knee by a fall, that for weeks she lay in the greatest agony. The doctor declared that dropsy would supervene, but the heavenly physician ful-filled those promises which will abide until the end of the world, and by prayer and the laying on of Dorothea's hands, the knee was cured in twenty-four hours, and the swelling vanished.*

One giving an account of her arraignment says:

> *During the course of the trial, authenticated cures were brought forward, it is said, to the number of some hundreds. There was one of a stiff knee, that had been treated in vain by the best physicians in France, Germany, and Switzer-land; and one of an elderly man who could not walk, and had also been given up by his physicians, but who soon dispensed with his crutches; a man came with a burned foot, and the surgeons said it was a case for "either amputa-tion or death," and he also was cured; one of the leading physicians of Wurtemburg testified to the cure of a hopeless patient of his own; another remained six weeks, and says he saw all kinds of sicknesses healed. Cancer and fever have been treated with success; epilepsy and insanity more fre-quently than any other forms of disease.*

Such was the ministry of healing and comfort carried on by this holy woman till the day when she fell asleep in Jesus, and such was the blessed example which she left behind her.

Travelers tell us of a deep and secluded lake in Switzerland in whose crystal mirror the reflection of distant mountains may be seen, though the mountains themselves are not visible to the eye. In the tranquil, hidden life of this Swiss peasant girl, the image of the invisible Savior was clearly mirrored, and how many of those who knew her in life, and of those who have read the story of her consecration since her death have therefrom caught a reflected glimpse of the unseen Redeemer, and been quickened with new love to Him, and a new sense of His present power.

## Samuel Zeller

Samuel Zeller took up the work at Mannedorf as it dropped from the dead hands of sister Dorothea. He is the son of the founder of a well-known boys' reformatory at Beuggen, near Basle, and brother-in-law of Gobat, late bishop at Jerusalem. He had been a co-laborer at the home before the death of its founder, and with much prayer that the gifts of faith and of healing might rest upon him, she had committed the work to his care. Since her death the institution has continued with no apparent loss of power or usefulness under his direction, he being aided by Miss Zeller, his sister, and by several devoted assistants. All the helpers, even to the servants, render their service as a labor of love, in grateful return, in most cases, for the recovery which they have received at this home.

Mr. Zeller is a fervent evangelist, going out in every direction preaching the word, as well as laboring "in season out of season" for the souls and bodies of those who come under his care. From two houses the home has grown to 10, and they are always filled with patients, from many nations. The same methods are employed as under his predecessor. He lays hands upon the sick; he anoints with oil in the name of the Lord, and pleads the promise given in James; and his reports published year by year are full of striking instances alike of healing and of conversion.

He entertains no extravagant views of his mission. Holding most tenaciously to the perpetuity of the promise: "*The prayer of faith shall save the sick*" (James 5:15), he yet strongly recognizes the sovereignty of God in the answer. To the question asked by a recent visitor, whether it is not God's will that all His children should be free from sickness, he replied that it is evidently the Father's will that some should overcome sickness, and he quoted significantly the words of Hebrews:

> *[Some] through faith subdued kingdoms, wrought*
> *righteousness, obtained promises, stopped the mouths of*
> *lions, quenched the violence of fire, escaped the edge of the*
> *sword, out of weakness were made strong, waxed valiant*
> *in fight, turned to flight the armies of the aliens. Women*
> *received their dead raised to life again: and others were*
> *tortured, not accepting deliverance; that they might obtain*
> *a better resurrection: And others had trial of cruel mockings*
> *and scourgings, yea, moreover of bonds and imprisonment:*
> *They were stoned, they were sawn asunder, were tempted,*
> *were slain with the sword: they wandered about in*
> *sheepskins and goatskins; being destitute, afflicted, tor-*
> *mented; (Of whom the world was not worthy:) they*
> *wandered in deserts, and in mountains, and in dens and*
> *caves of the earth. And these all, having obtained a good*
> *report through faith . . . (11:33–39)*

A visit to this home was made a few years later by several eminent German preachers and professors, and when one of these was asked his opinion of the work he answered, "Where the Holy Spirit speaks with so much power, we can do no other wise than listen to His teaching; critical analysis is out of the question." A quiet and deep spiritual life, a profound faith in the promises of God, and a humble and self-denying surrender to His Word and will are the traits which have characterized the work from the beginning until the present time. The cases of recovery at Mannedorf are so fully given in the report of the home that we need not here reproduce them.

## Pastor Blumhardt

Pastor Blumhardt exercising his ministry in the small Lutheran village of Mottlingen, in the heart of the Black Forest in Germany is another who was greatly honored of God in his prayers of faith. He died quite recently, but during many years of his active pastorate he was credited with extraordinary grace in praying for the sick. Like others of whom we have spoken, he had the ministry of healing thrust upon him.

He first became known for his unusual consecration, and for his zeal and ability in stirring up formal Christians to renewed activity. He prayed for the diseased with such efficacy, and such well-attested cures were reported from his intercessions, that very soon he was resorted to by the suffering from every direction. His home and neighborhood became a hospital, where not only invalids, but sorrowing and sin-sick souls came for counsel and help.

One writing of him says, "as regards Blumhardt and his work, it may emphatically be said that the pleasure of the Lord prospered in his hands." He seems to have taken no pains to report his success, having evidently learned the secret that "the way to have a strong faith is to think nothing of yourself." But others praised him, if not his own lips, and he became widely known throughout his country as a pastor who considered the sick bodies of his flock to be under his ministration as well as the sick souls.

We give one instance from the life of Blumhardt, to show the vast influence which a striking exhibition of miraculous power may exert upon the spiritual life of a people.

On commencing his ministry in Mottlingen he found the place fearfully given over to infidelity and sensuality. As his fervent preaching began to tell upon the community, Satan seemed to come in, with great wrath to resist him. A case occurred in the village which exactly resembled the instances of demoniacal possession recorded in Scripture. The woman thus afflicted endured the most excruciating agony. The pastor being called in was quite appalled, having never seen anything of the kind; and in his perplexity he was inclined to be excused from interfering with it. But some of his brethren in the church who had listened to his strong utterances on the subject of the prayer of faith, came to him saying, "If you do not wish to shake our belief in your preaching you cannot retreat before the evil one." After a moment's thought, and silent prayer he answered: "You are right; but to be in accord with the word of God you must also unite with me in supplication according to James v: 14." What followed appears from the following account by his friend Pastor Spittler. He says:

>Kindly permit me not to mention in this place the frightful details of her sufferings. The medical man who attended the person was perfectly at a loss as to the case. He said, "Is there no clergyman in this village who can pray? I can do nothing here." The minister (Blumhardt) who had then the spiritual care of the village felt the force of such a reproach, joined as it was to that of his believing people. He went to the house in the strength of faith. The more frightful the manifestations of the destroying power of Satan became, with the more unshaken faith in the all-overcoming power of the living God, that pastor continued to struggle against the assaults of the infernal powers, till at last, after a tremendous outcry of the words, "Jesus is Victor! Jesus is Victor!" heard almost throughout the whole little village, the person found herself freed from all the dreadful chains under which she had sighed so long, and often come to the very brink of death.
>
>That voice, "Jesus is Victor!" sounded like a trumpet of God through the village. After a week one man of very loose and deceitful character, whom the pastor on that account felt almost afraid of approaching, came trembling and pale to Blumhardt into his study, and said, "Sir, is it then possible that I can be pardoned and saved? I have not slept for a whole week, and if my heart be not eased, it will kill me." He made an astonishing confession of iniquity, which for the first time opened the pastor's eyes to the multitude and enormity of sins prevailing among the people. The pastor prayed with him and put Christ before him, in his readiness to pardon even the vilest of sinners that would come to him for mercy. When the man seemed completely cast down and almost in despair, Blumhardt found it his duty, as an ambassador of Christ, solemnly to assure him of God's mercy in Jesus Christ; and lo! immediately his

*countenance was changed, beaming with joy and gratitude.*

*The first thing which the man now did was to go to his fellow-sinners, from cottage to cottage, and tell them what he had just experienced. First they were astonished, and could not understand it; yet they saw the marvellous change in him. He urged them to go to the minister about their souls; some he even dragged as it were in triumph to the manse, till about twenty persons were in the same way convinced of sin, and found grace and forgiveness in Jesus.*[3]

Then follows the account of a most gracious and wide-spread revival. The whole village became a Bochim. With tears and lamentations the people came confessing their sins, and inquiring the way of escape from the wrath of God that was resting upon them. The Pastor's house was besieged from morning to night with penitents, so that within two months, as he declared, there were not 20 persons in the place who had not come to him bewailing their sins and finding peace in Jesus Christ.

The transformation which resulted was hardly less wonderful than that which occurred in Kidderminster under the preaching of Richard Baxter. The story gives a most striking indication of what might result even now, under the preaching of the gospel "with signs following."

"The soul is the life of the body; faith is the life of the soul; Christ is the life of faith"—so wrote the good John Flavel; and thus he traced very obviously and directly the course through which Christ the Redeemer acts upon the human body.

## Otto Stockmayer

Pastor Otto Stockmayer might be fitly named, the theologian of the doctrine of healing by faith. He has given some very subtle, not to say bold and startling expositions of the relation of sin and sickness. "The soul is the life of the body" and the Lord does not intend that His saving and sanctifying ministry shall stop with the regeneration and renewal of the soul is Stockmayer's strongly asserted doctrine. Attaching great weight to the words of Scripture which declare that Christ "healed all that were sick: That it might be fulfilled which was spoken by Esaias the prophet, saying, Himself took our infirmities, and *bare our sicknesses*" (Matthew 8:16b–17), he reasons that if our Redeemer bore our sicknesses it is not His will that His children should remain under the power of disease, any more than that having borne our sins it is His will that they should remain under condemnation and disobedience. He says:

> *Once understanding that it is not the will of God that his children should be sick (James v: 14-18), and that Christ has redeemed us from our sickness as from our sins, (Matt. viii: 16, 17), we can no longer look upon healing as a right which it would be lawful for us to renounce. It is no longer a question whether we wish to be healed, God's will must be fulfilled in our bodies as well as in our souls. Our beloved Lord must not be robbed of a part of the heritage of his agony.*
>
> *It is by virtue of a divine will that the offering of the body of Jesus Christ has sanctified us (Heb. x:10), which means that Christ by his death has withdrawn the members of our body, with our entire being, from every sacrilegious end or use. He has regained and consecrated them for his own exclusive and direct use.*
>
> *Wrested by Christ's ransom from all foreign power, from the power of sin or of sickness or of the devil, our members must remain intact, surrendered to him who has redeemed them.*
>
> *"Let my people go" was God's word to Pharaoh, and such is God's command to sin and sickness, and to Satan: "Let my people go that they may serve me." Thus God's children must not seek the healing of the body without taking at the same time by faith, all the new position which Christ's redemption gives us—and which is expressed in these words of Moses to Pharaoh: or better still in Paul's words (2 Cor. v: 14, 15), which amounts to this—Nothing more for self,*

*but all for Christ. Before seeking freedom from sickness we
must lay hold of the moral freedom which the Redemption
of Christ has obtained for us, and by which we are cut off
from any self-seeking: from the seeking of our own will, our
own life, our own interests, or our own glory. Our members
are henceforth Christ's, and neither for ourselves or for our
members, but for Christ and for his members we desire
health. We knew none other but Christ.*

This, in brief, is the doctrine of Pastor Stockmayer as set forth
in a tract entitled "Sickness and the Gospel,"[4] which has passed
through many editions and been very widely read. As the minister
of a Christian flock, his practice has conformed to his teaching.
He has used the same methods as those employed at Mannedorf;
and he has now a home in Hauptwiel Thurgan, Switzerland for
the reception of such as desire to be healed through prayer.

### Pastor Rein

Pastor Rein is another of the same group of primitive teachers
and ministers. He was greatly esteemed while living, and it is only
a few years since he fell asleep. He began his service in the gospel
as a decided formalist. But shutting himself up to the Bible and
determining to shape his ministry rigidly by its teachings without
regard to tradition, a great change came over him. He now
abandoned the habit of reading prayers at the bedside of the sick,
and began to pour out petitions directly from the heart. Later he
felt constrained to use the practice of laying hands on them while
praying, according to the word of the Lord in Mark 16. Still later
he began to anoint with oil in the name of the Lord in connection
with his praying for the sick, carrying out strictly the directions
given in the Epistle of James. His ministry seems to have been as
conspicuous for its humility as for its zeal and consecration; and
diligent care for the welfare of others so marked his course, that he
may be said to have illustrated the maxim that "true humility
consists not so much in thinking meanly of ourselves as *in not
thinking of ourselves at all.*"

From a very tender tribute to his life which recently appeared we make the following extract:[5]

> When sick people were brought to him he received them as sent by the Lord. Much blessing and consolation was found in the silence and retirement of the simple cure of Pastor Rein. He loved to work for the kingdom of God in self-renunciation, and always in silence, without show, and he always shrank from being spoken of. Oh how blessed it is when the word of God accompanied with prayer is used as the medicine of the body as well as soul.
>
> Rein never employed a doctor, believing in the words of Exodus xv: 26. "I am the Lord that healeth thee," or as it is in many translations "I am the Lord thy physician." When he was ill the elders of his Church or his friends laid hands on him, and prayed over him, and he was always better than if he had taken medicine; he was kept in a greater calm, and his communion with God was not interrupted by the doctors' visits, and by the continual occupation of punctually following their directions. He lived in such intimate relation with God that he asked him for all he wanted, the greatest and the least things alike. This was why he could not except even healing, and he shrunk from seeking any help but that which came directly from God.
>
> He was jealous for God that he alone should have the glory. That which grieved him deeply was to see how little glory is given to God in general, and especially in the cure of illness, which is attributed generally to doctors or to medicine. Thus he would not allow any remedy to come between him and his God, and he rejoiced with all his heart when he saw others leave the old track of this world's laws of prudence, to follow the path of an obedient and un-reserved faith.
>
> When he prayed over and laid hands on the sick he watched attentively for a knowledge of God's will regarding

*the person whom he was occupied with, and always be-sought him to reveal to him, whether the sickness was unto death, or whether it was rather a merciful visitation, sent to lead the subject of it to reflection; and he prayed accord-ingly.*

*This confidence in God, which made him renounce all human means in illness, caused him to be much criticised. But we must say to his honor, that Rein was extremely charitable towards others, never seeking to put a yoke upon them or to lay down the law to them, in that which he looked upon as a permission, a precious grace from on high.*

*He never regarded it as a sin in any one to take medicine, or to consult a doctor, when they had not the special faith to do without them; a faith which very precious as it is, is not necessary for salvation. Who can find fault with such as declare, like Rein, that they cannot do otherwise than commit themselves solely to God in all things, even for bodily health, and that they esteem as happy those who can do the same.*

*He was actuated by a holy jealousy, when he heard the signs which should follow them that believe, (Mark xvi: 17, 18), spoken of as belonging only to Apostolic times, instead of its being recognized, that it is owing to the decline of faith that these signs no longer exist. It has been said that "Faith is God's power placed at man's disposition." So he believed, and on this principle he acted.*

Several interesting incidents of recovery under his prayers are given in connection with this sketch of his life, but they are of the same type as those elsewhere recorded, and we will not reproduce them.

Among other evangelists and pastors abroad, who hold the same faith and practice as these we may mention Lord Radstock of England. A very devoted and deeply spiritual man he is known to be by all who have come in contact with him. And many who have never seen him have read with interest of his evangelistic work among the higher ranks especially in Russia and Sweden. Writing to the London "Christian" concerning his work in the latter country, he sends reports of several very striking instances of cure in answer to prayer and says:

> *One interesting feature of the Lord's grace in Stockholm is the obedience of faith with which several pastors and elder brethren have accepted their privilege of anointing the sick and praying over them in the name of the Lord. There have been many remarkable instances of God's gracious healing. I enclose details of a few cases, that God's children may be encouraged to see that God has not withdrawn the promise in James v: 15, and that it is better to trust in the Lord than to put confidence in man.*

In America there are several homes for healing conducted on the same principle as that of Miss Trudel. Quite a number of them are under the direction of pious women, who have learned the secret of the prayer of faith. We have only space to refer to one work which is most widely known through its published reports, and of which, from his near neighborhood to it, the writer has had an excellent opportunity to judge.

## Dr. Charles Cullis

Dr. Charles Cullis is at the head of what is known as the "Faith-work" in the city of Boston. The work has many branches, the Consumptive's Home; the Willard Tract Repository; homes for children; city mission work; foreign missionary work; schools among the freedmen, etc., all maintained upon the same principle virtually as the orphan work of Pastor George Muller, at Bristol in England. Anyone who has been made acquainted with a single department of this enterprise, as for example, that of the Consumptive's Home, can have no doubt as to the most beneficent and Christlike character of the labors there carried on.

Dr. Cullis has for several years been accustomed when applied to, to minister to the sick in the manner above described. And there are among us many unimpeachable witnesses to the answers which have been granted for the recovery from disease. The writer is well acquainted with quite a number of these, some of several years' standing, and has no hesitation in saying that they bear every evidence of genuineness. How Dr. Cullis was led to exercise this ministry is best told in his own words which we extract from his published report called "Faith Cures."

> *For several years my mind had been exercised before God as to whether it was not his will that the work of faith in which he had placed me, should extend to the cure of disease, as well as the alleviation of the miseries of the afflicted. I often read the instructions and promise contained in the fourteenth and fifteenth verses of the fifth chapter of the epistle of James.*
>
> *They seemed so very plain, that I often asked of my own heart, why, if I can rely on God's word, "whatsoever ye shall ask in my name, that will I do," and every day verify its truth in the supply of the daily needs of the various work committed to my care,—why can not I also trust him to fulfil his promises as to the healing of the body. "The prayer of faith shall save the sick, and the Lord shall raise him up?" I could not see why with such explicit and unmistakable promises, I should limit the present exercise of God's power. I began to inquire of earnest Christians whether they knew of any instances of answer to prayer for the healing of the body. Soon afterwards the "Life of Dorothea Trudel" fell into my hands, which strengthened my convictions, and the inquiry arose, "if God can perform such wonders in Mannedorf, why not in Boston?"*
>
> *At this time I had under my professional care a Christian lady, with a tumor which confined her almost continuously to her bed in severe suffering. All remedies were unavailing, and the only human hope was the knife: but feeling in my heart the power of the promise, I one morning sat down by her bedside, and taking up the Bible, I read aloud God's*

*promise to his believing children; "and the prayer of faith*
*shall save the sick, and the Lord shall raise him up; and if*
*he have committed sins, they shall be forgiven him."*

*I then asked her if she would trust the Lord to remove*
*this tumor and restore her to health, and to her missionary*
*work. She replied "I have no particular faith about it, but*
*am willing to trust the Lord for it."*

*I then knelt and anointed her with oil in the name of the*
*Lord, asking him to fulfil his own word. Soon after I left,*
*she got up and walked three miles. From that time the*
*tumor rapidly lessened, until all trace of it at length*
*disappeared.*

The work thus begun has gone on now, for quite a number of
years, and we think there can be no reasonable doubt that in
Boston as well as in Mannedorf and in Mottlingen there has been
a living and repeated demonstration that God is still pleased to
recover the sick directly and manifestly in answer to His people's
intercessions.

If these things be so, can any say that we have not reason to praise
God and rejoice with new joy in Him:

*Who forgiveth all thine iniquities,*
*Who healeth all thy diseases?*

"Any explanation but the admission of the miraculous" is the
cry which an unbelieving world raises when anything wonderful
happens. And Christians more solicitous for their caution than for
their faith, have sometimes joined in the cry. And thus the seal of
the supernatural has been assiduously withheld we fear, where it
should have been permitted to place its impress and testimony.
But we do not, so much call attention to these instances of healing
as to these examples of faith. There may be mistakes in the
estimates put upon the cures, but can there be any in the sure word
of promise? If any of these testimonies of recovery should prove
ill-founded, it would only demonstrate the ignorance of men. But

God hath in the last days spoken to us by His Son and "he that hath received his testimony *hath set to his seal that God is true"* (John 3:33).

## ENDNOTES

[1]Dorothea Trudel or *The Prayer of Faith*, (London: Morgan and Scott).

[2]*Consecrated Women,* (London: Hodder and Stroughton).

[3]*Pastor Blumhardt and His Work*, (London: Morgan and Scott).

[4]Partridge and Co., London.

[5]See *Israel's Watchman*, August 1878.

# CHAPTER

## 9

---

# *The Testimony of the Healed*

"One thing I know, that, whereas I was blind, I now see" (John 9:25). This confession of experience has always been regarded as the strongest that can be made. The "I know" indeed may seem to savor of egotism and assurance. But let us not forget that while the egotism of opinion is always offensive, the egotism of experience can never be rebuked. It is the highest attainment of mere human thought and speculation to know that one does not know. Hence, very fittingly we have the culture of our age graduating in agnosticism, which is knowledge culminating in ignorance, as the highest mountain peaks are lost in the clouds. On the other hand, when we read the opening words of John's first epistle, "That which was from the beginning, which we have heard, which we have seen with our eyes, which we have looked upon, and our hands have handled, of the Word of life" (1 John 1:1), we are not surprised at the writer's constant use of the words "we know," or that he is able to say "*Hereby we do know that we know him*" (2:3).

Experience is the surest touchstone of truth. It is not always infallible, indeed; especially when it deals with our spiritual states and conditions. For these are often deceptive and difficult to interpret. But certainly one ought to know when an infirmity which has long oppressed the body has been removed, or when a pain that has incessantly tortured the nerves has ceased. This is a kind of testimony which is not easily ruled out of court.

And there are many who stand ready to give in this witness. Ought we to refuse to hear it, or to dismiss it as visionary and idle talk? We are quite accustomed to accept what we call a religious experience as a test of fitness for church membership. Is it less difficult to recognize and interpret a physical experience?

## Miss Fancourt

Let us listen to the statements of some who have told the story of their bodily healing. We cite as our first example that of Miss Fancourt, of London, the daughter of an English clergyman, whose case created no small interest at the time of its publication.

The story of her sickness is too long to be given in detail. Suffice it to say that she was attacked with severe hip disease in November 1822. From this date until 1828 she was a constant sufferer, not only from the disease itself, but from the varied operations of leeches, blisters, bleedings and cuttings of the surgeon's knife, and all to no effect. From this period onward for two years she was a helpless cripple, for most of the time confined to her bed. The story of her recovery we give in her own words:

> *Thus it continued till the 20th of October, 1830, when a kind friend who had seen me about two months before had been led by God to pray earnestly for my recovery, remembering what is written, "Whatsoever ye shall ask in prayer, believing, ye shall receive." He asked in faith, and God graciously answered his prayer. On Wednesday night, my friend being about to leave the room, Mr. J. begged to be excused a short time. Sitting near me, we talked of his relations and of the death of his brother; rising, he said: "they will expect me at supper," and put out his hand. After asking some questions respecting the disease, he added, "it is melancholy to see a person so constantly confined." I answered "it is sent in mercy." "Do you think so? Do you not think the same mercy could restore you?" God gave me faith and I answered "yes." "Do you believe Jesus could heal, as in old times?" "Yes." "Do you believe it is only unbelief that prevents it?" "Yes." "Do you believe that Jesus could heal you at this very time?" "Yes."—Between these questions*

*he was evidently engaged in prayer.—"Then" he added,
"rise up and walk; come down to your family." He then
had hold of my hand; he prayed to God to glorify the name
of Jesus. I rose from my couch quite strong. God took away
all my pains, and we walked down stairs, Mr. J. praying
most fervently, "Lord have mercy upon us; Christ have
mercy on us." Having been down a short time, finding my
handkerchief left on the couch, taking the candle I fetched
it. The next day I walked more than a quarter of a mile;
and on Sunday from the Episcopalian chapel, a distance of
one mile and a quarter. Up to this time God continues to
strengthen me, and I am perfectly well. To Jesus be all the
glory. Nov. 13, 1830.*[1]

We have the added information that this long suffering invalid
continued to be well, and that the story of her healing, so soon as
it went abroad, drew down upon her and her family a most violent
storm of ridicule and obloquy. By the religious press which took
up the matter the story was treated as a gross scandal upon the
Christian faith, and so bitter were the reflections upon the parties
involved that the venerable father of the lady, though hitherto a
confessed disbeliever in modern miracles, felt called upon to
publish his emphatic confirmation of the story. The following is
the statement of Rev. Mr. Fancourt:

*Under this peculiar dispensation of mercy there rests on
my mind a solemn conviction that the glory of God and the
interest of religion are deeply involved in the publicity
which it will probably acquire. But without shrinking from
the responsibility attached to the declaration, I profess
myself ready to bear my open testimony to a notable fact,
namely; that as I view it God has raised an impotent
cripple, in the person of my youngest daughter, to instantaneous soundness of her bodily limbs by faith in the name
of Jesus, being taught by her mother church to know and
feel that there is none other name under heaven given to*

*man in whom and through whom she could receive health and salvation, but only the name of our Lord Jesus Christ. In this faith, through the instrumentality of the effectual fervent prayer of a righteous man (for God heareth not sinners), which availeth much, God has done exceeding abundantly above all that we could ask or think. I am aware that there are questions of difficult solution as to the instrumentality by which the benefit has been bestowed; but who would not tremble at the fearful conclusion which would result from a denial of the divine interposition? Deprecating such a thought, I feel persuaded that they are most on the side of truth and soberness who unite with us in telling the church that God hath done great things for us, whereof we are glad, which in their first communication made us like them that dream.*

We cannot help pausing upon the lesson suggested by this incident. Strange, it might be said, that the sufferer should be grudged her release from pain and helplessness. If a supernatural cure could not be admitted, it would seem that at least none would envy her the harmless illusion. Yet has it not been so from the beginning? "We must admit any solution rather than a miracle," said the "Christian Observer," commenting on this cure. And we remember that the wise Jews said about the healing of another cripple, "that indeed a notable miracle hath been done by them is manifest to all them that dwell in Jerusalem; and we *cannot deny it*" (Acts 4:16), as if to say "we have done our best to disprove it." Evidently our Lord anticipated this treatment of miracles of healing when He introduced them, for He said, "Go and show John again those things which ye do hear and see: The blind receive their sight, and the lame walk, the lepers are cleansed, and the deaf hear, the dead are raised up, and the poor have the gospel preached to them. And blessed is he, whosoever shall not be offended in me" (Matthew 11:4–6). The last thing, it would seem, at which the world should take offence: that the prison doors should be opened, and light and sound be let in upon poor immured and darkened souls; that lame feet wearily dragged by bodies which they were made to bear up should be rendered whole and elastic by the Healer's touch; that lepers should be released from their ghastly malady, and the dead be given back to their friends,—are these events that should give offense?

Alas! at what antipodes man's anger often stands to Christ's. The rulers of the synagogue "answered with indignation" (Luke 13:14) because on the Sabbath day the Lord had healed a suffering woman whom Satan had bound for 18 years.

We hear of the mighty indignation of Christ. At the tomb of Lazarus, Jesus was "indignant in spirit," for so they tell us the words mean (John 11:33). He saw the masterpiece of the devil, whose works He had come to destroy, spread out before Him—death and the tears, the anguish and the groans that follow in death's train; and His soul was stirred to holy wrath within Him. Do we well to be angry at the suggestion that even now the Lord of life may snatch from sickness, death's forerunner, those upon whom He has laid His hand?

## Rev. Morgan Edwards

We give the following instance which we find recorded and strongly indorsed by an eminent Baptist minister of the last century, Rev. Morgan Edwards, of New Jersey. We reproduce the story of the "miracle," as he names it in his own somewhat quaint and old-fashioned phraseology. It is in regard to Hannah Carman, who, he says, died in Brunswick, N. J., 1776. He says:

> *Of her I received the following piece of history, so well attested that the skeptic himself can have nothing to gainsay. I have before me three certificates of the fact, and the testimony of Squire N. Stout's lady, who was present at the time of the miracle. She was remarkable for piety and good sense from a child. About the 25th year of her age she got a fall from a horse, which so hurt her back that she was bowed down and could in no wise lift up herself. Her limbs were also so affected that she was a perfect cripple, not able*

*to walk nor to help herself in the smallest matters. One day the young woman who had the care of her (now Squire Stout's lady), seated her in an elbow chair, and went to the garden. She had not been long in the garden before she heard a rumbling noise in the house. She hastened in, thinking that the cripple had tumbled out of her chair; but how was she surprised and frightened to see the cripple in the far end of the room praising God who had made her whole every whit. Miss Ketcham (for that was the name of Squire N. Stout's lady, from whom I had the narrative) sent to her neighbor Bray (the signer of one of my certificates) who came in haste, and was equally astonished, for the cripple was all the while in an ecstacy, taking no notice of the company, but running about the house, moving chairs and tables from place to place, going to her bedroom, taking up her bed and walking about with it, and every now and then falling on her knees to praise God, who had made whole a daughter of Abraham, who had been bowed down for ten or a dozen years. It has been observed before that the cripple was alone in the house when the miraculous event occurred. The manner thereof must have come from herself, and was as follows: "While I was musing on these words, Aeneas, Jesus Christ maketh thee whole, I could not help breathing out my heart and my soul in the following manner: O that I had been in Aeneas' place! Upon that I heard an audible voice saying, Arise, take up thy bed and walk! The suddenness of the voice made me start in my chair; but how was I astonished to find my back strengthening and by limbs recovering their former use in that start. I got up, and to convince myself that it was a reality and not a vision, I lifted up my chair and whatever came in my way: went to my room and took up my bed, and put my strength to other trials, till I was convinced that the cure was real, and not a dream or delusion."*

Edwards adds:

*I doubt not but some witlings will find pleasantry in this*
*story. Let them; and be their pleasantry their reward. But*
*whoever believes in the power of ejaculatory prayer will be*
*benefited by it.*[2]

The witlings it would seem then made sport of this story of
healing, as of the one just before referred to. But, considering the
eminent character of the man who vouches for it, and the certificates to the truth of the narrative of which he speaks, is there not
a fair presumption at least in favor of its genuineness? We shall be
regarded as very simple, no doubt, for having reproduced the tale,
but no matter; simplicity is one of the soft and formative stages of
all true faith. The first announcements of the resurrection were
deemed as "*idle tales*" by those who heard them; and had it not
been for the credulity of the simple-minded women who first
reported this miracle, we might not soon have had the faith of the
strong-minded men who afterwards preached it.

Prof. Godet, alluding to alleged miracles among the French
Protestants which have precisely the same kind of documentary
evidence in their favor, strongly refuses to pronounce against them,
and quotes with approval the following weighty words:

*There was a time when men believed everything; in our day*
*they believe nothing. I think we should take a middle course;*
*we should not believe everything, but we ought to believe*
*some things. For this spirit of incredulity and strong-minded-*
*ness answers no good purpose, and I have not discovered its*
*use. Is it possible that God has so hidden Himself behind the*
*creatures of His hand and under the veil of secondary causes*
*that He will never lift the curtain at all? Let us conclude that*
*the credulity of our ancestors caused many fictions to be*
*received as good history, but also that incredulity causes good*
*history to pass in our day for worthless stories.*[3]

The following narrative of a well-known physician, Dr. R_____
Philadelphia, is certainly very striking. It is given in his own words

as published in *The Great Physician*, by Dr. Boardman. Being asked to give an account of the recovery of his son, Dr. R _____ said:

*I do not like to speak of it to people generally, they are so unbelieving; but I can tell you. The children were jumping off from a bench, and my little son fell and broke both bones of his arm below the elbow. My brother, who is a professor of surgery in the College at Chicago, was here on a visit. I asked him to set and dress the arm. He did so; put it in splints, bandages, and in a sling. The child was very patient, and went about without a murmur all that day. The next morning he came to me and said, "Dear papa, please take off these things." "Oh, no, my son! you will have to wear these things five or six weeks before it will be well." "Why, papa, it is well." "Oh, no, my dear child, that is impossible." "Why, papa, you believe in prayer, don't you?" "You know I do, my son." "Well, last night when I went to bed it hurt me very bad, and I asked Jesus to make it well, and he did make it well, and it is well."*

*I did not like to say a word to chill his faith. A happy thought came: I said, "My dear child, your uncle put the things on, and if they are taken off he must do it." Away he went to his uncle, who told him he would have to go as he was six or seven weeks, and must be very patient; and when the little fellow told him that Jesus had made him well, he said, "Pooh! pooh! nonsense," and sent him away. The next morning the poor boy came again to me, and plead with so much sincerity and confidence that I more than half believed that he was really healed, and went to my brother and said, "Had you not better undo his arm and let him see for himself? then he will be satisfied. If you do not, I fear, though he is very obedient, he may be tempted to undo it himself, and then it may be worse for him." My brother yielded, took off the bandages and splints, and exclaimed, "It is well, absolutely well," and hastened to the door for air to keep from fainting.*

*He had been a real, simple-hearted Christian, but in his student days wandered away; but this brought him back to the Lord. Strange if it had not. To all this I could say nothing, if I had been ever so much disposed, in the way of accounting for it, upon any other hypothesis than that of the little fellow himself, that Jesus had made him well.*

A marvelous story, you will exclaim, but is it not especially wonderful that we find the doctors of medicine as the witnesses to a miracle? They who handle human wounds with the callous fingers of science, cry out, "Lo, God was in this place!" while we theologians are such devotees to cause and effect that we fear we may commit sacrilege by bringing in the Cause of causes. But it may be that the physicians and physiologists are bolder than we in personalizing the mysterious agency which operates in the cure of sick. They call it the "*vis medicatrix,*" as if it were "some gentle feminine nurse hidden from the sight, whose office it is to expel the poisons, knit the fractures, and heal the bodies." Would that we were quite as bold to recognize sometimes, at least, the Holy Spirit as our healer, and to pay that only fee which He requires, our open acknowledgement and thanks to Him who has said, "I am the LORD that healeth thee" (Exodus 15:26). And we must express our decided conviction that, on the whole, Christian physicians are less skeptical on the question of miraculous healing than Christian ministers; at least we know more of them in our day who have orally or in writing given in their adherence to this doctrine than of preachers and theologians. In the narrative that follows next we have the beautiful sight of the beloved physician spending the night in prayer with a few friends who have come to ask the recovery of his long suffering patient.

In Dr. Boardman's book we read the tender story of an English physician, Dr. De Gorrequer Griffeth, leaving a little patient for whom his skill could avail nothing, and going down by the river side, whither he had been wont to resort, for communion with God, and there asking and receiving the recovery of the child. The two persons who have been most largely used in praying for the cure of the sick in our own city are educated and practicing physicians. We to whom are committed the oracles of God, do well to see to it that we are not more skeptical than they to whom are entrusted the pharmacopoeia of nature.

## Jennie Smith

We instance another cure, the story of which has been read by many, and heard by not a few from the lips of the emancipated sufferer herself. The remarkable history of Miss Jennie Smith of Philadelphia, is rehearsed in the little book *From Baca to Beulah.*[4]

Her disease, so mysterious and agonizing and long continued that her pastor pronounced it "a narrative of suffering rarely if ever equaled," cannot be described at length here. Suffice if to say that she was a helpless cripple for about 16 years, suffering much of the time the most extreme agony. One limb was subject to such violent and uncontrollable spasms that it had to be confined in a strong box, and often held down by heavy weights. During her extraordinary sufferings, her faith and consecration seem to have been brought into very lively exercise, so that making her couch a pulpit, she was greatly used for quickening the spiritual life of such as came within her reach. Meantime she began to lay hold of the promise of God for bodily healing, and getting tokens of His power in several partial reliefs, she was led on to ask and obtain entire recovery. The story of this we give in her own words. After a day of unusual suffering, a few Christian friends had gathered about her in the evening as she lay in her extension chair. She says:

> The evening was devoted to prayer, led by pastor Everett. After the first hour or more, some were obliged to leave. One brother, whom I had not met before, as he shook hands on leaving, said, "My sister, you are asking too much; you are too anxious to get well. The Lord can make better use of you upon your cot than upon your feet." I was thankful for the brother's words. I then looked searchingly into my heart. The blessed Lord knows I honestly answered, "No, I am not anxious to get well; I have gained the victory over

that. If the heat of the furnace was increased a thousand fold I could say, Thy will be done, and to feel pain would be sweet if fully shown to me that it is the Father's will that I should suffer. And I believe the time has come for me to know that will."

Up to this point of the meeting there was not that oneness of mind that I felt there must be. I said to those who remained, "can you tarry with me till the morning if need be? I feel that it must be by waiting that our Father will give us the blessing. Are we of one accord in this matter?" My physician, Dr. Morgan, was the first to say, "I will stay, and I fully agree with you."

They all gathered about my chair. Never can that little group forget that season. It was now after nine o'clock. We continued waiting before the Lord. Occasionally one or another would quote, with comment, an appropriate text of scripture, or engage in a brief prayer. For myself, I lay in quiet expectancy, still suffering, but with a remarkable sense of the divine presence. Much of the time I was almost oblivious to my surroundings, so engaged was I in communion with my heavenly Father. About 11 o'clock I was led to vocally offer myself to God in flesh consecration, saying:

"I give this body anew—these eyes to see, these lips to talk, these ears to hear, and, if it be thy will, these feet to walk—for Jesus. All that is of me—all, all is thine, dear Father. Only let thy precious will be done."

Up to this time there was no cessation from suffering or increase of strength. As before said, I was weaker than usual. After a brief silence there suddenly flashed upon me a most vivid view of the healing of the withered arm. It seemed to me I could see it being thrust out whole. At the same instant the Holy Spirit bestowed on my soul a faith to claim a similar blessing. It seemed as if heaven were at that moment opened, and I was conscious of a baptism of strength, as sensibly and as positively as if an electric shock had passed through my system. I felt definitely the strength *come into my back, and into my helpless limbs. Laying my hand on the chair-arms, I raised myself to a sitting posture. The Garrigues brothers, being seated on either side of the chair, naturally sprang forward and laid hold to assist me. This, however, was not necessary. Dr. Morgan, who was sitting near, stepped forward and let down the foot-board, and, while the hands of my friends were yet on my shoulders, I arose and stood upon my feet.*

*Sister Fannie could not remember ever having seen me standing up. She was so startled she threw up both hands and screamed, "Oh, Jennie, Jennie!" No words can express my feelings. My very being yet thrills with praise as I speak of that hour. As I stood Brother W.H.G. placed his hand upon my head, saying, "Praise God, from whom all blessings flow."*

*My first thought was "Can I kneel?" I asked to do so, and knelt as naturally as if I had been accustomed to it. There was so much of the divine presence that not a word was spoken. We poured forth our souls in silent thanksgiving and praise. I then arose and walked across the room with entire ease and naturalness; there were no prickling or otherwise unpleasant sensations. Sat down in a rocking-chair for some minutes. It seemed so wonderful that I did not have to learn to walk. My limbs and body seemed as if made new.*

A case so widely known as this has been could not fail to elicit considerable comment. How was such a rapid and complete recovery effected? Some said that it was doubtless owing to a sudden and powerful reassertion of the will; that as in many such obscure diseases the illness was probably nerves and largely imaginary, and their prayers and faith simply brought courage and reassurance. Indeed, and is it not a great thing even to find a physician who can discover that nothing ails us when all the doctors have pronounced it a desperate case? If this were all, which we do not for a moment admit, it would certainly be a vast triumph of faith-healing over medication. For it is not alone that our poor diseased humanity needs a physician with divine skill to remove our deep-seated sicknesses, but especially one with divine insight to fathom and uncover them. The doctor's eyes are often more at fault than his hand. He cannot cure because he cannot comprehend the secret of our plague. How wonderful is the insight of the Great Physician. His penetrating glance goes to the root of disease when ours can only see the symptoms.

Never was there healer with such vision as His.

> *He took our suffering human race,*
>   *He read each wound and weakness clear,*
> *He struck his finger on the place,*
>   *And said, thou ailest here and here.*

Blessed is the patient who has found a doctor whose healing touch is guided ever by that clear and unerring sight which knows what is in man, and needeth not that any should testify of him.

Of this instance we have the doctor's written statement, confirming in every particular the testimony of his patient, both as to the fearful character of her sickness and her sudden and complete recovery in answer to prayer. We might bring forward many more witnesses did space permit. The instances of drunkards, cured at once of long enthralling appetite, of the victims of opium saved from their bondage, and all traces of the habit taken away, are interesting as evidences of God's immediate action in taking away the consequences of sin, as well as forgiving the sin itself.

If one's eye is open, and his mind unprejudiced, how many of such traces of God's finger will he see in the world, events clear and unmistakable enough for him who is willing to believe, but questionable and uncertain enough for him who is determined to deny.

# ENDNOTES

[1] Mrs. Oliphant's *Life of Edward Irving*, p. 461.
[2] Materials for *History of the Baptists in New Jersey*, 1792, p. 63.
[3] *Defence of the Christian Faith*, p. 88.
[4] Philadelphia: Garrigues Bros., 1880.

# CHAPTER

## 10

---

# *The Verdict of Candor*

In summing up what has been brought forward in the preceding chapters, we wish to review briefly the theory, the testimony and the practice, which our discussion has involved.

As to the theory: Is it right for us to pray to God to perform a miracle of healing in our behalf? "The truth is," answers an eminent writer, "that to ask God to act at all, and to ask him to perform a miracle are one and the same thing."[1] That is to say, a miracle is the immediate action of God, as distinguished from His mediate action through natural laws. We see no reason, therefore, why we should hesitate to pray for the healing of our bodies any more than for the renewal of our souls. Both are miracles; but both are covered and provided for by the same clear word of promise.

Our hesitancy to ask for physical healing we believe to rest largely on a false and wide-spread error in regard to the relation of the human body to the redemption of Christ. It is taken for granted by many that this house of clay was never intended either to be repaired or beautified by the renewing Spirit. The caged-eagle theory of man's existence is widely prevalent—the notion that the soul is imprisoned in flesh, and is beating its bars in eager longing to fly away and be at rest—all of which may be very good poetry, but is very bad theology.

The Scripture teaches indeed that "we that are in this tabernacle do groan, being burdened" (2 Corinthians 5:4); but it does not therefore thrust death's writ of ejection into our hands as our great consolation, and tell us that our highest felicity consists in moving out of this house as quickly as possible. *"Not for that we would be unclothed, but clothed upon,* that mortality might be swallowed up of life" (5:4), is the inspired testimony concerning our highest hope of existence. The redemption of the body, not its dissolution, resurrection not death is set before us in the gospel as the true goal of victory. But because that great promise of the gospel, "Who shall fashion anew the body of our humiliation that it may be conformed to the body of his glory," has been so largely supplanted by the notion of a spiritual elimination taking place at death, in which a purified soul is forever freed from a cumbering body, all this has been changed in the creed of many. The heresy of death-worship has supplanted the doctrine of resurrection, with a multitude of Christians, because they have allowed the partial felicity, the departing to be with Christ, to take the place of the final victory, the coming of Christ, to quicken our mortal bodies by His Spirit that dwelleth in us.

It is easy to see now that when death gets established in the high esteem of Christians, sickness, his prime minister, should come to be held in great regard also. And so it is, that while very few enjoy being sick, very many are afraid seriously to claim healing, lest it should seem like rebellion against a sacred ordinance, or a revolt from a hallowed medicine which God is mercifully putting to their lips for their spiritual recovery. Those who have such a feeling should search the Scriptures to learn how constantly sickness is referred to as the work of the devil. From the day when "Satan [went] forth from the presence of the LORD, and smote Job with sore boils" (Job 2:7), to the hour when the Deliverer came and loosed "a daughter of Abraham, whom Satan hath bound, lo, these eighteen years" (Luke 13:16), he that "had the power of death, that is, the devil" (Hebrews 2:14), has been compelling our wretched race to reap the firstfruits of mortality, disease and pain and bodily decay. Alas, if the Lord's people shall be so deceived by him that they shall willingly accept sickness, the firstfruits of death, as their portion, instead of seeking for health, the firstfruits of redemption! If any shall insist indeed, that God often allows His servants to be sick for their good; or that He sometimes permits them to fall into sin for their chastening, on that account we shall not admit that sickness is God's agent any more than that sin is. An old divine probably spoke as truly as he did quaintly when he said that "the Lord sometimes allows his saints to be sharpened on the devil's grindstone," but we believe that in the comprehensive petition, "*Deliver us from the evil one*," is contained without question a prayer for rescue from all the ways and works of Satan—from sickness as well as from sin; from pain, the penalty of transgression, as well as from transgression itself.

## Why is recovery rare?

But, it is asked, if the privilege and promise in this matter are so clear, how is it that the cases of recovery through the prayer of faith are so rare? Probably because the prayer of faith itself is so rare, and especially because when found it receives almost no support in the Church as a whole. Prayer for such matters should be the outcome of the faith and intercession of the whole body of believers. So it was in the beginning. When Peter was delivered from prison, it was because "prayer was made without ceasing *of the church unto God* for him" (Acts 12:5). And when Paul knelt alone in the chamber of Publius to intercede for his father's recovery, it was equally true that his petition was an expression of what was the unanimous and concurring faith of the whole Church. But it is not easy for an individual prayer to make headway against the adverse sentiment of the great body of Christians. For example let an earnest soul pray for a revival in a church where the prevailing view is that of indifferent unbelief, or positive disbelief in revivals, and would he be likely to obtain the coveted blessing? The promise stands fast, indeed, "How much more shall your heavenly Father give the Holy Spirit to them that ask him" (Luke 11:13); but the condition, "They were all with one accord in one place" (Acts 2:1), is wanting. How shall one man move the great ship before the wind by holding up his pocket handkerchief to the breeze, when all the mariners refuse to spread the sails? And how shall one Christian's faith prevail against the non-consent of the whole Church? There may be scattered instances of blessing in such circumstances, but there can be no widespread exhibitions of divine power. They tell us that all the heat communicated to a cake of ice short of that which would bring it to the melting point becomes latent and disappears. Faith, likewise, may become inoperative and fruitless in the Church when multiplied a hundredfold by unbelief.

But there is another answer also to the question. It is as true here as in any other field that God acts sovereignly and according to His own determinate counsel. He sees it best to recover one person at the instance of His people's prayers, and He may see it best to withhold such recovery for the time from another.[2] And we would most strongly emphasize the importance of offering our supplications for this as for all mercies in the most loyal and hearty and unreserved submission to the will of our Father.

He has told us that "all things work together for good to them that love God" (Romans 8:28), but we are not to conclude that they all work in one direction. There are blessings and trials, joys and sorrows, pains and pleasures, sickness and health, falls and recoveries, advances and retrogressions, but the final issue and resultant of all these experiences is our highest good. This we conceive to be the meaning of the promise. And when we remember that God superintends all this complex system of providences, and foresees the final effect of each separate element in it, we see how becoming it is that we should bring every petition into subjection to the will of the Lord.

When Augustine was contemplating leaving Africa and going into Italy, his pious mother, fearing the effect which the seductions of Rome might have upon his ardent nature, besought the Lord with many tears and cries that he might not be permitted to go. He was suffered to go, however, and in Milan he found his soul's salvation. "Thou didst deny her," says Augustine in his confessions, "thou didst deny her what she prayed for at that time that thou mightest grant her what she prayed for always." This is a perfect illustration of the point which we are emphasizing. God may withhold the recovery which we ask today because He will give to us that "saving health" which we ask always. He may permit temporal death to come, in order that He may preserve His child unto life eternal. How little we can know what is best for us and what shall work our highest good!

Isaac Barrow, the eminent and devout theologian, was so wayward and wicked while a lad that his Christian father confessed that he had prayed "that if it pleased God to take away any of his children it might be his son Isaac." What would the Church have lost had this prayer been granted? On the other hand, the mother of Charles I., it is said, bent above the cradle of her infant boy when he had been given up to die, and refused to be comforted unless God would spare his life. His life was spared; but how gladly would that mother have had it otherwise could she have looked forward to the day when his head fell bleeding and ghastly beneath the stroke of the executioner's axe? Such illustrations open a broad field for reflection, and suggest the real limitation of the prayer of faith as related to healing, viz., the gracious and all-wise will of God.

And this is the same limitation which belongs to the entire realm of intercessory prayer. "Holding such views to the efficacy of prayer for recovery from disease, why should you have any sick persons in your flock?" is the question which a clerical critic propounds. We shall answer by propounding a much harder one. Holding such views in regard to the efficacy of prayer for the conversion of souls, and resting on the plain declaration of Scripture concerning God our Savior that He "will have all men to be saved, and to come unto the knowledge of the truth" (1 Timothy 2:4), why should our questioner allow any sinner to remain unconverted under his ministry? And yet is it not his sorrowful experience that of all that come under his word and prayers, only a few comparatively give evidence of being regenerated? Alas! that we must all concede that this is our observation. But because I have to admit that all will not hear, and all will not repent and be converted, shall I therefore refuse to persist in preaching and warning and rebuke and intercession, "that I might by all means save some" (1 Corinthians 9:22)? Indeed not! And since the sure word of promise is given to us on this matter also, let us hold fast our confidence without wavering, so that whether there be few or many who shall be recovered we may by all means heal some. Such we believe to be a candid verdict in regard to the promise concerning prayer for the sick.

And now what shall be said in regard to the testimony brought forward? It would be considered very weighty, we venture to believe, were it adduced in support of a generally accepted theory. When evidence and established conviction are put in the same scale they tip the beam very easily, but testimony against a heavy makeweight of unbelief and prejudice makes slow headway. If the story of Augustine, or Luther, or Livingston, or Fox, or Dorothea Trudel were found in the gospels how we should fight for its genuineness. "Ah, yes," you say, "because the gospels are inspired, and we should not dare to question any statement recorded on their pages." But miracles were given to accredit inspiration, and not inspiration to accredit miracles. The first miracles got themselves credited simply on human testimony, on the evidence of men and women like ourselves, who saw, and believed and reported. And when they had become established as facts, then their weight went to prove the divine origin of Christianity. It is easy for us to say that the works recorded in the gospels are supernatural, because the system to which they belong is supernatural. That is true; but it is reading backward. The first Christians could not reason in that way, because the premise from which we argue was not established in their day. No! The miracles of the New Testament became established in precisely the same manner as any alleged fact is proved today, by the evidence of honest, candid and truthful witnesses, who saw and bare record. If, therefore, our theologians choose to treat the narratives of such godly and truthful men as Augustine, and Luther, and Baxter as "silly tales" they must be careful that they do not build a portico to "the school of Hume," from which their pupils will easily and logically graduate from the denial of modern miracles to the denial of all miracles.

Nor does age have anything to do with determining the value of signs and wonders. A young miracle is entitled to the same respect as an old one, provided it bears the same credentials. And if we give way to the subtle illusion that the marvelous is to be credited just in proportion to its distance from us; if we show ourselves forward to admit that the Lord wrought great and mighty signs 1,800 years ago, and utterly averse to conceding that the same Lord does anything of the kind today, then we must be very careful again that we do not give countenance to the mythical theory of miracles, which has been so strongly pushed in this generation. Do we believe that the credibility of miracles depends on the magnifying power of distance; that antiquity must stand behind them as a kind of convex mirror to render them sufficiently large to be distinctly seen? How we revolt from such an imputation! Yet let us be cautious that we do not give occasion for it, by emphasizing, as we cannot too strongly, the great things that the Lord did by our fathers, while we utterly refuse to believe that He does any such things by their sons. Let us not forget that the Jews in Christ's day were condemned for denying the wonderful works wrought in their own generation, and not for disbelieving those done by Elijah and Elisha 900 years before. The defenders of New Testament miracles are numbered by hundreds, and there is no special danger of a breach in the ramparts of Christianity at that point. The question of God's supernatural working today and tomorrow is the one where havoc is being wrought.

Unbelief shading off from rationalism to liberal evangelicalism is doing its utmost to give away our most precious heritage. With how many is regeneration merely a repairing of the old nature by culture, instead of a miraculous communication of the divine life! How many regard the promised coming of Christ in glory as simply a new phase of providence effected by the turning of the kaleidoscope of history! To how many is Satan only a concrete symbol of evil, so that their denial of the reality of the infernal has issued in a disbelief in the supernal! To how many is inspiration only a higher state of intellectual exaltation, and resurrection an elimination or spiritual release, effected by the dissolving chemistry of death! To read the utterances put forth by Christian teachers in these directions within the last few years is enough to startle one and make him cry out in the strong words of Edward Irving: "Oh the serpent cunning of this liberal spirit, it is killing our children; it has already slain its tens and thousands; *this city is sick unto death*, and dying of the mortal wounds which she hath received from it." Therefore, let us be cautious that by taking up the current sneer about prodigies and wonders we do not get our eyes blinded and our ears dull of hearing so as to be utterly unable to discern any divine manifestations in case they should be made.

As to the practice involved in this discussion: Can it be of any service for authenticating the truth of Christianity today to show examples of men and women healed of sickness through faith in the Great Physician? So far as our observation goes, the most powerful effect of such experiences is upon the subjects themselves, in the marked consecration and extraordinary spiritual anointing which almost invariably attend them. We can bear unqualified testimony on this point. Of a large number within the circle of our acquaintance, who have been healed, or who have imagined themselves healed, we have never seen one who did not give evidence of having received an unusual enduement of spiritual power. It has seemed as though the double blessing of forgiveness and health had been followed by the bestowment of a double portion of the Spirit. If we could let the objectors to our doctrine witness some of the examples of alleged healing which have been under our eyes for several years—inebriates who, after half a lifetime wasted in desperate struggles for reform, declare that their appetite was instantly eradicated in answer to intercessory prayer; invalids lifted in an hour from couches where they had lain for years; and now their adoring gratitude, their joyful self-surrender, their burning zeal in the service of the Lord. If we could let our critics witness these things, we believe that the most stubborn among them would at least be willing that these happy subjects of—something—should remain under the illusion that they have had the Savior's healing touch laid upon them.

Such we believe to be the verdict of candor upon this whole question. We do not ask that the highest place in Christian doctrine be given to faith in supernatural healing. We readily admit that grace is vastly more important than miracles; but miracles have their place as shadows of greater things. We urge that they may hold this place, that we may be helped thereby the better to apprehend the substance.

When the Emperor Theodosius had on a great occasion given release to all the prisoners confined within his realm he exclaimed: "And now would to God I could open all the tombs and give life to the dead!" If we could sometimes see the Lord unlocking the prison-house of sickness and giving reprieve from the impending penalty of death to those long in bondage it might be a salutary pledge and reminder of our Redeemer's purpose to bring forth the prisoners from the tomb in that day when He shall quicken our mortal bodies by His Spirit that dwelleth in us; it might sound in our ears with repeated emphasis the Lord's word, "turn you to the strong hold, ye prisoners of hope: even today do I declare that I will render double unto thee" (Zecharaiah 9:12).

# ENDNOTES

[1] Jellet, *Efficacy of Prayer*, p. 41.

[2] "Nor are signs wrought continually, but as often as it shall have pleased God and seems necessary; whence it is evident that to work signs depends not on the option of man, but on the will of God." Bullinger.

# CHAPTER

## 11

---

# *The Verdict of Caution*

T he Church can no longer say, silver and gold have I none,"
said Pope Gregory to Thomas Aquinas. "No, nor can she say
any longer, 'In the name of Jesus Christ of Nazareth rise up and
walk,' " answered Thomas. A very deep wisdom, and a very fruitful
suggestion are contained in this answer of the theologian. As riches
increase, that close dependence on God, which is the fertile soil of
faith and trust, decreases. It is when we are most straightened in
ourselves that the bounty of God is most widely open to us; it is
when we have nothing that we find the key with which to enter in
and possess all things which are ours in Christ.

We are living in an age in which the Church enjoys very large
prosperity in an earthly direction; when she is "rich, and increased
with goods," and, therefore, in constant peril of saying "[I] have
need of nothing" (Revelation 3:17). It is not an era, therefore, in
which the greatest triumphs of faith and intercession may be
reasonably looked for. Every Christian knows in his own experience the difference between saying his prayers and supplicating
God for help under the stress of overwhelming need; and in the
Church we may well open our eyes to the fact that our prosperity,
and our rest from persecution and trial are sources of weakness and
enervation. We do not pray as apostles, and martyrs, and confes-
sors, and reformers prayed, because not pressed upon by enemies,
and thereby shut up to God as they were; and so we do not get
such answers as they received.

Our first caution, therefore, concerning this subject is that we do not demand too much of the Christian Church of today. We should ask great things and expect great things of God; but of men, weak and backslidden in heart, we ought not to be too exacting. Faith for healing cannot rise above the general level of the Church's faith. There are multitudes of prayers in these days, written prayers and extemporaneous prayers, prayers in the Church, and prayers in the family; but how many Christians out of the great mass have any very extensive record of direct, definite and unmistakable answers to their petitions? Of all who knock at the gates of heaven each day, how many wait and watch till the door is opened and their portion is brought to them? But it is not reasonable to expect that such as have no experience in prevailing prayers for other things should be able to wield at once the prayer of faith which saves the sick. In God's school it is no more true than in man's, that pupils can step immediately into the highest attainments with no previous study, or diligent mastery of the first principles of faith. If the conviction and assurance of the Church as a whole should rise to the height of this great argument, we might witness wonderful things; but, so long as it does not, we should not be made to doubt because of the meager conquests which we witness. It is for us to pray always and earnestly that the Lord would be pleased to restore to His Church her primitive gifts, by restoring her primitive endowments of unworldliness and poverty of spirit and separation unto God. If any organ of the body be weak and sickly, the only sure method of restoring it is to tone up the whole system, and bring it to the normal standard of health; so if the entire body of Christ were revived and reinvested with her first spiritual powers, these special gifts and functions of which we are writing would not fail to be in extensive exercise.

## *The need for balance*

Then again, we need to be very careful that we do not fall into heresy on this question. Heresy, as a thoughtful Christian writer has pointed out, means a dividing or a choosing; it is the acceptance and advocacy of one hemisphere of truth to the rejection of the other. Every doctrine is two sided; so that whichever phase commends itself to us we must remember its counterpart, and aim to preserve the balance of truth by holding fast to this also. In the matter before us, as in the whole doctrine of prayer, human freedom and the divine sovereignty are inseparably joined. Here are the two sides:

*Ask what ye will, and it shall be done unto you. (John 15:7)*

*If we ask anything according to his will, he heareth us. (1 John 5:14)*

In our assent to the doctrine of the divine sovereignty we must never forget the gracious privilege which is accorded to us of freely making known our requests to God, with the fullest assurance that He will hear and grant them. "Whatsoever ye shall ask in my name, that will I do" (14:13); we cannot lean too hard upon this promise or plead it too confidently. But at the same time we must be sure that beneath every prayer the strong, clear undertone of "thy will be done" is distinctly heard. Of course in saying this, we open a mystery and suggest a seeming contradiction which the wisdom of the ages has been unable to solve. But because we find both sides of this truth distinctly expressed in Scripture, we must be sure to emphasize both.[1]

Let us be very careful therefore that we do not proclaim the doctrine of divine healing in an unbalanced and reckless manner. If we are told that a brother in the Church is sick, let us not make undue haste to declare that he will certainly be restored if we carry his case to God. We must keep distinctly in mind both Melita and Miletum: remembering that at one place Paul healed the father of Publius by his prayers, and that at the other place he left Trophimus sick. Some commentators have conjectured the reason why the latter was not at that time recovered, viz., that he was to be thereby kept back from martyrdom which he would probably have met had he gone with Paul, and for which his time had not come in the purpose of God. Whether there is any truth or not in this conjecture, there was doubtless some good reason why this companion of the apostle should have been detained for the while under infirmity. The all-wise and gracious Lord, who is shaping our lives, must be allowed to choose such detentions for us, if He sees that He can thereby best forward our usefulness and advance His own glory. We should be cautious, therefore, that in this matter we do not push the element of human choice too strongly and rashly, to the ignoring of the divine, and so bring in the heresy of free will.

Let us take warning from those misguided teachers who are going to the other extreme, and bearing so hard upon the divine sovereignty as practically to deny man's freedom, to ask or expect miraculous healing. More than this, indeed, they seem to have pushed the sovereignty of God almost into an iron fixedness, where even the Almighty is not at liberty to work miracles any longer, as though under bonds to restrain this office of His omnipotence since the apostolic age. This we hold to be a far more serious error than the other, since it appears not only to shut up man's freedom of asking, but to limit God's freedom of giving. There have appeared in our religious newspapers, of late, extended deliverances, in which the possibility of any miraculous interventions in this age is most emphatically denied, and the attempt to apply the plain promise in James to present times and circumstances characterized as gross superstition. It is a rash responsibility for evangelical teachers to take in speaking thus, we should say. It is opening channels of denial respecting the supernatural, into which the swelling unbelief of our age will not be slow to pour, inevitably deepening those channels into great gulfs of skepticism.

"Ah, but it is you who are ministering to unbelief," it is replied, "by holding out promises in the fulfillment of which men will be disappointed, and thereby be led to doubt the Word of the Lord." That is an objection that can be urged equally against the whole doctrine of prayer, and it is one concerning which we can take no blame. It is for us simply to emphasize every promise which God has given, and to refrain from cumbering it with any conditions of ours. If such assent should promote unbelief in any, that is the Lord's responsibility who gave the promise. If instead of assent we give denial, that is our responsibility, and the consequences must lie at our door.

Let us on our part, therefore, avoid heresy by keeping these two great elements of prayer in equilibrium, believing strongly but asking submissively, holding up in one hand of our supplication a "Thus saith the Lord," and in the other a "The will of the Lord be done."

## Do not fall into fanaticism

It requires great caution also in this subject that we do not fall into fanaticism. As we have already indicated, fanaticism is not necessarily a sign of error. It is more likely to be a healthful than a fatal symptom. It is often the proud flesh and fever heat which indicate that healing is going on in some fractured bone or ligament of the system of doctrine. Nevertheless, it must be subdued and kept down lest the truth may suffer reproach. And in this field especially do we need to guard against it.

Nowhere does zeal require to be so carefully tempered by knowledge as here. Novices, lifted up with pride, will lay hold of this doctrine, and with the enthusiasm which the discovery of some long-neglected truth is apt to engender, they will parade their faith and make extravagant claims concerning it. Nothing needs to be held with such quietness and reserve as this truth. To press it upon the undevout and uninstructed is only to bring it into contempt. Those who have the most wisdom in such matters will be found speaking in very hushed tones, and without assumption or ostentation. One who has the habit of parading this theme on all occasions, and haranguing it at every street corner, gives clear evidence of his unfitness to handle it. Here is a serious peril, as we distinctly foresee; but the best truth has always had to run such risks. Dry and lifeless tradition is the only thing which has invariably been exempt from them.

The more careful, therefore, should all be, who desire to see God's word prevail, to pray much and argue little, that the Spirit, who can alone discover the deep things of God, may reveal His true will to the Church concerning this important question. And most especially is all undue forwardness in attempting to exercise this ministry to be avoided. We are persuaded that there is no deeper or more difficult question which can come within our reach. If anyone is sincerely desirous of being used of the Lord in this direction let him give diligent heed to be taught of God concerning it. We are persuaded that there is no school on earth which is competent to graduate one in this divine science. Therefore we would commend our readers neither to books nor to theologians, but to the personal instructions of the Spirit of God. We admire the candor with which one eminent doctor of theology, Professor Godet, has confessed the true secret of knowledge in this field. He says:

> *A single prayer answered, a single case of living contact with the power of the Father, a single exertion of the strength of Christ over the weakness that is in us will teach us more on the subject of miracles than all that I have been able in this lecture to say to you upon this great subject.*

Let it be distinctly borne in mind that this is no easy art, no surface-truth to be picked up by any religious adventurer who may desire to exhibit some novel accomplishment. Unless one is ready for the most absolute self-surrender and the most implicit obedience let him not even enter this school of inquiry with any hope of learning its secrets. It is told of Pastor Blumhardt, who knew as much of this subject, we believe, as any man in recent times, that after the promise for healing was first brought powerfully to his mind he passed two years in repeated prayers and fastings and searchings for the mind of the Spirit before he had the assurance that he should lay hands on the sick for their recovery. We know that others who have been greatly owned of God in this direction have had a similar experience. Therefore we would interpose a strong caution against rashness or forwardness in this matter. We need less praying for the sick rather than more; only that the less shall be real, and deep, and intelligent, and believing. What a revelation is contained in the fact that some of the disputants in this controversy, after boldly denying that miraculous healing is possible in this age of the world, have then added "of course we ought to pray for the sick." That is, being fairly interpreted, after becoming thoroughly convinced that God will not interpose supernaturally for their restoration, then we should offer our supplication for their healing. It seems to us, on the contrary, that such a conviction furnishes a good reason why we should refrain from praying till we have acknowledged our unbelief and forsaken it.

The strongest and most enlightened faith, oneness of heart in all uniting to pray, minute and obedient submission to every condition named in Scripture are what are absolutely essential in this field. With the utmost tenderness and deference we would allude to a memorable instance of praying for the sick, which is fresh in mind. A call issued by the secular authorities; a day of prayer in which believers and formalists alike unite incense of the Romish mass ascending with the intercessions of the Protestant prayer meeting; the Jew and the Christian offering up, each according to his kind. The helpless and imprisoned patient meantime shut out from the ministry of grace and shut in to the ministry of drugs and stimulants so that any lucid exercise of faith or of prayer in the Holy Spirit would seem to be well-nigh impossible. What shall we say of this? God forbid that we should by the slightest criticism seem to mock the grief of a suffering nation, or to disparage a call to prayer from the rulers who did the best they knew in a great crisis, and we have no light as to how the Lord may have regarded such an offering. But in simple candor and loyalty to the word of God we must decline to have this event established as a prayer gauge, as many are insisting on making it. It was simply a national fast day, concerning which we proffer no remark. But the prayer of faith, by the elders of the Church, offered at the special request of the sick person, made in the name of Jesus, the one mediator between God and man, and in the Holy Ghost the Comforter, and all rendered up in obedience to every known condition of faith and oneness of mind enjoined in Scripture—this is the kind of prayer for the sick which we are discussing in this volume, and no other. Here is a service which belongs to the Holy of holies of the Christian Church, and which cannot be brought out into the court of the Gentiles.

A caution against dogmatism and pride of opinion in a field where we know only in part, may well close what we have to say. Alas! how little we truly understand of this whole matter. We believe strongly because we have promises that are "yea, and in him Amen, unto the glory of God by us" (2 Corinthians 1:20). And so we have presented as best we could the doctrine, the history and the experience of the Church upon this great question. How little we can speak of actual use of these gifts. But in the oft-quoted words of a good man, we are "very confident that the Lord has more truth yet to break forth out of his holy word"; on this subject especially, because so many of God's people are "searching diligently what or *what manner of time* the Spirit of Christ" did signify when He penned these great promises. If God has anything to reveal by any instrument whatever, let us be open to receive it. If such instruments shall prove to be, as we quite believe, the "poor of this world rich in faith" (James 2:5); the servants of Christ, who after long endurance of the bondage of pain have traced the promises of healing line by line in their own experience; and the obedient children, who have faced the world's doubt and scornful denial for the joy of answering God's challenge, "Prove me now herewith," let us take heed that we do not despise even such teachers and light bearers. And in all our urgency for the truth of God in this matter, let us not forget that miracles are but signs, not the substance. In prayer, in preaching, in tears and persuasions over perishing souls, in bearing the cross and counting all things as loss for the excellency of the knowledge of Christ Jesus the Lord, let us for the present be diligently employed, until the day dawn and the shadows flee away; until the harvest be gathered and the firstfruits shall be needed no more; until that which is perfect shall come, and that which is in part shall be done away.

## ENDNOTES

[1]"The only way for a believer, if he wants to go rightly, is to

remember that truth is always two-sided. If there is any truth that the Holy Ghost has specially pressed upon your heart, if you do not want to push it to the extreme, ask what is the counter-truth, and lean a little of your weight upon that; otherwise, if you bear so very much on one side of the truth, there is a danger of pushing it into a heresy. Heresy means selected truth; it does not mean error: heresy and error are very different things. Heresy is truth; but truth pushed into undue importance to the disparagement of the truth on the other side."—William Lincoln.

# CHAPTER

## 12

---

# *Conclusion*

The prayer of faith, when really understood and exercised, will be confessed to be the very highest attainment of the Christian life. And yet it is an attainment which comes from unlearning rather than from learning; from self-abnegation rather than from self-culture; from decrease towards spiritual childhood rather than from increase towards the stature of intellectual manhood. The same condition holds for opening the kingdom of heaven for others as for entering it ourselves, viz., that we "become as little children." To reach down and grasp the secret of simplicity of faith and implicitness of confidence is far more difficult than to reach up and lay hold of the key of knowledge. Hence, how significant it is that in the Scriptures children are made the heroes of faith. "This is the victory that overcometh the world, even our faith" (1 John 5:4). And who then are the overcomers? Who are they that have laid hold of the mighty secret of this spiritual conquest? "Ye are of God, *little children, and have overcome them*" (4:4). And why? "Because greater is he that is in you, than he that is in the world" (4:4). Yes; and just in proportion as we are emptied of self, and schooled back into that second childhood which should follow the second birth, will God be in us most fully and act through us most powerfully.

There is a passage in the life of an eminent Christian philosopher which is well worth pondering deeply and seriously in this age of superficial praying. A friend of Coleridge says that standing by his bedside not long before his death he was commenting on the

Lord's prayer, when he suddenly broke out: "Oh my dear friend, *to pray, to pray* as God would have us; to pray with all the heart and strength; with the reason and the will, to believe vividly that God will listen to your voice through Christ and verily do the thing He pleaseth thereupon—this is the last, the greatest achievement of the Christian's warfare on earth. Teach us to pray, O Lord!" "And then," says the narrator, "he burst into a flood of tears, and begged me to pray for him." The greatest achievement indeed! And yet it is not by might nor by power. Wisdom cannot compass it; learning cannot master it. "To pray with all the heart and strength;" which should mean with the heart submerged in the heart of Christ, and with the strength transformed into "the irresistible might of weakness," with the reason brought into complete captivity to the cross of Christ, and with the will surrendered up to the will of God, this is indeed the secret of power.

Let it be noted that we are speaking of one of the highest attainments of Christianity now, and not of its rudiments. The faith which saves us is the simplest exercise of the heart; the prayer of faith which saves the sick is the most exacting. The one is merely receptive, the other is powerfully self-surrendering. Do you wish to be saved, the Master will only say to you "Take the cup of salvation and call upon the name of the LORD" (Psalm 116:13). Do you wish to be mightily used of the Lord in the office of raising the sick from their beds, and giving life to those who are dead in sin, you will hear Him asking the searching question, "Are ye able to drink of the cup that I shall drink of, and be baptized with the baptism that I am baptized with?" (Matthew 20:22). In the faith by which we are converted and delivered from the wrath to come we do naught but *receive Jesus Christ*; in the faith by which we are consecrated and made vessels "meet for the master's use, and prepared unto every good work" (2 Timothy 2:21), we *give ourselves, soul, body and spirit to Jesus Christ.*

### Three conditions

That we may see how strenuous and searching the requirements for prevailing prayer are, let us note three explicit conditions laid down in Scripture, to which are attached the promise of what-soever we ask:

*If ye abide in me, and my words abide in you. (John 15:7)*

*Because we keep his commandments, and do those things that are pleasing in his sight. (1 John 3:22)*

*If we ask anything according to his will. (1 John 5:14)*

The first requirement, "If ye abide in me . . ." is that of intimate and unbroken communion with the Lord. Our justification depends upon our being *in* Christ. Our power and fellowship depend upon our *abiding in* Christ. And this last implies the most constant and uninterrupted intimacy of the soul with the Savior. It is the entering into His life and having His life so entering into us, that the confession of the apostle becomes realized in us—"I live; yet not I, but Christ liveth in me" (Galatians 2:20). Such abiding will stand in exact proportion to our detachment from the world.

The "double minded man" who is trying to make the most of both worlds, grasping for earth's riches and pleasures and yet wishing to secure the highest prizes of the kingdom of heaven, will inevitably waver; and to such a one the Scripture speaks expressly, "Let not that man think that he shall receive any thing of the Lord" (James 1:7). It is a hard saying, but one which in some form or other is constantly repeated in the Word of God. "Know ye not that the friendship of the world is enmity with God?" (4:4) asks the Apostle James; and the converse is hardly less true for believers, that the enmity of this world is friendship with God. When, for any cause, a Christian finds his earthly affections sundered, so that they do not draw him down, he will at least learn how much easier it is to set his affections on things above. Never do we find the heart of God opening so widely to us as when the heart of the world is closed against us. There is a homely wisdom, therefore, in the lines of an old poet, Henry Vaughan, when for his "soul's chief health" he prays for these three things:

*A living faith, a heart of flesh,*
 *The world an enemie;*
*The last will keepe the first two fresh,*
*And bring me where I'de be.*

How easy it is to understand the secret of Paul's, "I live, yet not I," after he has told us of the double crucifixion which he has endured—"By whom the world is crucified unto me, and I unto the world" (Galatians 6:14). Some become dead to the world through the pain or trial or privation which cuts them off from all communion with it, though the world is still there; to others the world becomes dead because of the cutting off of friends, and comforts, and fortune, in which their world consisted. In either case, if there be a heart which truly longs for God, it will find a wonderful release towards Him. We are advocating no morbid asceticism, but simply interpreting Scripture; and we must add, also, interpreting the secret of power in those who have been mightily prevalent in intercession. For in tracing the lives of those most eminently successful in the prayer of faith, as they have passed in review in this volume, we have found that, almost without exception, they have been those remarkably separated from the world, either through their own voluntary consecration or through persecutions, and trials, and sufferings endured for Christ's sake.

The next condition which we have noted: "If we keep his commandments, and do those things which are pleasing in his sight," needs to be emphasized not less strongly. Implicit obedience, a painstaking attention to the smallest and the greatest requirements of the Lord, is what is enjoined. Rather, we might say, a fidelity in service which admits no distinction of small or great when handling the commandments of the Lord. For true obedience knows no such discriminations as essential and non-essential in the divine requirements; it has no test fine enough for distinguishing things indifferent from things vital. Among the sayings of Christ, our perfect exampler in praying as in living, we find these two professions which we do well to read together.

*I do always those things that please him. (John 8:29)*

*I know that thou hearest me always. (11:42)*

Here again we touch the heart of this great secret. To obey well is to pray well; for not only does God love the willing and the obedient, but such know His mind and understand how and what to ask as no others can. One step in compliance with the Father's will will carry us further in knowledge than 10 steps in mere studious search into the mystery of His ways. Wonderfully do the mind and purposes of God open themselves to the obedient soul. Who "by searching can find out God" (Job 11:7)? But "if any man will do his will, he shall know of the doctrine" (John 7:17).

Therefore, should we study to exercise the most minute and diligent obedience to the Lord's requirements. "Whatsoever he saith unto you, do it" (2:5). In keeping this commandment there is great reward and the surest entrance into the promise of Christ, "Whatsoever ye shall ask the Father in my name, he will give it you" (16:23).

In all our Christian life and practice let us beware of saying, concerning any command of God, that it is only a form, and therefore it does not matter. Forms are sometimes given, no doubt, as tests of our fidelity, as when Naaman is enjoined to wash seven times in the Jordan for his healing, or when the elders are commanded to anoint the sick with oil for their recovery. Forms are nothing, to be sure; but the obedience which responds to those forms in every minute particular, for the love of Christ, is most precious in the sight of God. Hence, significantly, Paul thanks God concerning the Roman Christians that they had "obeyed from the heart *that form* of doctrine which was delivered [them]" (6:17).

And, finally, "if we ask anything according to his will"; which means "that we should be of a truth purely, simply and wholly at one with the One Eternal Will of God, or altogether without will, so that the created will should flow out into the Eternal Will, and be swallowed up and lost therein, so that the Eternal Will alone should do and leave undone in us."[1] And let us not be alarmed at this requirement, as though it meant pains, racks, tortures, the loss of our lives, the death of our children and everything else which is dreadful to contemplate. Why is it that we have associated such things with the prayer, "Thy will be done"? Let us search the Scriptures and see what God's revealed will is. "For this is the will of God, *even your sanctification*" (1 Thessalonians 4:3). "And this is the will of him that sent me, that every one that seeth the Son, and believeth on him, *may have everlasting life*" (John 6:40). "Who will have *all men to be saved, and to come unto the knowledge of the truth*" (1 Timothy 2:4). These and many other texts, if we had space to quote them, point in one direction, and indicate that the will of God is our health and not our hurt; our weal and not our woe; our life and not our death. It must be the will of God that all that is contrary to Him should be destroyed. "Every plant, which my heavenly Father hath not planted, shall be rooted up" (Matthew 15:13). Sin, sickness and death are contrary to God; they are not plants of His planting, but tares which the enemy has sown in His field. Therefore, they are to be plucked up, and we may be certain that we are working in the line of His will when we are seeking to eradicate them.

What, then if we should chiefly aim in our ministry at the sick bed to set forth this blessed disposition and purpose of the divine will? What if, instead of laying such stress on patient submission to pain and bodily disorder as things inevitable, we should seek to lift the sufferer up into harmony with God, in whom there is no sickness and no disorder? And then when we pray "Thy will be done" we shall mean let sickness be destroyed; let the sufferer be delivered from the racks and tortures of pain's inquisition; let sin and the bitter fruit of sin in these poor tormented bodies be plucked up together. In praying thus, we must surely be setting our faces in the right direction. For looking upward for the key of our petition, "Thy will be done on earth," we hear "as it is in heaven." But in heaven there is certainly no sin, sickness or death; and so we are enjoined to ask and strive and labor that there be none on earth. And looking forward to the predicted consummation of Christ's redemptive work, when God's will shall be actually done on earth, we read the glowing words: "And there shall be *no more death, neither sorrow, nor crying, neither shall there be any more pain*" (Revelation 21:4). Here then is the clearly defined pattern, above us, and before us; and amid all the tangled mysteries of evil, we should set our faces like a flint to pray it out and work it out into blessed fulfillment. And while we recognize the doctrine of the divine sovereignty, to which we have elsewhere referred, this should no more prevent our asking in faith for the healing of our bodies, than the doctrine of election should prevent our asking with the fullest assurance for the salvation of our souls. These observations in this closing chapter, let it be remembered, are especially for such as may be called to exercise the ministry of healing. If there are those who desire this office, we believe they should seek with all their heart, the consecration, the separation from the world and the surrender to God's will, which the Scriptures enjoin as conditions of prevailing prayer.

To the sick, sensible of their lack of these attainments, and fearing that their case cannot be reached on that account, we would speak a different word, even the word of the Master—"Be not afraid, only believe" (Mark 5:36). Christ comes to the sinner, helpless, guilty, lost, and saves him just as He finds him. And so with the sufferer, when he lies stripped of his raiment, wounded and half dead. As the good Samaritan "*came where he was . . .* and bound up his wounds, pouring in oil and wine" (Luke 10:33–34), so Jesus will take the patient just where he is, if he takes Him at all. We have not to make ourselves better in order to be healed, either spiritually or physically. Therefore, let the sufferer take courage and lift up his weary head. Oh, ye unnumbered subjects of pain and bodily torture, with hands and feet which you would use so diligently and swiftly in the service of your Lord if they were only released from the fetters which bind them! Oh ye countless victims of pain and disorder, who have never consecrated either your souls or your bodies to the service of Him who made them, hear all of you that voice of Him who speaketh from heaven, saying, "I am the LORD that healeth thee" (Exodus 15:26). And if the promises of God and the teachings of Scripture and the testimonies of the healed set forth in this book might throw one ray of hope or alleviation into your sick chambers, it would repay amply the pains we have taken in its preparation, and more than compensate us for any reproach we may incur for having borne witness to a doctrine of which many, as yet, can hear only with impatience and derision. And to this last word we would join a prayer which has come down to us from a very ancient liturgy, "Remember, O Lord, those who are diseased and sick, and those who are troubled by unclean spirits; and do Thou who art God, speedily heal and deliver them."

## ENDNOTES

[1] *Theologia Germanica,* p. 90.

# The Testimony of the Fathers

Those who have never had their attention called to the statements of the Christian fathers respecting the continuance of miracles in their day, will doubtless be surprised at this conclusion of Uhlhorn. But other eminent writers on the early history of the church are equally emphatic. And we are persuaded that no one who has looked carefully into the subject will consider it an easy task to refute this conclusion.

The most ingenious attempt to break the force of the patristic testimony on this subject, which we have met, is that of Rev. Dr. Geo. W. Samson, in an article, "Are there Miracles of Healing?" in *The Christian at Work*, June 1st, 1882. His position is that "no evidence of the continuance of miracles after the apostolic age is presented by the early Christian writers." And his theory is, that the seeming testimonies to such continuance are written in a kind of historical present tense, the real reference being to the days of the apostles, and not the times of the writers. He applies this method somewhat plausibly to the statements of Irenaeus, but refrains, we think very wisely, from using it upon the other witnesses. When, as in the testimony of Tertullian and Augustine, for example, names and places are given, it is clearly quite impossible to throw the allusion back to apostolic times. We insert a few additional testimonies from the fathers, and ask the candid reader to see how impossible it is to make them refer to the times of the apostles.

Tertullian says:

*Even Severus himself, the father of Antonine, was gra-*
*ciously mindful of the Christians. For he sought out the*
*Christian Proculus, surnamed Torpacion, the steward of*
*Euhodias, and in gratitude for his once having cured him*
*by anointing, he kept him in his palace till the day of his*
*death. (Ad. Scap. 4.)*

We believe no one can candidly read the paragraph in which this
sentence stands without being persuaded that the reference is to
healing by supernatural means.

Origen, commenting on the words, "the demonstration of the
Spirit and of power," says:

*Of "power" because of the signs and wonders which we*
*must believe to have been performed, both on many other*
*grounds and on this, that traces of them are still preserved*
*among those who regulate their lives by the precepts of the*
*gospel. (Contra Celsum, B, I, Chap. II.)*

Again, he says:

*And there are still preserved among Christians traces of*
*that Holy Spirit which appeared in the form of a dove. They*
*expel evil spirits, and perform many cures and fore-see*
*certain events according to the will of the Logos. (Id. B. I,*
*xivii.)*

Once more:

*We assert that the whole habitable world contains*
*evidence of the works of Jesus, in the existence of those*
*churches of God which have been founded through Him by*
*those who have been converted from the practice of in-*
*numerable sins. And the name of Jesus can still remove*
*distractions from the minds of men and expel demons, and*
*also take away diseases. (Id. B. I, lxvii.)*

Who can deny that these are plain assertions of the continuance of miracles in the writer's day?

Chrysostom, in his *Libra Contra Gentiles*, commenting on John 14:12:

> *"He that believeth on me, the works that I do shall he do also, and greater works,"* etc., *appeals to the miracles recorded in the Acts of the Apostles in proof of the truth of this promise, and then adds: "But if any one assert that these are mere smoke and a fictitious wonder unworthy of credit,* LET US VIEW THOSE OF THE PRESENT DAY, *which are calculated both to stop and to put to shame the blaspheming mouth, and to check the unbridled tongue. For throughout our whole habitable world, there is not a country, a nation, or a city, where these wonders are not commonly spoken of, which, if figments, would never have occasioned so much admiration. And you yourselves, indeed, might testify for us to this. For we shall have no occasion to receive confirmation of what we assert from others, seeing that you yourselves, our opponents, supply us therewith." (Logos pros Hellenas—Ed. Par, 1621, Tom I, p. 728–732.)*

We now reproduce the famous paragraph from Irenaeus entire, that the reader may judge whether the writer is speaking of his own or of apostolic times:

> *If, however, they maintain that the Lord, too, performed such works simply in appearance, we shall refer them to the prophetical writings, and prove from these both that all things were thus predicted regarding Him, and did take place undoubtedly, and that He is the only Son of God. Wherefore, also, those who are in truth His disciples, receiving grace from Him, do in His name perform (miracles), so as to promote the welfare of other men, according to the gift which each one has received from Him.*

*For some do certainly and truly drive out devils, so that those who have thus been cleansed from evil spirits frequently both believe [in Christ] and join themselves to the church. Others have foreknowledge of things to come; they see visions, and utter prophetic expressions. Others, still, heal the sick by laying their hands upon them, and they are made whole. Yea, moreover, as I have said, the dead even have been raised up, and remained among us for many years. And what shall I more say? It is not possible to name the number of the gifts which the church, [scattered] throughout the whole world, has received from God, in the name of Jesus Christ, who was crucified under Pontius Pilate, and which she exerts day by day for the benefit of the Gentiles, neither practising deception upon any, nor taking any reward from them [on account of such miraculous interpositions]. For as she has received freely from God, freely also does she minister [to others].*

*Nor does she perform anything by means of angelic invocations, or by incantations, or by any other wicked, curious art; but directing her prayers to the Lord who made all things, in a pure, sincere and straightforward spirit, and calling upon the name of our Lord Jesus Christ, she has been accustomed to work miracles for the advantage of mankind, and not to lead them into error. If, therefore, the name of our Lord Jesus Christ even now confers benefits, and cures thoroughly and effectually all who anywhere believe on Him, but not that of Simon, or Menander, or Carpocrates, or any other man whatever, it is manifest that when He was made man He held fellowship with His own creation and did all things through the power of God, according to the will of the Father of all, as the prophets had foretold. (Adv. Haer B. I, xxxii.)*

We have in this case, as in the other quotations, used the translation of the Ante-Nicene Christian Library, T. & T. Clark, Edinburgh.

Mosheim, referring to the alleged cures and expulsion of demons in the second century, says:

> *That those gifts of the Spirit which are commonly termed miraculous, were liberally imparted by Heaven to numbers of the Christians, not only in this, but likewise in the succeeding age, and more especially to those who devoted themselves to the propagation of the gospel among the heathen, has, on the faith of the concurrent testimony of the ancient fathers, been hitherto universally credited throughout the Christian world. Nor does it appear that in our belief as to this we can with the least propriety be said to have embraced anything contrary to sound reason. Only let it be considered that the writers on whose testimony we rely were all of them men of gravity and worth, who could feel no inclination to deceive; that they were in part philosophers; that in point of residence and country they were far separated from each other; that their report is not grounded on mere hearsay, but upon what they state themselves to have witnessed with their own eyes; that they call on God in the most solemn manner to attest its truth (vid Origen contra Celsum, L. I, p. 35), and lastly that they do not pretend to have themselves possessed the power of working miracles, but merely attribute it to others; and let me ask what reason can there possibly be assigned that should induce us to withhold from them our implicit confidence. (Historical Commentaries, Century II, sect. 5, Note.)*

The extended note of Mosheim from which we make this extract is well worth the reader's examination in full. It contains the strong avowal that the opinion above quoted of the continuance of miracles is the Catholic view; and it criticizes at length the opposite theory as propounded by his contemporary Middleton, which he says the author was compelled in a later work practically to retract.

## NOTE B. (P. 169)

---

## Practice of the Early Baptists

Rev. Morgan Edwards, in *Materials towards a History of American Baptists*, Vol. I, p. 23, speaking of Rev. Owen Thomas, once pastor at Welch Tract, Del., says:

> *Mr. Thomas left behind him the following remarkable note: "I have been called upon three times to anoint the sick with oil for recovery. The effect was surprising in every case; but in none more so than in that of our brother, Rynallt Howell. He was so sore with the bruises of the wagon when he was anointed that he could not bear to be turned in bed otherwise than with the sheet; the next day he was so well that he went to meeting. I have often wondered that this rite is so much neglected, as the precept is so plain and the effects have been so salutary."*

On page 28 of the same work Mr. Edwards says, referring to Rev. Hugh Davis, pastor of Great Valley church:

> *Some years before his death he had a severe pain in his arm, which gradually wasted the limb and made life a burden. After trying many remedies he sent for the elders of the church to anoint him with oil, according to James v: 14-17. The effect was a perfect cure, so far that the pain never returned. One of the elders concerned (from whom I had this relation) is yet alive [1770], and succeeds Mr.*

*Hugh Davis in the ministry, viz, Rev. John Davis.*

He gives several other like incidents, and makes the following observation upon the custom:

> *The present generation of Baptists in Pennsylvania and the several other colonies (German Baptists excepted) have somehow reasoned themselves out of the practice of anointing the sick for recovery, not believing that the same kind of reasoning would lead them to discontinue every positive rite, as it actually led Barclay and thousands besides. Our pious forefathers in this province practiced the rite frequently and successfully, as might be shown. (See Examples, pp. 23, 28.) The same may be said of the Baptists of Great Britain and Ireland. Their progenitors also used the salutary unction, whereof some narrations have been made public.*

## NOTE C. (P. 133)

# *A Disputed Text*

Since the first edition of this work was published some of its critics have sharply arraigned it because of its failure to discredit the last part of Mark's Gospel, viz., the 16th chapter, from verse 9 to the end.

After an extended examination of the whole question, it seemed to the author that the doubts which have been thrown upon the passage have so rapidly diminished, and have now so nearly reached the vanishing point, that it was hardly worthwhile to disturb the reader's mind with them. It is a grave consideration as to how much of questioning in regard to such texts the preacher or the writer is justified in raising. It seems to us that unless the evidence against them considerably preponderates, it is best to say nothing about the uncertainty. In this case, we believe that the evidence in favor of the genuineness of the passage vastly outweighs that against it. We have not room to set forth the grounds of this conviction, but would refer the reader to Olshausen's very strong and to us very conclusive defence of this side of the question. The fact that so early a writer as Irenaeus quotes this passage as a part of Mark's Gospel, both Olshausen and Lange consider to be a powerful argument in its favor. When we consider that Irenaeus was only a step removed from the apostles, being a disciple of Polycarp who was the disciple of John, we shall see how important a consideration this is. The view of Olshausen, that this part was accidentally torn off from some ancient manuscript and the loss perpetuated by the transcribers, is far more reasonable, it seems to us than that it was an addition by a later hand.

For a full and satisfactory discussion of the whole question, we would refer the reader to the fresh and able Commentary of Morrison. His conclusion in regard to the matter is as follows: Speaking of the view that this passage is spurious, he says: "This notion has grown into a romance of criticism which has thrown a spell of doubt over spirits that have not the least sympathy with Biblical skepticism. But we have shown in a full discussion of the subject in the body of the Commentary *that the romance has culminated. There would appear to be no good reason for questioning the authority of the passage.*"—Introduction to Commentary on Mark.

## NOTE D. (P. 221)

*Pastor Blumhardt*

We cannot too strongly commend the biography of this excellent man, from which we have made this brief extract. It is the most remarkable exemplification of the power of faith and of the possibilities of intercessory prayer which we have ever met. At the same time it is a life the farthest removed from anything of extravagance, and high assumption. We give one or two further extracts from it for the benefit of such as may not be able to read the entire book. The first is a reference to the remarkable instance which we have cited:

> *"It was especially," he writes, "in that awful case of sickness that I discovered how the testamentary words of our Lord Jesus Christ, 'They shall lay hands on the sick, and they shall recover,' are not quite out of power, if applied with an humble, penitent, and believing heart. Everything concerning illnesses in my parish began to be changed. Seldom did a medical man appear in it; the people would rather pray. Certain diseases especially among newborn children, seemed entirely to cease, and the general state of health became better than it was before.*
>
> *"Yet never in the least did Blumhardt urge the people to give up medical means; they did it all of their own accord. Nor did he consider his personal presence and mediation necessary. Hundreds and thousands that came, in course of time, from all parts of Europe—yea, from the remotest parts*

*of the globe—or applied to him, either through friends and relations or by letter, were directed by him to search themselves before the Almighty, to repent, to give themselves entirely to God, with all their families, and He would then, in answer to a child-like petition as to their peculiar necessities do according to His holy pleasure. But others without number came or were brought to Mottlingen, especially on days of public worship; scores of them were accommodated inside the church, outside in the church-yard, or listened to the sermon from neighboring houses. From early in the morning till after the third service, in the evening, Blumhardt had scarcely a minute of rest. Hundreds came, one after another, desiring to lay their spiritual and bodily complaints in particular before him.*

*"I myself," continues Mr. Spittler, "was an eye-witness during eighteen months. Two years after the beginning of the revival, one Sunday morning, a friend and I counted more than a hundred towns and villages of Wurtemburg and the Grand Duchy of Baden, from which either a few or whole bands of thirty or fifty had come to hear the Word of God, or to receive release from diseases. It would take me hours to testify what the Lord has, through a series of years, done for many a distressed family or individual, who, when all human means seemed to fail, looked up to God as a compassionate and merciful Father. God knows the cases, and those who are concerned know them, and will praise Him here on earth as long as their breath is within them. Blumhardt's daily prayer and sigh before the Lord was, 'Oh that all people would learn again to pray and bring all their matters before their Heavenly Father!' "—pp. 30–32.*

*Pastor Blumhardt did not like to dilate on these answers to prayer. Still they were known. He held that the signs mentioned by our risen Saviour (Mark xvi.18) embraced a promise for all times, and that if the signs were now lacking it was through a want of faith in the Church. He took the Lord at his word. Many a captive who had been enthralled bodily and mentally by Satan went away from Bad Boll rejoicing in a liberty wherewith Christ had, in both respects, made him free. Often, as those who had left wrote to tell of their healing, and of the change that had passed over their life, Blumhardt would say with energy, "Thank God, the God of our fathers still lives."*

*An esteemed professor of the school of medicine at the University of Tubingen, resolved, during one of his vacations, to go and make personal inquiries about these cases of healing. Curiosity mainly moved him. He asked the pastor to give him some proofs of the reality of these cures. Blumhardt said, "Give yourself time, and take out of these drawers of my writing-table the letters I have received. Take out as many as you please. Examine the testimony of others as to the answers to prayer for healing. I know of no other proof I can give." We give the words of an intelligent visitor at Bad Boll: "This professor has often since related to me that Blumhardt, (not at all wishing to bias his judgment) left him alone to peruse the letters. He confessed that during the reading of these letters, some of which he thought to be 'most remarkable,' his astonishment grew more and more, and it became difficult to him to continue to doubt, as he had done, the reality of these things, and still more difficult knowing the man whose communication made the deepest impression upon him to be a thoroughly open and honorable character, and least likely to lend himself to anything approaching a selfish fraud." pp. 59–61*

# THE GOSPEL
# OF HEALING

A.B. Simpson

# PREFACE

---

The first half of this volume has been issued in many successive editions as a series of tracts on the gospel of healing. The testimony of many persons that the tracts have been greatly blessed of God, and the desire often expressed to have them in permanent form, have induced the author to reissue them in a book with the addition of several fresh chapters. It is hoped that this simple volume may now be found to be a compact and more useful channel of scriptural instruction upon this important subject.

The views expressed have been carefully weighed in the balance of the divine Word. They have been confirmed by much experience and careful observation.

The importance of this subject and the emphatic way in which God's Holy Spirit is pressing it upon the attention of His people demand for it the most careful and thorough scriptural study. Effectual faith can only come through thorough conviction.

In spite of the cold and conservative and sometimes scornful unbelief of many, this doctrine is becoming one of the touchstones of character and spiritual life.

It is revolutionizing, by a deep, quiet and divine movement, the whole Christian life of thousands. It has a profound bearing upon the spiritual life. No one can truly receive it without becoming a holier and more useful Christian.

It is most important that it should be ever held in its true place in relation to the other parts of the gospel. It is not the whole gospel, or perhaps the chief part of it, but it is a part, and in its due relationship to the whole it will prove to be, like the gospel itself, "the power of God . . . to every one that believeth."

Albert B. Simpson

# CHAPTER

## 1

---

# *The Scriptural Foundation*

Man has a twofold nature. He is both a material and a spiritual being. And both natures have been equally affected by the Fall. His body is exposed to disease; his soul is corrupted by sin. How blessed, therefore, to find that the complete scheme of redemption includes both natures. It provides for the restoration of physical as well as the renovation of spiritual life!

The Redeemer appears among men with His hands stretched out to our misery and need, offering both salvation and healing. He offers Himself to us as a Savior to the uttermost; His indwelling Spirit, the life of our spirit; His resurrection body, the life of our mortal flesh.

Jesus begins His ministry by healing all who have need of healing; He closes it by making full atonement for our sin on the cross. Then, on the other side of the open tomb, He passes into heaven, leaving the double commission for "all nations" and "alway, even unto the end of the world" (Matthew 28:19–20).

He says, "Go ye into all the world, and preach the gospel to every creature. He that believeth and is baptized shall be saved, but he that believeth not shall be damned. And these signs shall follow them that believe; In my name shall they cast out devils; . . . they shall lay hands on the sick, and they shall recover" (Mark 16:15–18).

This was "the faith . . . once delivered unto the saints" (Jude 3). What has become of it? Why is it not still universally taught and realized? Did it disappear with the apostolic age? Was it withdrawn when Peter, Paul and John were removed? By no means! It remained in the church for centuries and only disappeared gradually in the church's growing worldliness, corruption, formalism and unbelief.

With a reviving faith, with a deepening spiritual life, with a more marked and scriptural recognition of the Holy Spirit and the living Christ and with the nearer approach of the returning Master Himself, this blessed gospel of physical redemption is beginning to be restored to its ancient place. The church is slowly learning to reclaim what she never should have lost. But along with this there is also manifested such a spirit of conservative unbelief and cold, traditional theological rationalism as to make it necessary that we should "earnestly contend for the faith which was once delivered unto the saints."

## *Faith must rest on the Word*

First, we must be sure of our scriptural foundations. Faith must always rest on the divine Word. The most important element in the "prayer of faith" is a full and firm persuasion that the healing of disease by simple faith in God is a part of the gospel and a doctrine of the Scriptures.

The earliest promise of healing is in Exodus 15:25–26: "There he made for them a statute and an ordinance, and there he proved them, and said, If thou wilt diligently hearken to the voice of the LORD thy God, and wilt do that which is right in his sight, and wilt give ear to his commandments, and keep all his statutes, I will put none of these diseases upon thee, which I have brought upon the Egyptians: for I am the LORD that healeth thee."

The place of this promise is most marked. It is at the very outset of Israel's journey from Egypt, like Christ's healing of disease at the opening of His ministry.

It comes immediately after Israel passed through the Red Sea. This event is distinctly typical of our redemption, and the journey of the Israelites in the wilderness is typical of our pilgrimage: "These things happened unto them for ensamples: and they are written for our admonition, upon whom the ends of the world are come" (1 Corinthians 10:11).

This promise, therefore, becomes ours as the redeemed people of God. And God meets us at the very threshold of our pilgrimage with the covenant of healing. He declares that, as we walk in holy and loving obedience, we shall be kept from sickness, which belongs to the old life of bondage we have left behind us forever.

Sickness belongs to the Egyptians, not to the people of God. And only as we return spiritually to Egypt do we return to its malarias and perils. This is not only a promise; it is "a statute and an ordinance." And so, corresponding to this ancient statute, the Lord Jesus has left for us in James 5:14 a distinct ordinance of healing in His name, as sacred and binding as any of the ordinances of the gospel.

In Psalm 105:37 we read of the actual fulfillment of that promise: "He brought them forth also with silver and gold: and there was not one feeble person among their tribes." Although they did not fulfill their part in the covenant, God kept His word. And so, although our faith and obedience are often defective, if Christ is our surety and if our faith will claim His merits and His name, we too shall see the promise fulfilled.

### Satan the source

The story of Job is one of the oldest records of history. It gives us a view of the source from which sickness came—in this case, Satan (Job 1–2). It also reveals the course of action that brings healing— that is, taking the place of humble self-judgment at the mercy seat. If ever a sickroom was unveiled, it was that of the man of Uz. But we see no physician there, no human remedy, only a looking unto God as his Avenger. And when Job renounces his self-righteousness and self-vindication and takes the place where God is seeking to bring him—that of self-renunciation and humility—he is healed.

The psalms of David are a record of many afflictions. But God is always the deliverer, and God alone: "Bless the LORD, O my soul, and forget not all his benefits: who forgiveth all thine iniquities; who healeth all thy diseases" (Psalm 103:2–3). We see no human hand. The psalmist looks to heaven as directly for healing as he does for pardon, and in the same breath he cries:

"Who forgiveth all thine iniquities; who healeth all thy diseases."
It is a complete healing—*all* his diseases—as universal and lasting
as the forgiveness of his sins. And how glorious and entire that was
is evident enough: "As far as the east is from the west, so far hath
he removed our transgressions from us" (103:12). But here, as in
the case of Job, there is an intimate connection between sickness
and sin, and both must be healed together.

Asa was a king who had begun his reign by an act of simple,
implicit trust in God when human resources utterly failed him. By
that trust he won one of the most glorious victories of history (2
Chronicles 14:9–12). But success corrupted him. It taught him to
value too highly the arm of flesh. In his next great crisis, Asa formed
an alliance with Syria and lost the help of God (16:7–8). He refused
to take warning from the prophet and rushed on to the climax of
his earthly confidence.

Asa became sick. Here was a greater foe than the Ethiopians, but
again he turned to man: "And Asa in the thirty and ninth year of
his reign was diseased in his feet, until his disease was exceeding
great: yet in his disease he sought not to the LORD, but to the
physicians" (16:12). The outcome could not be more sad or
sarcastic: "And Asa slept with his fathers" (16:13).

## The Old Testament evangel

It was Isaiah who delivered the great evangelical vision, the gospel
in the Old Testament, the very mirror of the coming Redeemer.
And at the front of his prophetic message, prefaced by a great
Amen—the only "surely" in the chapter—is the promise of healing: "Surely he hath borne our griefs, and carried our sorrows . . .
and with his stripes we are healed" (Isaiah 53:4–5). It is the
strongest possible statement of complete redemption from pain
and sickness by Christ's life and death. And these are the very words
Matthew quotes afterward, under the inspired guidance of the
Holy Spirit (Matthew 8:17), as the explanation of Jesus' universal
works of healing.

Our English version of Isaiah does only imperfect justice to the
force of the original. The translation in Matthew is much better:

"Himself took our infirmities, and bare our sicknesses." A literal translation of Isaiah would be: "Surely he hath borne away our sicknesses and carried away our pains."

Any person who will refer to such a familiar commentary as that of Albert Barnes on Isaiah, or to any other Hebrew authority, will see that the two words denote respectively *sickness* and *pain*. And the words for "bear" and "carry" denote not mere sympathy but actual substitution and the utter removal of the thing borne.

Therefore, as Jesus Christ has borne our sins, He has also borne away and carried off our sicknesses, yes, and even our pains. Abiding in Him, we may be fully delivered from both sickness and pain. Thus "by his stripes we are healed." Blessed and glorious gospel! Blessed and glorious Burden-Bearer!

And so the ancient prophet beholds in vision the Redeemer coming first as a great Physician and then hanging on the cross as a great Sacrifice. The evangelists have also described Him so. For three years He was the great Healer, and then for six hours of shame and agony He was the dying Lamb.

## Jesus fulfills prophecy

Matthew, inspired by God, quotes Isaiah 53:4–5 as the reason why Jesus healed all who were sick: "He . . . healed all that were sick: that it might be fulfilled which was spoken by Esaias the prophet, saying, Himself took our infirmities, and bare our sicknesses" (Matthew 8:16–17).

It was not that Jesus might give His enemies a vindication of His Deity, but that He might fulfill the character presented of Him in ancient prophecy. Had He not done so, He would not have been true to His own character. If He did not still do so, He would not be "Jesus Christ the same yesterday, and to day, and for ever" (Hebrews 13:8). These healings were not occasional but continual, not exceptional but universal. Jesus never turned any away. "He . . . healed all that were sick." "As many as touched him were made whole." He is still the same.

This was the work of Jesus' life, and God would not have us forget that His Son spent more than three years in deeds of power and love before He went up to Calvary to die. We need that living Christ quite as much as we need Christ crucified. The Levitical types included the meal offering as much as the sin offering. And suffering humanity needs to feed upon the great loving Heart of Galilee and Bethany as much as on the Lamb of Calvary.

It would take entirely too long to examine in detail the countless records of Jesus' healing power and grace. He cured the leper, the lame, the blind, the paralytic, the impotent, the fever-stricken—all who "had need of healing." He linked sickness often with sin and forgave before He spoke the restoring word. He required their own personal touch of appropriating faith and bade them take the healing by rising up and carrying their beds.

His healing went far beyond His own immediate presence to reach and save the centurion's servant and the nobleman's son. How often He reproved the least question of His willingness to help and threw the responsibility of man's suffering on his own unbelief.

These and many more such lessons crowd every page of the Master's life and reveal to us the secret of claiming His healing power. What right has anyone to explain these miracles as mere types of spiritual healing and not as specimens of what He still is ready to do for all who trust Him? Such was Jesus of Nazareth.

## Jesus empowers others to heal

But was this blessed power to die with Jesus at Calvary? Jesus does not so indicate. "Verily, verily, I say unto you, He that believeth on me, the works that I do shall he do also; and greater works than these shall he do; because I go unto my Father" (John 14:12). Jesus makes it emphatic—"verily, verily"—as if He knew it was something mankind was sure to doubt. It is no use to tell us that this meant that the church after Pentecost was to have greater spiritual power and do greater spiritual works by the Holy Spirit than Jesus Himself did, inasmuch as the conversion of the soul is a greater work than the healing of the body. Jesus says, "The works that I do shall he do also," as well as the "greater works than these." That is, Jesus' followers are to do the same works that He Himself did and greater also.

Even during His life on earth Jesus sent out the 12 apostles. Then He sent out the 70 as forerunners of the whole host of the Christian eldership (for the 70 were in effect the first elders of the Christian age, corresponding to the 70 elders of Moses' time) with full power to heal. And when Jesus was about to leave the world, He left on record both these commissions in the most unmistakable terms.

## A twofold commission

> *Go ye into all the world, and preach the gospel to every creature. He that believeth and is baptized shall be saved; but he that believeth not shall be damned. And these signs shall follow them that believe; In my name they shall cast out devils; they shall speak with new tongues; they shall take up serpents; and if they drink any deadly thing, it shall not hurt them; they shall lay hands on the sick, and they shall recover. (Mark 16:15–18)*

Here is the commission of the twofold gospel given to them and the assurance of Christ's presence and unchanging power. What right have we to preach one part of the gospel without the other? What right have we to hold back any of God's grace from a perishing world? What right have we to go to unbelievers and demand their acceptance of our salvation message without these signs following? What right have we to explain their absence from our ministry by trying to eliminate them from God's Word or to consign them to an obsolete past?

Christ promised the signs, and they followed as long as Christians continued to believe and expect them. It is important to observe Young's translation of verse 17: "Signs shall follow them that believe these things." The signs shall correspond to the extent of their faith.

By such mighty "signs and wonders" the church was established in Jerusalem, Samaria and unto the uttermost parts of the earth.

The unbelief of the world needs these signs today as much as in the apostolic times. During the apostolic age these manifestations of healing power were by no means confined to the apostles. Philip and Stephen were as gloriously used as Peter and John.

In First Corinthians 12:9, "the gifts of healing" are spoken of as widely diffused and universally understood among the endowments of the church. But the apostolic age was soon to close; were the gifts to be continued, and if so, by whom? By what limitation was the church to be preserved from fanaticism and presumption? By what commission was healing to be perpetuated to the end of time and placed within the reach of all God's suffering saints?

The answer is in James 5:14, to which we turn again with deep interest: "Is any sick among you? let him call for the elders of the church; and let them pray over him, anointing him with oil in the name of the Lord: and the prayer of faith shall save the sick, and the Lord shall raise him up; and if he have committed sins, they shall be forgiven him."

Notice first who gives this commission. It is James—James, who had authority to say, in summing up the decrees of the council at Jerusalem, "My sentence is . . . ". He is the man who is named first by Paul himself among the pillars of the church (see Galatians 2:9).

Observe to whom this power is committed. Not to the apostles, who are now passing away; not to men and women of rare gifts or difficult to contact. It was given to the elders—the men most likely to be within reach of every sufferer, the men who are to continue till the end of the age.

Notice the time at which this commission is given. It was not at the beginning, but at the close of the apostolic age. It was not for that generation, but for the one that was just rising and all the succeeding ages. Indeed, these New Testament letters were not widely circulated in their own time, but were mainly designed "for our admonition, upon whom the ends of the world are come."

Again, observe the nature of the ordinance enjoined. It is "the prayer of faith" and the "anointing . . . with oil in the name of the Lord." This was not a medical anointing, for it was not to be applied by a physician, but by an elder. It must, naturally, be the same anointing we read of in connection with the healing of disease by the apostles (for instance, Mark 6:13).

Any other interpretation would be strained and contrary to the obvious meaning of the custom as our Lord and His apostles observed it. In the absence of any explanation to the contrary, we are bound to believe that it was the same—a symbolic religious ordinance expressive of the power of the Holy Spirit, whose peculiar emblem is oil.

The Greek Orthodox church still retains the ordinance, but the Roman Catholic church has changed it into a mournful preparation for death. It is a beautiful symbol of the divine Spirit of life taking possession of the human body and breathing into it God's vital energy.

## Divine healing is a command

Divine healing ceases to be a mere privilege. It is the divine prescription for disease, and no obedient Christian can safely ignore it. Any other method of dealing with sickness is unauthorized. This is God's plan. This makes faith simple and easy. We have only to obey in childlike confidence; God will fulfill.

Once more, we must not overlook the connection of sickness with sin. There is here the suggestion that the trial has been a divine chastening and requires self-judgment, penitence and pardon. There is the blessed assurance that both pardon and healing may be claimed together in His name.

If more were needed than the testimony of James, then John, the last of the apostles and the one who best knew the Master's heart, has left a tender prayer: "Beloved, I wish [pray] above all things that thou mayest prosper and be in health, even as thy soul prospereth" (3 John 2). By this prayer we may know our Father's gentle concern for our health as well as for our souls. When God breathes such a prayer for us, we need not fear to claim it for ourselves. But as we do, we must not forget that our health will be even as our soul prospers.

In Ephesians 5:30 we note a union between our body and the risen body of the Lord Jesus Christ: "We are members of his body, of his flesh, and of his bones." We have the right to claim for our mortal frame the vital energy of Christ's perfect life. He has given His life for us, and it is all-sufficient.

"If the Spirit of him that raised up Jesus from the dead dwell in you, he that raised up Christ from the dead shall also quicken your mortal bodies by his Spirit that dwelleth in you" (Romans 8:11). This promise cannot refer to the future resurrection. That resurrection will be by the "voice of the Son of God" (John 5:25), not the Holy Spirit. This is a present dwelling in and a quickening by the Spirit. And it is a quickening of the "mortal body," not the soul.

What can this be but physical restoration? The physical restoration is the direct work of the Holy Spirit, and only they who know the indwelling of the divine Spirit can receive it. It was the Spirit of God who wrought the miracles of Jesus Christ on earth (Matthew 12:28). And if we have the same Spirit dwelling in us, we shall experience the same works.

## Not simply healing but health

Paul expressed his physical experience this way: "Always bearing about in the body the dying of the Lord Jesus, that the life also of Jesus might be made manifest in our body. For we which live are alway delivered unto death for Jesus' sake, that the life also of Jesus might be made manifest in our mortal flesh" (2 Corinthians 4:10–11).

Paul knew constant peril, infirmity and physical suffering— probably by persecution and even violence. But it came in order that the healing, restoring and sustaining power and life of Jesus might be the more constantly manifest in his very body. And this for the encouragement of suffering saints—"for your sakes" (4:15). His life was a constant miracle that it might be to all persons a pledge and monument of the promise made to him for all who might thereafter suffer. This life, he tells us, was "renewed day by day" (4:16). The healing power of Christ is dependent on our continual abiding in Him and, like all God's gifts, is renewed day by day.

Christ did not say, "I *will be* with you alway." That would have suggested a break. He said, "I *am*"—an unchanging now, a presence never withdrawn, a love, a nearness, a power to heal and save as constant and as free as ever, even unto the end of the world. "Jesus Christ the same yesterday, and to day, and for ever."

Thus have we traced the teachings of the Holy Scriptures from Exodus to Patmos. We have seen God giving His people the ordinance of healing at the very outset of their pilgrimage. We have seen it illustrated in the ancient dispensation in the sufferings of Job, the songs of David and the sad death of Asa. We have seen Isaiah's prophetic vision of the coming Healer. We have seen the Son of man coming to fulfill that picture to the letter; we have heard Him tell His weeping disciples of His unchanging presence with them. We have seen Him transmit His healing power to their hands. And we have seen those followers hand down this gospel of healing to us and to the church of God until the latest ages of time.

What more evidence can we ask? What else can we do but believe, rejoice, receive and proclaim this great salvation to a sick and sinking world?

# CHAPTER

## 2

---

## *Principles of Divine Healing*

There are certain principles underlying the teachings of the Holy Scriptures with respect to healing that are important to understand. When rightly comprehended, they are most helpful to intelligent faith.

The causes of disease and suffering are distinctly traced to the Fall and the sinful state of man. If sickness were part of the natural constitution of things, then we might meet it wholly on natural grounds and by natural means. But if it be part of the curse of sin, it must have its true remedy in the great Redemption. That sickness is the result of the Fall and one of the fruits of sin, no one can surely question. Death, we are told, has passed upon all, for all have sinned, and the greater includes the less.

Sickness is named among the curses that God was to send for Israel's sin (Deuteronomy 28:58–61). Again, sickness is distinctly connected with Satan's personal agency. He was the direct instrument of Job's suffering; and our Lord definitely attributed the diseases of His time directly to satanic power. It was Satan who bound the paralyzed woman "these eighteen years." It was demonic influence that held and crushed the bodies and souls of those Christ delivered. If sickness is the result of a spirit agency, it is most evident that it must be met and counteracted by a higher spiritual force and not by mere natural treatment.

And on the supposition that sickness is a divine discipline and chastening, it is still more evident that its removal must come not through mechanical or medical appliances, but through spiritual channels. It would be both ridiculous and vain for the arm of man to presume to wrest the chastening rod from the Father's hand by physical force or skill. The only way to avert God's stroke is to submit the spirit in penitence to His will and seek in humility and faith His forgiveness and relief.

From whatever side we look at disease, it becomes evident that its remedy must be found in God alone and the gospel of redemption.

Since disease is the result of the Fall, we may expect it to be embraced in the provisions of redemption. Therefore, we naturally will look for some intimation of a remedy in the preparatory dispensation to Christ's coming and the preaching of the gospel.

We are not disappointed. The great principle that God's care and providence embrace the temporal and physical as well as the spiritual needs of His people runs all through the Old Testament. Distinct provision for divine healing is made in all the ordinances of Moses. And the prophetic picture of the coming Deliverer is that of a great Physician as well as a glorious King and gracious Savior.

The healing of Abimelech, Miriam, Job, Naaman and Hezekiah; the case of the leper; the incident of the brazen serpent; the statute at Marah; the blessings and curses at Ebal and Gerizim; the terrible rebuke of Asa; the message of Psalm 103 and Chapter 53 of Isaiah—all leave the testimony of the Old Testament clear that the redemption of the body was the divine prerogative and purpose.

## The ministry of Christ

The personal ministry of Jesus Christ is the next great stage in the development of the principles of divine healing. In Christ's life on earth, we see a complete vision of what Christianity should be. From Jesus' words and works, we may surely gather the full plan of redemption. And what was the testimony of His life to physical healing? He went about their cities healing all manner of sickness and disease among the people. He healed all who had need of healing, "that it might be fulfilled which was spoken by Esaias the prophet, saying, Himself took our infirmities, and bare our sicknesses" (Matthew 8:17).

This was not an occasional incident. It was a chief part of Jesus' ministry. He began His work by healing the sick. He continued to heal to the close of His life. He healed on all occasions and in a great variety of cases. He healed without leaving any doubt or question of His will. He distinctly said to the doubting leper, "I will." He was only grieved when people hesitated to trust Him fully.

In all this Jesus was unfolding the real purpose of His great redemption and revealing His own unchanging character and love. He is still "the same yesterday, and to day, and for ever" (Hebrews 13:8). Surely we have a principle to rest our faith on as secure as the Rock of Ages.

## *Healing is centered in the atonement*

Redemption finds its center in the cross of our Lord Jesus Christ. There we must look for the fundamental principle of Divine healing, which rests on Jesus' atoning sacrifice. This necessarily follows from the first principle we have stated: If sickness is the result of the Fall, it must be included in the atonement of Christ, which reaches as "far as the curse is found."

Peter states of Christ, "his own self bare our sins in his own body on the tree, . . . by whose stripes ye were healed" (1 Peter 2:24). In His own body He has borne all our bodily liabilities for sin, and our bodies are set free. In that one cruel "stripe" of His—for the word is singular—was summed up all the aches and pains of a suffering world. There is no longer need that we should suffer what Christ has sufficiently borne. Thus our healing becomes a great redemption right that we simply claim as our purchased inheritance through the blood of Christ's cross.

## *Beyond the cross*

But there is something higher even than the cross. It is the resurrection of our Lord. There the gospel of healing finds the fountain of its deepest life. The death of Christ destroys sin—the root of sickness. But it is the life of Jesus that supplies the source of health and life for our redeemed bodies. The body of Christ is the living fountain of all our vital strength. He who came forth from Joseph's tomb with the new physical life of the resurrection is the Head of His people for life and immortality.

Not for Himself alone did Jesus receive the power of an endless life. He received it as our life. God "gave him to be the head over all things to the church, which is his body" (Ephesians 1:22–23). "We are members of his body, of his flesh, and of his bones" (5:30). The risen and ascended Christ is the fountain of our strength and life. We eat His flesh and drink His blood. He dwells in us and we in Him. As He lives in the Father, so he who eats Him shall live by Him. This is the great, vital, precious principle of physical healing in the name of Jesus. It is "the life also of Jesus . . . made manifest in our mortal flesh" (2 Corinthians 4:ll).

## Healing is new life

It follows that this life must be wholly a new life. The death and resurrection of the Lord Jesus have made an infinite gulf between the present and the past of every redeemed person. Henceforth, "if any man be in Christ, he is a new creature: old things are passed away; behold, all things are become new" (2 Corinthians 5:17). The death of Jesus has slain our old self. The life of Jesus is the spring of our new life.

This is true also of our physical life. God does not restore the old natural strength. He does not build up our former constitution. We must let go all the old dependencies. Our natural strength may fail. The life of Jesus is a strength that "out of weakness [is] made strong." It is a life that has no resources to start with. Creation-like, it is made out of nothing; resurrection-like, it comes out of the tomb and the failure of all previous hope and means.

This principle is of immense importance in the practical experience of healing. So long as we look for healing in the old natural life, we shall be disappointed. But when we cease to put confidence in the flesh and look only to Christ and His supernatural life in us for our strength of body as well as spirit, we shall find that we "can do all things through Christ which strengtheneth [us]."

It follows from this that the physical redemption that Christ brings is not merely healing but also life. It is not the readjustment of our life on the old basis, leaving it to go like a machine upon the natural plane. It is the imparting of a new kind of life and strength; therefore, it is as fully within the reach of people in health as those who are diseased. It is simply a higher kind of life—the turning of life's water into His heavenly wine.

It is only kept by constant abiding in Jesus and receiving from Him. It is not a permanent deposit but a constant dependence, a renewing of the inward man day by day. It is a strength that comes only as we need it and continues only while we dwell in Him.

## *A sacred life*

Such a life is a very sacred thing. It gives a peculiar sanctity to every look, tone, act and movement of the body. We are living on the life of God, and we must live like Him and for Him. A body thus divinely quickened adds power to the soul and to all the service of the Christian life. Words spoken in this divine energy and works done through the life of God will be clothed with a positive effectiveness which must make others feel that our bodies as well as our spirits are indeed the very temple of the holy God.

The great Agent in bringing this new life into our life is the Holy Spirit. The redemption work of the Lord Jesus is not completed without His blessed ministry. Not as a visible physical presence does the Savior of sinners and of the diseased now meet the sick and halt and blind, but through the Spirit. All the old physical power is there. All the ancient results upon the suffering frame are produced, but the approach is spiritual, not physical.

The presence of Christ must be brought to our consciousness. But the contact of our need with His life must come through the Holy Spirit. So Mary had to learn in the very first moment of the resurrection. "Touch me not . . . I ascend." Thus, henceforth, must she know Him as the Ascended One. So Paul had ceased to know Christ Jesus "after the flesh."

Our Lord, when speaking to the disciples at Capernaum of the living Bread—the Source of healing—added: "What and if ye shall see the Son of man ascend up where he was before? It is the spirit that quickeneth; the flesh profiteth nothing" (John 6:62–63). This is the reason why many find it hard to meet the Healer. They do not know the Holy Spirit. They do not know God spiritually.

The sun in the heavens might as well be a ball of ice were it not for the atmosphere that attracts its warmth and light to us and diffuses them through our world. And Christ's life and love only reach us through the Holy Spirit, the Light, the Atmosphere, the divine Medium who brings and sheds abroad His life and light, His love and presence in our being. He takes of the things of Christ and shows them to us, extracting His life and sweetly diffusing it through every part of our being. He is the great Quickener.

It was through the Holy Spirit that the Lord cast out devils on earth. And now, "if the Spirit of him that raised up Jesus from the dead dwell in you, he that raised up Christ from the dead shall also quicken your mortal [body] by his Spirit that dwelleth in you" (Romans 8:11).

## Free grace . . .

This new life must come, like all the blessings of Christ's redemption, as the free grace of God, without works and without distinction of merit or respect of persons.

Everything that comes through Christ must come as grace. There can be no works mingled with justifying faith. So our healing must be wholly of God, or not of grace at all. If Christ heals, He must do it alone. This principle ought to settle the question of using "means" in connection with faith for healing. The natural and the spiritual, the earthly and the heavenly, the works of man and the grace of God cannot be mixed any more than a person could expect to harness a tortoise with a locomotive. They cannot work together.

The gifts of the gospel are sovereign gifts. God can do the most difficult things for us Himself. But He does not help our self-sufficiency to do the easiest. A hopeless case is, therefore, much more hopeful than one where we think we can do something ourselves. We must venture on Him wholly.

If healing is to be sought by natural means, let us obtain all the best results of skill and experience. But if it is to be received through the name of Jesus, it must be by grace alone.

## . . . freely given

It follows also in the same connection that if healing is a part of the gospel and a gift of Christ, it must be an impartial one, limited only by the great "whosoever" of the gospel. It is not a special gift of discriminating favoritism, but a great and common heritage of faith and obedience. It is "whosoever will, let him take the water of life freely." It is true that all who come must conform to the simple conditions of obedient faith. But these are impartial, without respect of persons and within the reach of all who trust and obey.

The simple condition of this great blessing—the condition of all the blessings of the gospel—is faith without sight. Grace without works and faith without sight must always go together as twin principles of the gospel. The one thing God asks from all who are to receive His grace is that they shall trust His simple Word. But this must be real trust. We must believe and doubt not. If God's Word be true at all, it is absolutely and utterly true.

With its living roots, a very small seed can split open great rocks and mountains, but the germ must be intact. One little laceration may kill its life. One doubt will destroy the efficacy of faith; therefore, it must begin by our taking God simply at His Word. A faith that is going to wait for signs and evidence will never be strong. Plants that begin by leaning will always need support. Indeed, the "faith" which rests upon seeing is not faith. "Blessed are they that have not seen, and yet have believed."

Abraham had to believe God and take the new name of faith and fatherhood before there was any indication of the answer. Indeed, every natural sign contradicted and stultified the promise. It is beautiful to notice the form of expression in Genesis 17. First Abraham was told, "Thou shalt be a father of many nations" (17:4). Then came the change of his name from Abram ("exalted father") to Abraham ("father of many"). It was the profession of his faith and the acknowledgment before a scorning world that he believed God.

Then follows God's next word. And how wonderful! The tense is changed. It is no longer a promise but an accomplished fact: "A father of many nations have I made thee" (17:5). Faith has turned the future into the past, and now God calls "things which are not" as though they were (see 1 Corinthians 1:28). So we must believe and receive the healing life of Jesus and all the blessings of the gospel.

## More than an option

Are we under an obligation to seek divine healing of the body? Is it an optional matter with us how we shall be healed—whether we shall trust God or look to man?

Is this not "a statute and an ordinance" for us, too, and a matter of simple obedience? Is it not God's great prerogative to deal with the bodies He has redeemed, and an impertinence for us to choose some other way than His? Is not the gospel of salvation a commandment as well as a promise, and is not the gospel of healing of equal authority?

Has God not chosen to legislate about the way in which the plague of sin that has entered His world shall be dealt with? Have we any business to interfere with His great health promise? Has He not at enormous cost provided a remedy for the bodies of His children as part of His redemption, and is He not jealous for the honor and rights of His dear Son's name in this matter?

Does He not claim to be the Owner of His children's bodies, and does He not claim the right to care for them? Has He not left us one great prescription for disease, and is not any other course unauthorized and followed at our own risk? Surely these questions answer themselves. They leave but one course open to every child of God to whom He gives the light to see that His Word is "yea" and "Amen."

## God's fixed principles

The order of God's dealings with our souls and bodies is

regulated by certain fixed principles. The Bible was written to state
them in plain language for the wayfaring man. God works from
within outward, beginning with our spiritual nature and then
diffusing His life and power through our physical being.

Many persons come to God for healing whose spiritual life is
wholly defective and wrong. God does not always refuse the
healing. He begins in the depths of the soul, and when the soul is
prepared to receive His life, He may begin to heal the body.

There is a close relation between the state of the soul and the
body. John prays that Gaius "mayest prosper and be in health, even
as thy soul prospereth" (3 John 1). A little cloud of sin upon the
heart will leave a shadow upon the brain and nerves and a pressure
upon the whole frame. A malicious breath of spiritual evil will
poison the blood and depress the whole system. But a clear, calm
and confident spirit will bring vigor into all the physical life. It will
open the way for all the full pulses of the Lord's life in us.

Hence, also, healing will often be gradual in its development as
the spiritual life grows and faith takes a firmer hold of Christ. The
principle of the divine life, like the natural, is "first the blade, then
the ear, after that the full corn in the ear." Many people want the
head of wheat while the blade is yet tender. But it would only
overwhelm us by its weight. We must have deep and quiet strength
to sustain our higher blessing.

Sometimes this preparation is completed beforehand. Then God
can work very rapidly. But in each case He knows the order and
process best adapted to the development of the whole man. That
is ever His great end in all His workings in us.

## Some limitations

Any limitations there may be of healing are also fixed by certain
principles. Some enter not into this promised land because of
unbelief and because they are a stiff-necked generation. Sometimes
someone asks, "Why should people ever die if Christ will always
heal?" Because faith can only go as far as God's promise, and God
has nowhere promised that we shall never die during this dispensation. It is not immortal life that God promises in connection

with the healing of the mortal body. The promise is fullness of life and health and strength up to the measure of our natural life and until our life work is done. True, it is the life of the resurrection that we have; but it is not the whole of it—only the firstfruits.

In speaking of our immortal life the apostle says: "Now he that hath wrought us for the selfsame thing is God, who also hath given unto us the earnest of the Spirit" (2 Corinthians 5:5). That is, as our earnest was a handful of the very soil of the purchased farm, but only a handful, so God has given us now by His Spirit in our new physical life a handful of the very life of the resurrection. But it is only a handful, and the fullness will not come until His coming. But that handful is worth more than all the soil of earth.

Shall we have strength for all kinds of supernatural exploits and extraordinary exertions? We have the promise of sufficient strength for all the will of God and all the service of Christ. But we shall have no strength for mere display and certainly none to waste in recklessness or spend in selfishness and sin.

Within the limits of our God-appointed work—and these limits may be very wide, much wider than any mere natural strength—we "can do all things through Christ which strengtheneth [us]." We may fearlessly undertake all labors, self-denials and difficulties in the face of exposure, weakness, conditions of climate and the most engrossing demands upon strength and time, where Christ clearly leads and calls us. We shall have His protecting power and find that "God is able to make all grace abound toward [us]; that [we], always having all sufficiency in all things, may abound to every good work" (2 Corinthians 9:8).

But let us touch the forbidden fruit, wander out of the sacred circle of His will or spend our strength on self or sin, and our life will lose its strength like Samson's arm and wither like Jonah's gourd. Yes, it must be true, always true, in our life as Paul says in Romans 11:36: "Of him, and through him, and to him, are all things: to whom be glory for ever. Amen."

# CHAPTER

## 3

---

## *Popular Objections*

There are currently a number of objections to the glad tidings that He who "forgiveth all [our] iniquities" as truly and as fully also "healeth all [our] diseases." I shall refer to some of the more forcible.

Objection 1: *The age of miracles is past.* This is commonly assumed as an axiom and almost quoted as a Bible text.

In reply let me ask, What age are we in? There have been, and shall be, various ages and dispensations. There was the Edenic, the Patriarchal, the Mosaic. There will be the Millennial, the Eternal. We are presently in the Christian era.

But perhaps there is more than one Christian age: one for Christ and His apostles and one for us. Yet Paul says he lived in "these last days." He speaks of the people of his generation as those on whom "the ends of the world are come." And Peter, in his sermon on the day of Pentecost, claims for his day a prophecy of Joel for the latter days.

We must then be in the age of Christ and Christianity. And if this is not the age of miracles, then what is it?

But perhaps there was to be a great gulf between the first and last periods of this age. Perhaps it was only to begin with special manifestations of divine power and then shade down into sober commonplace. Why then should Joel say that the signal outpouring of the Holy Spirit should be "in the last days"? Why should he say that the supernatural signs and wonders both in earth and heaven should be especially "before the great and the terrible day of the Lord come"—that is, toward the close of the Christian age and prior to Jesus' second advent?

Why also should Paul so strongly insist that Christ's Church is one body, not two, and that the gifts of every part belong to the whole (see 1 Corinthians 12)? If there is an essential difference between the apostolic and a later age, then the church is not one body but two; then the gifts of those members do not flow into our members; then the glorious figure and powerful reasoning of that chapter are false and delusive. If we are the same body, we have the same life and power.

## Were the apostles different?

What made the apostles more mighty than ordinary men? It was not their companionship with Jesus; it was the gift of the Holy Spirit. Have we not the same? And do we not exalt the men and disparage the Spirit that made them what they were when we speak of their power as exceptional and transient?

Peculiar and exceptional functions they indeed had as witnesses of Christ's resurrection and the organizers of the church on earth. But to show to men that the miraculous gifts of the church were not confined to them, these gifts are specially distinguished from the apostleship in First Corinthians 12. They were conferred in preeminent degree on Stephen, Philip and others who were not apostles at all, and they were committed by James to the ordinary and permanent eldership of the church. No, our dear Master never contemplated or proposed any post-apostolic gulf of impotence and failure.

Mankind's unbelief and sin have made such a gulf. The church's own corruption has caused it. But Christ never desired it. See Him standing on the Galilean mountain midway between earth and heaven. See Him looking down to our century with a love as tender, a grace as full and a power as available as He exercised in the first. Hear Him speaking in the present tense, as though we were all equally near to Him who would never be separated from us: "All power is given unto me in heaven and in earth. . . . Lo, I am with you all the days, even unto the end of the age" (Matthew

28:18–20, Greek).

## Just one age

It was to be one age, not two, and Christ's "all power" has never been withdrawn. He was to be a perpetual I Am, to be as near at the end as at the beginning. The work we are to do is to be the complement of His own. In fact, it *is* His own work, for Luke says He "began both to do and teach" (Acts 1:1). He must, therefore, be continuing His work still.

This is just what Jesus said our work would be: "He that believeth on me, the works that I do shall he do also" (John 14:12)—that is, these works shall be Christ's and ours, in partnership. Neither shall they be in any way diminished by His seeming absence, for "greater works . . . shall he do; because I go unto my Father."

Indeed, as long as the ancient church retained in even limited measure the faith and holiness of the first days, the same works were uniformly found. In the second, third and fourth centuries, fathers as famous as Irenaeus and Tertullian bore testimony to the prevalence of many undoubted miracles of healing and even the raising of the dead in the name of Jesus. And as late as the fifth century supernatural events were attested by authorities as high as Procopius and Justinian on evidence so strong that the sober editor Mosheim declared that he who would doubt it must be ready to question all the facts of history.

## We are in the age of miracles

The age of miracles is not past. The Word of God never indicated a hint of such a fact. On the contrary, miracles are to be among the signs of the last days. The very adversary himself is to counterfeit them and send forth unto the kings of the earth demon spirits working miracles. The only defense against the false miracles will be the true.

We are in the age of miracles, the age of Christ, the age that lies between the two advents. Underneath the eye of a ceaseless divine Presence, this is the age of power, the age which above all other ages of time should be intensely alive.

Objection 2. *The same results as are claimed for faith in the healing of disease are also said to follow the practices of spiritism, animism, clairvoyance and the like.* Although some of the manifestations of spiritism are undoubted frauds, we will not deny that many are unquestionably supernatural, produced by forces for which physical science has no explanation.

It is no use to try to meet this monster of spiritism with the hasty and shallow denial of the facts. It is no use to try to explain spiritism as trickery. These manifestations often are real and superhuman. They are "the spirits of devils, working miracles" (Revelation 16:14). They are the revived forces of the Egyptian magicians, the Grecian oracles, the Roman haruspices, the Indian fakirs. They are not divine. They are less than omnipotent, but they are more than human.

Our Lord has expressly warned us of them and told us to test them, not by their power but by their fruits—their holiness, humility and homage to the name of Jesus and the Word of God. Their very existence renders it imperative that we should be able to present against them—like the rod of Moses that swallowed the magicians' rods and at last silenced their limited power—the living forces of a holy Christianity in the physical as well as the spiritual world.

Objection 3. *The miracles of Christ and His apostles were designed to establish the facts and doctrines of Christianity; we do not need their continuance.* But the critics continue to call in question the existence of these facts and the credibility of these writings. And how are the inhabitants of new countries to know the divine origin of these oracles? What access have they, or indeed the great masses of men everywhere, to the archives of learning or the manuscripts of the Bible?

## We need to see a living Christ

No, every generation needs a living Christ, and every new community needs these "signs following" to confirm the Word. And we have sometimes seen the plausible and persistent agnostic, whom no reason could satisfy, silenced and confounded when brought face to face with some humble, unlettered woman as she told him with glowing, convincing honesty that she had been raised up from lifelong helplessness by the Word and name of Jesus only.

Until Christ returns, the world will never cease to need the touch of His power and presence. "God also bearing them witness, both with signs and wonders . . . and gifts of the Holy Ghost, according to his own will" (Hebrews 2:4).

There is also a current misapprehension about the full design of Christ's miracles that takes away half their beauty and value. They are looked upon mainly, even solely, as special testimonies to Christ's power and deity. But if this had been all, a few special and marked cases would have been sufficient. He would not then have healed the thousands who daily thronged Him. But we are told, on the contrary, that they were not isolated and occasional but numerous and almost universal.

## Jesus had to be true to His character

Christ healed all who had need of healing and all who were sick. This was not only a proof of His power, but a demonstration of what He now wished them to know—His boundless love. Jesus healed to fulfill the ancient prophetic picture of the Messiah: "Himself took our infirmities, and bare our sicknesses." But if it was necessary then for Him to fulfill that character, it is as much so now. He must never cease to be true to the picture God drew of Him and which He also drew of Himself.

If this is not true still for us, then Jesus Christ is not "the same yesterday, and to day, and for ever." If this is not still true for us, then—perhaps—the other promises of the Scriptures are also not true for us, and He has not borne our sins any more than our sickness and suffering. No, His heart is still the same.

Objection 4. *Christ's last promise in Mark embraces much more than healing; if you claim one, you must claim all.* If you expect the healing of the sick, you must also include the gift of tongues and the power to overcome malignant poisons. We cheerfully accept this severe logic. We cannot afford to give up one of the promises.

We admit our belief in the presence of the Healer in all the *charismata* of the early church. We see no reason why a humble servant of Christ, engaged in the Master's work, may not claim in simple faith the power to resist malaria and other poisons and malignant dangers. To a greater or less extent the gift of tongues has been continuous in the church of Christ and, along with many counterfeits, has undoubtedly been realized in the present generation.

Objection 5. *Glory accrues to God from our submission to His will in sickness; the results of sanctified affliction are blessed.* Perhaps no objection is more strongly urged. And if those who urge and claim to practice this suggestion would really accept their sickness and lie passive under it, they would at least be consistent. But do they not send for a doctor and do their best to get out of this "sweet will of God"? Is this meekly submitting to the affliction? Does not the submission usually come when the result is known to be inevitable?

## Christian discipline is misunderstood

We do not deny the happy results of many a case of painful sickness in turning the soul from some forbidden path and leading it into deeper experiences. Nor do we question the fervent piety of many an invalid who cannot trust God for healing. But we are sure there is an immense amount of vague and unscriptural misunderstanding with respect to the principles of Christian discipline.

The Word says, "For this cause many are weak and sickly among you, and many sleep. For if we would judge ourselves, we should not be judged" (1 Corinthians 11:30–31). Here is a definite and unchangeable law of God's dealings with His dear children. When we are judging ourselves, we shall not be judged. While we hearken and obey, He "will put none of these diseases" upon us that He "brought upon the Egyptians" (Exodus 15:26). The normal state for God's faithful children is soundness of spirit and soul and body (see 1 Thessalonians 5:23).

God's desire for His children is that they may "be in health and prosper even as [their] soul[s] prosper" (3 John 1). His will for them is to act in these things according to His Word. He wants for them "the good pleasure of his goodness" (2 Thessalonians 1:11) and "that good, and acceptable, and perfect, will of God" (Romans 12:2). "Many," it is true, "are the afflictions of the righteous." But it is also true that "the LORD delivereth him out of them all. He keepeth all his bones: not one of them is broken" (Psalm 34:19–20).

## Affliction and sickness are not the same

Between "affliction" and "sickness" there is a very clear distinction. At Marah the children of Israel drank bitter water that God purified (Exodus 15:23ff.), just as many a trial is sanctified and blessed. It was *there* that He made a statute and an ordinance of healing. He told the people that if they would obey Him they should not be sick, for He would be their constant Healer. In exact parallel, James says to us (5:13): "Is any afflicted? let him pray"— that is, for grace and strength. But (5:14), "Is any sick among you? let him call for the elders of the church" to pray for healing.

Affliction is suffering with Christ, and He was not sick. Jesus warned, "In the world ye shall have tribulation" (John 16:33). All the more we need a sound, strong heart to bear and overcome.

Objection 6. **We are presumptuous to claim the healing of disease absolutely.** Rather, the model of all true prayer is Christ's language in the Garden: "Not as I will, but as thou wilt" (Matthew 26:39). Bowing to the divine will is the believer's best course, but these objectors have forgotten that Jesus also said on that occasion in Gethsemane, "Save me from this hour: but for this cause came I unto this hour. Father, glorify thy name" (John 12:27–28).

Indeed, there are many who believe that our Lord's prayer in Gethsemane was answered by the Father, saving Him from Satan's attempt to take His life prematurely in the Garden. In Hebrews we are told He "was heard in that he feared" (5:7). Certainly, in any such circumstances, when prompted by extreme distress to ask for something for which we have no clear warrant, promise or favorable intimation of the divine will, we ought ever to refer the matter to the arbitration of that unknown will.

## God has made known His will

But when we know from God's own Word to us that a blessing is in accordance with His will, that it is provided for, purchased and promised, is it not really evasive to come to Him in doubt and uncertainty? Is it not very much the same as if a son at college should continue to write, asking his father's permission for things for which he had already been given the fullest directions in his father's first letter?

Did Christ thus pray when he asked for things He knew to be consistent with God's will? At Bethany, prior to raising Lazarus, He said, "Father, I thank thee that thou hast heard me" (John 11:41). Is it not as lawful for us to imitate Him in His prayer at Bethany as in His prayer at Gethsemane?

When God's will is clearly made known, may we not pray even as Christ prayed? Jesus told His disciples, "If ye abide in me, and my words abide in you, ye shall ask what ye will, and it shall be done unto you" (John 15:7). Do we pray in indefiniteness when we ask forgiveness? We take it, we claim it, and being strong in faith we thus glorify God.

Objection 7. *There are many cases of failure; look at Paul and his companions who were ill.* Paul's thorn is inevitably kept as a precious relic to torment doubting Christians, and Trophimus and Epaphroditus are dragged forward on their couches to encourage the willing patient in the Hospital of Doubting Castle.

With regard to Paul's thorn we must say four things:

> *(1) It is not at all certain that it was disease. It was a messenger of Satan to buffet him—some humiliation, perhaps stammering.*
>
> *(2) It was so far healed and more than healed, whatever it was, that it brought the power of Christ to rest upon Paul so mightily that he was abundantly enabled for all his labors and duties. He longed for more such provocations of bless-*

*ing. And he who can see in this a feeble invalid laid aside from work is afflicted with spiritual cross-eyes!*

*(3) Before people can claim that their sickness is a heavenly visitation like Paul's to keep them from being exalted above measure, they would need to have been up in the third heaven with him and to hear things unlawful for a person to utter!*

*(4) Paul does give us elsewhere the account of his healing (see 2 Corinthians 1:8–11). It was unmistakably by believing prayer and mighty faith in "God that raiseth the dead."*

As for Epaphroditus, he was healed through God's mercy. Trophimus may also have been healed, although his healing was delayed.

## Healing is not always instantaneous

Healing, even by faith, is not always instantaneous. There are "miracles" and "gifts of healing," the one sudden and stupendous, the other simple and probably gradual. That Trophimus should have been to blame for his illness or slowness of faith is not remarkable. But that there should be only two such cases in all these inspired personal sketches is most remarkable!

There are still instances of failure, but perhaps they may be accounted for through defective knowledge or unbelief, or through disobedience to God in some way. There may be failure to follow consistently the teachings of the Word and the Spirit, or the sickness may be for a deeper spiritual discipline. And there are failures in the spiritual life from the same or similar causes. These failures in no way disprove the reality of the divine promises or the sufficiency of Christ's grace. "Let God be true" even if "every man a liar" (Romans 3:4).

Objection 8. *If these things are so, people should never die.* Why not? Why should faith go further than the Word? Anything beyond that is presumption.

The Word places a limit to human life, and all that scriptural faith can claim is sufficiency of health and strength for our life work and within its fair limits. It may be longer or shorter, but we need not, like the wicked, live out less than half our days (see Psalm 55:23). Our life should be complete, satisfying and long enough for the work God has given us to do. And then, when the close comes, why need it be with painful and depressing sickness, as the rotten apple falls in June from disease and with a worm at its core?

Why may it not rather be as that ripe apple would drop in September—mature, mellow and ready to fall without a struggle into the gardener's hand? So Job pictures the close of a good man's life "in a full age, like as a shock of corn cometh in his season" (Job 5:26).

Objection 9. *Did not God make all these "means," and does He not want us to use them?* Indeed, is it not presumption for us to expect God to do anything unless we first do all we can for ourselves? In reply I answer, God has nowhere prescribed medical "means," and we have no right to infer that drugs are ordinarily His "means." They are not again and again referred to, like food, as necessary or enjoined for our use.

## The Bible mentions few doctors

It is a singular, unanswerable fact that in the whole history of the patriarchs no reference is made to the use of medicines. In the story of Job, so full of vivid details, everyone else is described but the doctor, and everything in the universe but medications. There is no physician in attendance or surely we should have caught a glimpse of him. When Job recovers, it is wholly from God's direct hand after Job finds his true place of humility to God and love to man.

In the still more elaborate prescriptions and prohibitions of Leviticus, even including procedures for dealing with the disease of leprosy, there is not even a remote intimation of a doctor or a drugstore. It is not until after the time of Solomon and the importation, no doubt, of Egypt's godless culture and science that we find the first definite case of medical treatment. There King Asa, the patient, dies—and dies under the stigma of unbelief and declension from God.

In the New Testament, medical practice is referred to in terms not at all complimentary when the woman who touched the hem of Jesus' garment is described. Luke abandoned his practice as a physician for evangelistic work. While he was present with Paul in Melita at the healing of the father of Publius, it was Paul who "laid his hands on him [Publius] and healed him" (Acts 28:8). Surely this was so the Lord Jesus should have all the glory. Moreover, it was so His saints in these latter days should have the comfort of knowing that the healing was done in the presence of a physician whose medical skills were never used—as far as the record goes—after his conversion.

Without going further, this much at least is clear: (1) God has not prescribed medicine. (2) God has prescribed another way of healing in the name of Jesus, has provided for it in the atonement, has appointed an ordinance for its application, has commanded and enjoined it.

All the provisions of grace are by faith, not by works or "means." The use of remedies, if successful, usually gives the glory to man, and God will not permit that. If the healing of sickness is one of the purchases of Christ's atonement and one of His prerogatives as our Redeemer, then He is jealous for it, and we should also be jealous.

## *Recognize the "law of faith"*

If healing is part of the plan of salvation, then we know that the whole plan is framed according to the "law of faith." If the language of James is a command, then it excludes the treatment of disease by human remedies as much as the employment of one physician would exclude the treatment of another at the same time and for the same case.

If that is God's way of healing, then other methods must be man's ways, and there must be some risk in deliberately repudiating the former for the latter. We do not imply by this that the medical profession is sinful or the use of means always wrong. There may be—there always will be—instances where faith cannot be exercised. And if natural means have—as they do have—a limited value, there is ample room for their employment in these cases. But for the trusting and obedient child of God, there is the more excellent way that His Word has clearly prescribed. By it, God's name will be ever glorified afresh and our spiritual life continually renewed.

Our age is one of increasing rationalism. Unbelief is constantly endeavoring to eliminate all traces of direct supernatural working from the universe and to explain everything by second causes and natural development. For this very reason, God wants to show His immediate working wherever our faith will afford Him an opportunity. Higher criticism is industriously taking the miraculous from our Bibles, and a lower standard of Christian life is busy taking all that is divine out of our lives.

Let all who believe in a living God be willing to prove to a scoffing generation that "the everlasting God, the LORD, the Creator of the ends of the earth, fainteth not, neither is weary" (Isaiah 40:28). Let them proclaim that "in him we live, and move, and have our being" (Acts 17:28) and that still there is nothing too hard for the Lord.

Objection 10. *Divine healing unduly exalts the physical body and directs the minds of people from the transcendent interest of the immortal soul, promoting fanaticism and leading to other evils.* The same objection might be brought against the years of our Lord's ministry on earth, when the healing of the body was made an avenue to reach men's souls and a testimony of His spiritual teachings. The doctrine of Christ's healing power is closely linked with the necessity of holiness and the deeper truths and experiences of the spiritual life. It tends, in a preeminent degree, to promote purity and earnestness.

The power that heals the body usually imparts a much richer baptism of the Holy Spirit to the heart. The retaining of this divine life and health requires constant fellowship with God and prompts consecrated service for the Master. The spiritual results far outweigh the temporal.

Divine healing is one of the most powerful checks and impulses in the lives of those who have truly received it. The abuses complained of will usually be found connected with false teaching and unscriptural perversions that rash or ambitious persons disseminate for their own ungodly ends.

## A humbling, holy truth

The true doctrine of healing through the Lord Jesus Christ is most humbling, holy and practical. It exalts no man; it spares no sin; it offers no promises to the disobedient; it gives no strength for selfish indulgence or worldly ends. Rather, it exalts the name of Jesus, glorifies God, inspires the soul with faith and power, summons to a life of self-denial and holy service. It awakens a slumbering church and an unbelieving world with the solemn signals of a living God and a risen Christ.

Extravagances, perversions and counterfeits we know there are. Unauthorized and self-constituted healers and mercenary impostors abound. There are rash and indiscriminate anointings of persons that discredit the truth. But the truth of God is not chargeable with human error, and the counterfeit is often a startling testimony to the existence of the genuine.

Let the ministers of the Lord Jesus answer these evils by claiming and exercising, in the power of the Holy Spirit, the gifts and offices once delivered to them. In the words found in Malachi 3:18, let the people of God in these perilous times "discern between the righteous and the wicked, between him that serveth God and him that serveth him not."

# CHAPTER

## 4

## *Practical Directions*

Together we have considered the scriptural grounds of the doctrine of healing by faith in God. The practical question arises next: How can a person who fully believes in the doctrine receive the blessing and appropriate healing?

I suggest seven steps.

### *Be fully persuaded*

First, *be fully persuaded of the Word of God in this matter of divine healing*. The Word is the only sure foundation of rational and scriptural faith. Your faith must rest on the great principles and promises of the Bible or it can never stand the testings that are sure to come. You must be so sure that this is part of the gospel and the redemption of Christ that all the reasonings of the best of men and women cannot shake you.

Most of the practical failures of faith in this matter result from defective or doubtful convictions concerning the divine Word. A woman who had fully embraced this truth and accepted Christ as her Healer was immediately strengthened very much both in spirit and body. Her overflowing heart was only too glad to tell the good news to all her friends. Among others, she met her pastor and told him of her faith and blessing.

To her surprise, he immediately objected to any such views. He warned her against this new fanaticism and told her that these promises on which she was resting were not for us but only for the apostles and the apostolic age. She listened, questioned, yielded and abandoned her confidence. In less than one month, when I saw her again, she had sunk to such depression that she scarcely knew whether she even believed the Bible.

If those promises were for the apostles, she argued, why might not all the other promises of the Bible also be for them only? I invited her to spend time examining the teaching of the Word of God. We carefully compared the promises of healing from Exodus to James. Every question we calmly weighed until the truth became so manifest and its evidence so overwhelming that she could only say, "I know it is here, and I know it is true, even if all the world should deny it!"

Then she knelt and asked the Lord's forgiveness for her weakness and unbelief. She renewed her solemn profession of faith and consecration and claimed again the promise of healing and the baptism of the Holy Spirit. From that day she has been restored and blessed with all spiritual blessings. The very pastor who caused her to stumble has been forced to own that this is the finger of God. But the starting point of all her blessing was the moment when she fully accepted and rested in the living Word.

God countenances not the slightest departure from His Word. When God said to Moses, "Speak ye unto the rock," Moses used "means" and with his rod "smote the rock twice" (Numbers 20:8,11). God declared, "Because ye believed me not, to sanctify me in the eyes of the children of Israel, therefore ye shall not bring this congregation into the land which I have given them" (20:12).

Moses suffered severely for his departure from instructions, but God in His own way was sanctified.

## Be assured of God's will

Second, *be fully assured of the will of God to heal you.* Most persons are ready enough to admit the power of Christ to heal. The devil himself admits this. True faith implies equal confidence in the willingness of God to answer the prayer of faith. Any doubt on this point will surely paralyze your prayer for definite healing. If there is any question of God's will to heal *you,* there can be no certainty in your expectation.

A mere vague trust in the possible acceptance of your prayer is not faith definite enough to grapple with the forces of disease and death. The prayer for healing, "if it be Thy will," carries with it no claim for which Satan will quit his hold. This is a matter about which you ought to know His will before you ask, and then you must will and claim it because it is His will.

Has God given you any means by which you may know His will? Most assuredly. If the Lord Jesus has purchased healing for you in His redemption, it must be God's will for you to have it, for Christ's whole redeeming work was simply the executing of the Father's will. If Jesus has promised it to you, it must be His will that you should receive it, for how can you know His will but by His Word?

More than that, if the Lord Jesus has bequeathed healing to you in the New Testament, which is simply His last will and testament, then it is one of the bequests of your Savior's will, secured to all the blood-bought heirs of God and joint-heirs with Christ. If you are to partake of any of the benefits, you must observe all the terms of His Testament. Therefore, all questions of your wishes or desires in the matter must end when the will of God is defined and proved.

The Word of God is forever the standard of His will, and that Word has declared immutably that it is God's greatest desire and unalterable principle of action to give to every person according as he or she will believe. Especially has He promised to save all who will receive Christ by faith and to heal all who will receive healing by similar faith. No one thinks of asking for forgiveness "if it be Thy will." Nor should you throw any stronger doubt on His promise of physical redemption. Both are freely offered to every trusting person who will accept them.

Some of us prayed with and anointed for healing a woman quite prominent in Christian work. She returned in a few weeks saying that she was no better. Asked if she had believed fully, she replied, "I believed that I should be healed if it was His good pleasure, and if not, I am willing to have it otherwise."

"But," I responded, "may we not know God's pleasure in this matter from His own Word and ask with the full expectation of the blessing? Indeed, ought we to ask anything of God until we have reason to believe that it is His will? Is not His Word the intimation of His will; and, after He has so fully promised it, is it not a vexation and a mockery to imply a doubt of His willingness?"

She went away, and the very next morning she claimed the promise. She told the Lord that now she not only believed that He could, but would and did remove the trouble. In less than half an hour an external tumor of considerable size had wholly, visibly disappeared.

Often there is much subtle unbelief in the prayer, "Thy will be done." That blessed petition really expresses the highest measure of divine love and blessing. No kinder thing can come to us than that will. And yet we often ask it as if it was the iron hand of a cruel despot and an inexorable destiny. This leads us to say with Job: "Though he slay me, yet will I trust in him."

One doctor who really believed the Bible to be the inspired Word of God actually put his belief to the test by first saying to every patient at the first interview, "Are you a Christian?" If the patient answered affirmatively, his reply was, "I cannot prescribe any medicine for you because it is not medical healing that will cure you. Are you willing to put your case in the hands of the Lord Jesus Christ?" If the answer was still yes, he would pray and explain to the patient how he or she could have healing from the Lord. He would treat with medicine only those who said they were not Christians.

It should be added that that doctor was the most successful medical practitioner for miles around. He always had more patients than he could deal with personally.

## Are you right with God?

Third, *be careful that you are right with God.* If your sickness has come to you on account of any sinful cause, be sure that you thoroughly repent of and confess your sins and make all restitution as far as it is in your power. If sickness has been a discipline designed to separate you from some evil, at once present yourself to God in frank self-judgment and consecration and claim from Him the grace to sanctify you and keep you holy.

An impure heart is a constant fountain of disease. A sanctified spirit is in itself as wholesome as it is holy. At the same time, do not let Satan paralyze your faith by throwing you back on your unworthiness, telling you that you are not good enough to claim healing. You never can deserve any of God's mercies. The only plea is the name, the merits and the righteousness of Christ. But you can renounce known sin and you can walk so as to please God.

You can judge yourself and put away all that God shows you to be wrong. The moment you do this you are forgiven. "If we would judge ourselves, we should not be judged" (1 Corinthians 11:31). "If we confess our sins, he is faithful and just to forgive us our sins, and to cleanse us from all unrighteousness" (1 John 1:9). Do not wait to feel forgiveness or joy, but let your will be wholly turned to God, and believe at once that you are accepted. Then "draw near with a true heart in full assurance of faith, having [your heart] sprinkled from an evil conscience, and [your body] washed with pure water" (Hebrews 10:22).

It is quite vain for you to try to exercise faith for yourself or others in the face of willful transgression and in defiance of the chastening that God has meant you should respect and yield to. But when you receive His correction and turn to Him with humble and obedient heart, He may then graciously remove the pain and make the touch of healing the token of His forgiving love. "The prayer of faith shall save the sick, and the Lord shall raise him up; and if he have committed sins, they shall be forgiven him. Confess your faults one to another, and pray one for another, that ye may be healed" (James 5:15–16).

Often sickness is a moral malaria contracted by infringing on Satan's territory. You cannot be healed until you step away from the forbidden place and stand again on holy ground. Thus this question of your personal state, while not a condition of healing, is a very important element in it.

The great purpose of God in all His dealings with us is our highest welfare and our spiritual soundness. To the suffering Christian, therefore, there is no better counsel than the old exhortation: "The LORD is good unto them that wait for him. . . . He doth not afflict willingly nor grieve the children of men. . . . Let us search and try our ways, and turn again to the LORD" (Lamentations 3:25, 33, 40).

## Commit and claim

Fourth, having become fully persuaded of the Word of God, the will of God and your own personal acceptance with God, now *commit your body to God and claim by simple faith His promise of healing in the name of Jesus.* Do not merely ask for it, but humbly and firmly claim healing as His covenant pledge, as your inheritance, as a purchased redemption right. Claim it as something already fully offered you in the gospel and waiting only your acceptance to make good your possession.

There is a great difference between asking and taking, between expecting and accepting. You must take Christ as your Healer— not as an experiment, not as a future benefit, but as a present reality. You must believe that He does now, according to His promise, touch your life with His almighty hand and quicken the fountains of your being with His strength. Do not merely believe that He will do so, but claim and believe that He does now touch you and begins the work of healing in your body. And go forth counting it done, acknowledging and praising Him for it.

It is a good thing to prepare for this solemn act of committal and appropriating faith. It ought to be a very deliberate and final step. In the nature of things it cannot be repeated. Like the marriage ceremony, it is the signalizing and sealing of a great transaction. It depends for its value upon the reality of the union that it seals.

Before you take this step you should weigh each question thoroughly and then regard it as forever settled. You should step out solemnly, definitely, irrevocably on new ground, on God's promise, with the deep conviction that it is forever. This gives great strength and rest to the heart. It closes the door against a thousand doubts and temptations.

From that moment, doubt should be regarded as absolutely out of the question and even the thought of retreating to old "means" inadmissible. God has become the Physician, and He will not give His glory to another. God has healed, and all human attempts at helping would imply a doubt of the reality of the healing.

When God makes it plain that death is approaching, it would not appear to be unscriptural to call in a doctor, as the state officer lawfully appointed by the powers that be, to whom we are instructed to be obedient.

The more entirely the act of faith can be a complete committal, the more power will it have. If you have any question about your faith for this, make it a matter of special preparation and prayer. Ask God to give you special faith for this act. All your graces must come from Him, and faith is among them. You have nothing of your own, and even your very faith is but the grace of Christ Himself within you. You can exercise faith, and thus far your responsibility extends. But God must impart faith, and you simply put it on and wear it as from Him. This makes the exercise of strong faith a very simple and blessed possibility.

Jesus does not say to you, "Have great faith yourself." But He does say, "Have the faith of God." God's faith is all-sufficient, and you can have it and use it. You can take Christ for your faith as you took Him for your justification, for your victories over temptation, for your sanctification. You may then rest in the assurance that your faith has not failed to meet the demands of the promise, for it has been Christ's own faith.

You simply come in His name and present Him as your perfect offering, your plea, your faith, your advocate, your righteousness. Your very faith itself is nothing but simply taking His free gift of grace. Come and claim His promise. And, having done so, believe according to His Word that you have received it.

### Act your faith

Fifth, *act your faith.* To the paralyzed man, Jesus commanded, "Arise, and take up thy bed, and go thy way" (Mark 2:11). Not to show your faith or display your courage, but *because of* your faith begin to act as one who is healed. Treat Christ as if you trusted Him by attempting in His Name and strength what would be impossible in your own. He will not fail you if you really trust Him and continue to act your faith consistently and courageously. But it is most important that you not do this on human faith or word.

Do not rise from your bed or walk on your lame foot because somebody tells you to do so. That is not faith but impression. God will surely tell you to do so, but it must be at His Word. If you are walking with Him and trusting Him, you will know His voice. Your prayer, like Peter's, must be, "Lord, . . . bid me come unto thee on the water," and He will surely bid you if He is to heal you. But in this great and solemn work, you must know and see the Lord for yourself.

Remember the Lord's words to Peter when he began to sink: "O thou of little faith, wherefore didst thou doubt?" (Matthew 14:31). When you do go forth to act your faith, be careful not to begin to watch the result or look at the symptoms or see if you stand.

You must ignore all symptoms and see only God there before you, almighty to sustain you and save you from falling. The gardener who digs up his seed to see if it is growing will very soon kill his plants at the root. The true farmer trusts nature and lets the seed grow in silence. So trust God, willing even to see the answer buried like that seed and dying in the dark soil of discouragement. You can know that "if it die, it bringeth forth much fruit" (John 12:24).

## Be prepared for trials

Sixth, *be prepared for trials of faith*. Do not look necessarily for the immediate removal of the symptoms. Do not think of them. Simply ignore them and press forward, claiming the reality back of all symptoms. Remember the health you have claimed is not your own natural strength, but the life of Jesus manifested in your mortal flesh. Therefore, the old natural life may still be encompassed with many infirmities, but back of it and over against it is the all-sufficient life of Christ to sustain your body. "Ye are dead, and your life is hid with Christ in God" (Colossians 3:3). But Christ is your life (3:4), and "the life [you] now live in the flesh [you] live by the faith of the Son of God, who loved [you], and gave himself for [you]" (Galatians 2:20). Do not, then, wonder if nature fails you. The Lord's healing is not nature. It is grace. It is by the power of the risen Lord.

It is Christ who is your life. Christ's body is for your body as His Spirit was for your spirit. Therefore, do not wonder if there should be trials. They come to show you your need of Christ and to throw you back upon Him. To know this and so to put on His strength in your weakness and live in it moment by moment is the way of perfect healing. Then, again, trials always test and strengthen faith in proportion as it is real. Faith must be shown to be genuine so that God can vindicate His reward of it before the whole universe.

It is thus that God increases your faith by laying larger demands upon it and compelling you to claim and exercise more grace. "As an eagle stirreth up her nest" and tumbles out her young in midair to compel them to reach out their little pinions, so God may push you off all your own props and confidences to compel you to reach out your wings of faith. But for the sacrifice of Isaac, Abraham might never have attained, as he did, to the faith of the resurrection.

Whatever the symptoms, you must steadily believe that back of them all, God is working out His own great restoration. "For which cause we faint not; but though our outward man perish, yet the inward man is renewed day by day" (2 Corinthians 4:16).

## Use your new health for God

Seventh, *use your new strength and health for God, and be careful to obey the will of the Master.* This Christ-given strength is a very sacred thing. It is the resurrection life of Christ in you. And it must be spent as He Himself would spend it. It cannot be wasted on sin and selfishness. It must be given to God as "a living sacrifice" (Romans 12:1). The strength will fail when it is devoted to the world, and sin will always bring bodily chastisement. You may expect to "prosper and be in health, even as [your] soul prospereth."

Nor is it enough for you to use this healing for yourself. You must testify of it to others. You must tell it to the world. You must be a fearless and faithful witness to the gospel of full redemption. This is not a faith that you can hold to yourself. It is a great and solemn trust. In receiving it you must unite with others to use it for the glory of God, for a witness to the truth and for the spread of the gospel.

These wonderful manifestations of the power of God that we are beginning to see are perhaps significant signals of the end— forerunners of Christ's great appearing. As they marked the period of His presence on earth, so they will attend His return. And they bid us prepare solemnly and earnestly for His advent. Our eyes must no longer be on the grave but on the opening heavens. Our hearts must feel already some of the pulses of that resurrection life. It is ours to watch and work as none others can. We must not hold ourselves back in anxious self-care, but work in His great might, in season and out of season. And we shall find it true even as Christ said, "Whosoever will lose his life for my sake shall find it" (Matthew 16:25)—shall find it unto life eternal.

Thus let us claim and keep and consecrate this great gift of the gospel and the grace of God. In the words of Paul in First Thessalonians 5:23–24: "The very God of peace sanctify you wholly; and I pray God your whole spirit and soul and body be preserved blameless unto the coming of our Lord Jesus Christ. Faithful is he that calleth you, who also will do it."

# CHAPTER

## 5

---

## *Testimonies from Scripture*

The value of Scripture testimonies to the subject of divine healing cannot be questioned. They bring the gospel message down to the personal level and into contact with the sufferer as mere abstract teaching cannot do. Shall we glance at some of them?

### *The patriarch Job*

Job's physical affliction is the earliest fully detailed in the Scriptures. The sickness came from Satan, whose direct responsibility for some sicknesses our Lord distinctly taught. Satan's power is yet undiminished.

Job's sickness was divinely permitted. It was designed to lead him to search his heart and to see his utter need of sanctification.

Job's sickness did not at first sanctify him. It rather led to deeper exhibitions of self-righteousness. Sickness does not purify anyone, although it may lead a person to see his need of holiness and to receive that holiness from God.

Job's sickness was removed when he saw his sin and acknowledged it before God. This revelation came to him from God Himself. Job cried, "Now mine eye seeth thee. Wherefore I abhor myself, and repent in dust and ashes" (Job 42:5–6). Then came his complete justification and with it a spirit of forgiveness and love for others. As he prayed for his friends, the Lord turned his own captivity.

When we become right with God, and as we pray for others, greater blessing will come to us. Job's healing made all things new, and all his blessings were doubled. No doubt the spiritual blessing was the deepest of all.

How instructive to watch Job in the hands of God! Finally he is ready to learn his spiritual lesson and then receive from God's own hand life and restoration.

## Israel and the brazen serpent

Israel murmured in the wilderness between Egypt and the Promised Land, and God gave Israel something to murmur about. He sent "fiery serpents among the people, . . . and much people of Israel died" (Numbers 21:6). It is a serious thing to complain, for complaining may bring upon us what we fear, or worse. As Job remarked in his affliction, "The thing which I greatly feared is come upon me" (Job 3:25).

Israel's sickness came from Satan—from the serpent. So still he stings our life and poisons our blood. It was a fiery serpent. The Hebrew words are "the serpents, the seraphim." All our spiritual adversaries are not groveling worms. Many of them are lofty and transcendently wise.

The remedy was in the likeness of the disease—a figure of the serpent with the poison extracted. It was a striking intimation to the suffering camp and a sin-stricken world that Satan is robbed of his sting. Sickness and sin are, under the providence of God, mere shadows of their former selves.

There was also in that brazen serpent the thought of Christ made sin for us. Christ assumed the vile and dishonored name of sinful man. Christ was counted by God and treated by men as if He was indeed a serpent and a criminal. Thus for us has He taken the sting from Satan, sin and death. He hung upon the uplifted cross the trophy of victory. "As Moses lifted up the serpent in the wilderness, even so must the Son of man be lifted up: that whosoever believeth in him should not perish, but have eternal life" (John 3:14–15).

Is it not strange that if medical science is right for the saints, the most striking type of Christ on the cross as shown by Himself is one that was for the healing of the mortal body?

The healing came by looking at the brazen serpent. There is

unspeakable power in a look. A look of evil chills the soul. A look of purity and love transfigures it. The eye brings into the soul the object of vision. Looking unto Jesus brings His life into our whole being.

This was physical life. The same life still comes from the risen Christ for spirit, soul and body.

## Naaman, the leper

Naaman's leprosy was a classical instance of disease. Leprosy typified the physical effects of sin, destroying the body. The instrument of his cure was, first, a Hebrew maid. In her helpfulness we learn how God can use a very humble messenger and an incidental word. Indeed, Naaman's own servants, a little later, saved his blessing for him by their wise counsel.

The lesson of humble, obedient faith must next be learned. The proud self-will of Naaman must die before his body can be healed by the divine touch. And so Elisha meets his splendid entourage with quiet independence. He sends him a simple, direct message: wash seven times in the Jordan River and be clean.

The sick are often deeply wounded by God's seeming indifference, but God sometimes thus teaches them the lowliness of faith. He takes their thoughts off themselves and others. Naaman, like all other proud sinners, at first refused the cross. He was about to lose his blessing when a word of honest frankness from his servants brought him to his senses, and he went to the Jordan.

The faith of Naaman consisted in his doing just what the prophet told him. When he took God's way without qualification, and persevered in it, a perfect cure came. Perhaps the first or second or sixth time there was no sign of healing, but he pressed on. At length the wondrous blessing came—flesh like a little child's. Then and there he acknowledged and worshiped the great Jehovah he had found.

His request for a gift of earth from the place of his healing was a beautiful foreshadowing of that greater Gift whom we also receive—the Holy Spirit. Naaman took home with him some of Canaan's soil. We, in our healing, receive the pledge of the Spirit, a part of heaven begun on earth.

It is instructive to see how Elisha sent Naaman away leaning only on God. To his question about bowing in the house of Rimmon, Elisha gave no direct answer. Rather, he threw him on God alone and bade him go in peace. How little man appears in all this and how glorious is God!

## King Hezekiah

Hezekiah's was a hopeless case. All men's reasonings about the part the remedy had in curing Hezekiah ought to be set at rest since he was beyond the reach of every remedy. Even God had said that he should die. Man and means could, therefore, have nothing to do with Hezekiah's cure. It was wholly divine.

Hezekiah turned to God in humility. He made no attempt to find help from man. He threw himself helplessly on the mercy of the Lord. His prayer was not a very trustful one, but God heard his cry and sent deliverance.

The answer to his prayer was definite and clear: 15 years more of life from God Himself. It was sent to Isaiah and communicated to Hezekiah by him. Hezekiah at once believed it and began to praise God.

Hezekiah's healing was accompanied by a sign—a reversal of the sundial 10 degrees. Although Isaiah directed a poultice of figs to be applied, both in Second Kings 20 and Isaiah 38 we read that the healing had already been given by God. The poultice was applied on the authority of Isaiah, not on the authority of a "Thus saith the LORD," as in the case of the healing. With all the wealth of detail given in both records, there is no mention of a physician. God has told us to use the anointing oil and the prayer of faith; nothing else is obedience.

## The nobleman's son

Jesus' healing of the nobleman's son (John 4:46–53) speaks peculiarly to our own times. It teaches us that we do not need the physical and visible presence of our Lord to heal us. Jesus was far from this sick child. He simply spoke a word of power that crossed the intervening space with Almighty energy, even as that power still reaches from heaven to earth.

"Oh, if Jesus were only here!" you say. No, this great miracle was performed from a distance. It came about by simple faith without sight or signs. The Lord Jesus led this man away from all but His own word. "Except ye see signs and wonders," He exclaimed, "ye will not believe." And then He tested the man's faith by a command and a promise: "Go thy way; thy son liveth." The nobleman accepted the hard lesson, believed the naked word and his son was made whole. He showed his faith by quietly returning home, ceasing to clamor for the Lord to visit his son.

This healing began at a fixed moment and developed quietly and gradually, just as so many now are healed. "Then enquired [the nobleman] of [his servants] the hour when he began to amend." The boy was then convalescent. So still the dear Master works for all who trust Him. Faith has both its instants and its hours. We must learn to accept both: to count the death-blow struck at the moment of our believing, and then to follow on as it works out all its stages of blessing.

## *The healing of Peter's mother-in-law*

Christ had just come from the synagogue, where, amid the astonishment of the people, He had cast out a demon (see Mark 1:21ff.). Peter's wife's mother was lying sick of fever. It was a case of ordinary disease. And yet our Lord distinctly recognized another agency behind the fever. "He rebuked the fever," the Bible says, and this implies a personal, evil agent causing the fever. Jesus would not rebuke a mere natural law. There is no blame where there is no personal will. Indeed, the fever was the blistering touch of a demon's hand, and this demon was what Jesus rebuked.

Next, Peter's mother-in-law took hold of the healing power which Jesus stood over her to administer. Jesus took her by the hand and lifted her up, and she arose. There was His mighty touch, His almighty help. But there was also the woman's obedience, shown by her receiving His extended hand, and her action in rising. Thus we must meet His help and power.

Then there was the use of her new strength in ministering to Jesus and those with Him. This was the best proof of healing—and the best use of it, too. So must we ever give our new life to God. In ministering to others and forgetting ourselves, we shall find our own strength continually renewed. As we give our lives, we shall save them; as we serve others, Jesus will minister to all our needs.

It is a blessed exchange of responsibility and care to find that we have nothing to do but live for God, while He promises to "supply all [our] need according to his riches in glory by Christ Jesus" (Philippians 4:19). Good health is the richest material blessing of our physical lives. And, as everyone recognizes, it is one of our greatest needs.

## The healing of the multitude

We read in Matthew 8:16 of a large number of people being healed by Jesus the evening of the Sabbath on which He healed Peter's mother-in-law. They had been gathering all day long, waiting until the Sabbath was past. As soon as sundown came, they pressed upon Him from every side in great numbers. "And [He] healed all that were sick."

Note that they waited until the Sabbath was past. How exactly their prevalent ideas of healing resembled those of our own secular age! They considered the body, and all that pertained to it, to be purely secular. Healing, therefore, was secular work, unfit for the holy Sabbath. Is not this just what modern unbelief has taught the churches of Christendom? The cure of the body is a matter for natural laws and remedies, for secular physicians. It is a profession to be studied and used for profit, like any other business. In no sense is it sacred and holy as is the salvation and culture of the soul.

For the present, our Lord met them on their own ground, but the day soon came when He deliberately healed on the Sabbath day, that He might repudiate this absurd and godless idea and demonstrate that the body was as sacred as the soul. The body's restoration was also part of God's redemption; in no sense was it to be left to mere professional treatment. Jesus considered it to be His own prerogative and business to heal the body. Healing was as holy and sacred a work for the Sabbath as worship at the temple or the salvation of the soul.

Note also the universality of Jesus' healing. He healed all who had need. He wished to show that healing was not for favorite ones such as the mother-in-law of an apostle. Healing was for all sinful, suffering ones who could trust Him.

The highest and most helpful of all the lessons in this episode is the way in which these healings are linked with the prophecy of Isaiah announcing the character of the Messiah as one who would bear our sickness and infirmity. It was with no special and exceptional display of His power as the Son of God that Jesus was healing these sufferers. It was rather the real purpose and design of His Messiahship. And so those in all the ages can come to Jesus and lay upon Him their burdens and their pains.

How deep and full are these words: "Himself took our infirmities, and bare our sicknesses." Himself. Not Himself and physicians, but Himself alone. Not Himself and us, but He takes the whole burden and leaves us utterly free. If Himself, then the healing cannot be had apart from having Him. It is all wrapped up in Jesus—His life in us, His indwelling. "Himself took"—not merely once, but forever—"our infirmities." He not only lifted them once, but He carries them still. Blessed healing! Blessed Healer!

## The man with leprosy

Soon after the above-mentioned healings, in one of Christ's journeys through Galilee, He healed a man suffering from leprosy. The request of this man—"If thou wilt, thou canst make me clean" (Mark 1:40)—points up the mental attitude of the average Christian. The man had full confidence in the power of Christ to heal, but he was very uncertain about Jesus' willingness.

If a friend is going to doubt me at all, I should much rather he would doubt my ability to help than my willingness. I would rather he said, "I am sure you would help me if you could," than "I know you have it in your power to aid me, but I have little confidence in your disposition to do so." When will we see that this glib talk about God's will involves the most subtle and offensive distrust?

Christ's answer to the man was explicit and emphatic. It ought to settle forever the question of His will to heal the sincere, trusting sufferer: "I will; be thou clean." There is no evasion or ambiguity, no hesitation or conditioning. It is a great, prompt, kingly answer. In it we all may hear His word.

The touch of Jesus meant much to a leper. It was long since a hand of love had touched the man. Jesus' touch was not cold or mechanical. He was "moved with compassion." His heart of love and His very life were in it. Yes, Christ helps us not because His promise compels Him, but because His love overflows toward us.

The cleansed man was to go to the priest at Jerusalem and make a proper acknowledgement and testimony. He was to hold back all other testimony until he had borne witness before the religious authorities of the nation. So we must bear witness of Jesus' mighty works in us. We must do so where He wants us to witness, perhaps in the very hardest place for us and in the very face of religious pride and opposition. For the healed man it was a long journey from Galilee to Jerusalem. If our testimony requires as great a sacrifice for Him, is not His love worth it all?

## The paralyzed man

In healing the paralyzed man let down through the roof (Mark 2:1–12), our Lord indicated the connection between sin and sickness and assumed the right on earth to forgive sins. And from that moment He was regarded as a blasphemer.

Four of the paralyzed man's friends brought the sufferer for healing, but the Lord saw a deeper need that must first be met. The spiritual life must precede the physical. And so Jesus first speaks the word of pardon: "Son, thy sins be forgiven thee." So we must ever begin. And how many have been led to the very thought of salvation by their need of healing!

Then follows the man's physical healing. But this, too, must be taken by himself in the exercise of bold, obedient faith. He was not healed prostrate on his mat. He must rise, take up his bed and walk. We, too, must arise and step out upon Jesus' strength.

The paralytic was not healed, as is commonly supposed, through the faith of the men who brought him to Jesus, but through his own faith. Their faith laid him at the feet of Jesus and brought to him the word of forgiving mercy. But his own faith had to claim the healing. And it must have been a real faith that could rise up before the throng and carry his bed. The faith of others can do much for us, added to our own, but an unbelieving heart can have nothing from the Lord. (Incidentally, it seems clear from this episode that believers in divine healing should be careful not to assume the responsibility of preventing anyone from seeking medical advice.)

The purpose of healing, as a token of forgiveness and a sign of Christ's saving power, is very solemn. He healed this man that the throng might "know that the Son of man hath power on earth to forgive sins." Christ is ever wanting to convince the world of the reality of His gospel by His physical miracles. How can we expect men to believe that His spiritual gifts are real when we do not permit Him to manifest sufficient power to overcome the physical evils of our life? What right has any man to be sure that any part of his religion is real when his faith has never had enough vigor to accomplish any really difficult thing in his practical life?

## The lame man at Bethesda

Jesus healed the lame man at the Bethesda pool (John 5:2–9) openly and deliberately on the Sabbath. He purposely intended to refute the idea even then current that disease and the healing arts were secular in nature. He designed to show people that healing was sacred enough to be done on the Sabbath and that it was really an essential part of His spiritual ministry. Many persons are still afraid of unduly exalting the importance of the body, forgetting that whatever Christ touches He makes sacred and holy.

The next lesson here has reference to the folly of the things men depend on for healing. When the Lord undertook to heal the lame man, He paid no attention to Bethesda or any other "means." Rather, He spoke a single word of power and bade the helpless man go forth in the strength of God.

There is a lesson, too, for the waiting ones who are just hoping for some day of help to come. When Jesus healed the lame man, He dispelled his dreamy hope of future healing. He started him on the practical road of present decisions. Hope is often mistaken for faith. But faith is always in the present. It takes the blessing now.

Another most important lesson is the futility of leaning on others. "Sir, I have no man . . . to put me into the pool" expresses the languid dependence of hundreds still. They expect healing through the help of others. All their own strength and power through faith in God is paralyzed by their looking to "means" or to someone else's faith and prayers. Others cannot help us until we firmly believe for ourselves. If we cling to others, our hands only bind and impede them, like the clinging of a drowning man to his rescuer. Both may sink together.

Jesus' "Wilt thou be made whole?" expresses the real element of effectual faith. It acts through a firm and decided will. Faith is not mere willpower, but its seat is the will. Will is the mightiest thing God has given to mankind. No person can receive much from God without making a firm and decided choice. He or she must first see that it is God's will to make whole and then claim that wholeness with uncompromising tenacity.

One more lesson this sufferer must teach us. Jesus warned him, "Sin no more, lest a worse thing come unto thee" (5:14). Not always, yet often, such long and terrible disorders are the direct result of sinful indulgence. Many today are physically powerless because of secret, youthful sins. There must, therefore, be a distinct recognition, confession and repudiation of all sin. And the redeemed life, if it would retain Jesus' sacred life, must be pure and vigilant.But there is no touchstone so searching as the healing life of Christ. There is no cord that binds the soul more sacredly on the altar of holiness than "I am the LORD that healeth thee."

This miracle should not be separated from Jesus' discourse that follows on the life He has come to give. It was just an illustration of that blessed life. Christ's healing is neither more nor less than His own divine life breathed into us, quickening our souls and bodies—beginning eternal life now. This is just what He teaches here: "The Son quickeneth whom he will. . . . The hour is coming, and now is, when the dead shall hear the voice of the Son of God: and they that hear shall live" (5:21, 25).

## *The man with the withered hand*

The healing of the man with the withered hand (Matthew 12:10–13) was a repetition in Galilee of the bold lesson about healing on the Sabbath that Jesus had taught in Jerusalem. In Jerusalem, Jesus healed the powerless man at Bethesda on the Sabbath. Likewise, He healed the man with the withered hand on the Sabbath. Both healings emphasize the same great principle respecting the freedom of the Sabbath, the sanctity of the body and the sacredness of its cure.

They both also teach the same great lesson about the necessity of active and aggressive faith in order to receive Christ's healing power. This man was powerless, too, in his diseased hand. He could not in himself lift it. But he must, nonetheless, put forth an effort of will and an act of force. This he had to do in good faith, really expecting to succeed. And as he did so, the divine power quietly and fully met his obedient act and carried him through into strength and victory.

Thus faith must do things we have no strength to do. As faith is exercised, new strength will come. Just as the priests, in leading Israel across the Jordan River into Canaan, had to step into the water before it parted, so our feet must even touch the cold waters. In passive waiting there can come no life or power from God. We must put our feet on the soil of Canaan, we must stretch forth our hands and partake of the tree of life. "The spider taketh hold with her hands, and is in kings' palaces" (Proverbs 30:28). So many Christians have no grip in their fingers, no stamina in their will, no hold in their faith. Hear Jesus' voice, you who are listless: "Stretch forth thine hand."

In His ensuing arguments with the Pharisees, Jesus leaves no room to doubt the will of God to heal. He ridicules their prejudices against His healing a sufferer on the Sabbath. He declares the healing of this man was an act of simple human compassion—no more than any man would do for an ox or a sheep that had fallen into a pit. Moreoever, it was morally right. To heal is to do good, to save life. Not to heal is to do evil, to destroy life. Certainly Jesus did not treat sickness as a great boon.

Yet such gentle, merciful teaching only exasperated the Pharisees. When they saw God's power vindicate His teachings and the man stand forth before their eyes healed, they were filled with madness. They consulted how they might destroy Jesus. So prejudice still blinds men to the truth and love of God. Still today people oppose Christ's healing ministry because of the hardness of their hearts.

## The woman with a spirit of infirmity

Another of Christ's "Sabbath miracles" was the healing of the woman who had a spirit of infirmity (Luke 13:10–20). Because her healing supplements and enforces the same principles of the two other Sabbath healings we looked at, we will introduce it here.

Her disease was a case of helpless paralysis and deformity. She was bowed together and could not lift herself up. She had been 18 years in this condition. She was, therefore, about as difficult a chronic case as could be brought to the great Healer.

The cause of her disease demands special note. Here Jesus throws a ray of marvelously clear light upon the whole question of disease. The Lord distinctly declared that the woman's troubles had come not through natural causes, but through an evil spirit. Her body was bound by "a spirit of infirmity." And Jesus afterward declared that "Satan hath bound [her], lo, these eighteen years." This was not a case of providential discipline but the direct hand of the devil upon the woman's frame.

The question of God's will is also made clear. There is no greater word in Christian ethics than *ought*. It is a word of conscience, of law, of everlasting right. It is a cable that binds both God and man. When God says "ought," there is no appeal, no compromise, no alternative—nothing but an absolute obligation to obey. It does not mean that a thing is possible or permissible or perhaps to be done. It means that it is *necessary* to be done. Not to do it would be wrong.

And Christ said to these evil men who would put their petty prejudices before God's beneficent will and His people's happiness, "Ought not this woman, being a daughter of Abraham, . . . be loosed from this bond?" That should settle the question of how God regards our healing.

But there is one more principle, the greatest of all, and it conditions and limits this "ought" and everything else. It is the woman's faith. The Lord expressly calls her a child of faith, "a daughter of Abraham." The status of the woman makes her healing a matter of "ought." "Ought not this woman, being a daughter of Abraham, . . . be loosed from this bond?" It is the will of God to heal all who believe. More is meant by the expression "a daughter of Abraham" than mere faith. It signifies a very strong faith. Abraham believed without sight and in the face of seeming impossibilities.

Is there evidence of such faith on the woman's part? Yes. We are told that Jesus called her to Him and said, "Woman, thou art loosed from thine infirmity." In the Revised Version it reads, "He called her." It implies that Jesus required her to come to Him first. This would necessitate supernatural exertion and faith. She must have made the attempt to come before He touched her.

Then, as she came, He declared the work done: "Woman, thou art loosed from thine infirmity." He laid His hands on her and completed the work. But her faith had to take the initiative. Like Abraham, she had to step out on the naked word of God. Then the work could be counted done. "Thou art loosed"—and then the full results began to follow.

## *The centurion's servant*

In the healing of the centurion's servant (Matthew 8:5–13), we note the high commendation Christ gave to the faith of a Gentile who possessed little opportunity to know God and enjoy light. The Bible's most solemn lesson about faith is that it was most strongly developed in those who had but little light. Conversely, the greatest advantages were usually accompanied by the most unreasonable unbelief.

They who do not promptly use the light they have are not likely to make a good use of more. This centurion had very little more light than he had learned from his own profession and the smattering of Jewish teaching he may have gathered. But he had been true as far as he knew his duty. He had shown his love to God's people by building them a synagogue at his own expense.

His strong faith showed itself first in his recognizing Christ's absolute control over all the forces of the universe, even as he controlled his disciplined soldiers. Second, he recognized the sufficiency of Christ's word to stop the disease. He asked no more than one word from the Lord of heaven and earth. That one word he accepted as final as the decree of the Caesars.

The centurion recognized the authority of Christ's word. It passes over this universe like a resistless mandate. Even in the hands of a little child it is mighty with Christ's own omnipotence. How tremendous the force of law! Let a single human voice speak the sentence of the court, and all the power of wealth and influence are helpless to hold back the man from a prison cell. The word that Christ has spoken to us is a word with power. When faith claims it, all the powers of hell and earth dare not resist it. This is the province of faith—to take that imperial word and use its authority against the forces of disease and sin.

The humility of this centurion is a beautiful accompaniment of his faith. He felt deeply his unworthiness of Christ's visit. It was not often that a proud Roman acknowledged himself unworthy of a visit. But this man felt he was standing before One greater than his emperor, and his spirit bowed in lowly reverence and worship.

We can come nearer. Not only will Christ come under our roof, but He will make our heart His home forever.

# CHAPTER

## 6

*More Testimonies from Scripture*

L et us consider further testimonies to divine healing preserved for us in the Word of God. Like the others, these too bring the gospel of healing down to the personal, applicable level.

### The demented Gadarene

We turn first to the demon-possessed man of Gadara (Mark 5:2–17). There seems no reason to doubt that cases of insanity and diseases of the mind are still the same in character and cause as they were when Christ was on earth. Our Lord distinctly attributed the causes of these disorders to satanic agents. The power that held this man was sufficient to destroy a great herd of swine. What fearful forces one human heart can hold! The power that the evil spirits exerted upon the man's body enabled him to break any chain that the hand of man could place upon him. That gives us some idea of how spirit agents may affect the body either for good or evil.

All physical strength is spiritual in its cause. This wretched man seems to have been conscious of two principles within him. One was his own will, feebly struggling for freedom; the other, the evil spirits controlling him, crushing his will under theirs.

The Lord met this man with deep compassion. He regarded him as the victim of a power he could not resist. By a word of command He set him free. Immediately his whole appearance was changed. The wild and dreaded maniac suddenly was sitting at the feet of Jesus "clothed, and in his right mind."

The extent of the power that had possessed him was soon apparent in the destruction of the swine. He himself clung to his Deliverer and desired to go with Him. But Jesus knew that he needed to be pushed out into the discipline of confession and service. Jesus sent him at once to stand alone and spread the tidings in his home territory. Every new advance would give him new assurance and strength.

Before long the whole region of the Ten Cities was stirred by his testimony. This prepared the way for the Master's visit and a mighty work that closed with the miraculous feeding of four thousand people. So must we often trust the young disciple with the most bold and difficult service.

The treatment of the insane is one of the most important questions connected with the subject of faith. The true remedy is the power of Christ. No doubt it is a subject of much difficulty. In many instances there are long and severe trials of faith. But the little that has been attempted has shown how much may be done with holy wisdom and courageous faith.

## The woman who touched Jesus' garment

The healing of the woman who touched Jesus' garment (Luke 8:43–48) is contained within the heart of another: the raising of Jairus' daughter. In these twin miracles the Lord wrote, in one striking lesson, two finely illustrated principles. One was the fact of God's absolute power even to work where there is nothing but death. The other is faith's absolute power to take everything from God.

They emphasize the two wonderful omnipotences that Christ has linked together: "With God all things are possible" and "All things are possible to him that believeth." The helpless nature of the woman's disease and the failure of human physicians are underscored with great plainness of speech. There is no attempt to apologize for the medical profession. We are told frankly that all that had been done for her had only made her worse. Luke, once a physician himself, paints a most vivid picture of all this.

The process of the woman's faith and healing is very striking.

There were three stages. First, she believed that she would be healed. She said, "If I may but touch his garment, I shall be whole" (Matthew 9:21). Second, she reached and touched. She did something. The personal and vital element in faith is here brought out very vividly. Faith is more than believing; it is a living contact with a living Savior. It is the outreaching of a conscious need in us, feeling after and finding its supply in God. It is not a mere outward approach, not even a mere mental approach. Hundreds thronged Jesus, but only one touched Him.

Third, the woman consciously received the answer after believing and touching. Immediately her flow of blood was staunched; she felt in her body that she was whole of her plague. She did not feel first and then believe, but she believed and then she felt.

Her blessing, however, had to be confessed. Christ will not allow us to hold His gifts without acknowledgment. We cannot long enjoy and retain them in secret. Like plants, they need the light of day. And so her womanly sensitivity must be laid aside. Her shrinking heart must tell its blessings at Jesus' feet, in the hearing of all. How much we lose by reluctance and silence!

And how much she gained by that confession! Jesus assured her, "Daughter, be of good comfort: thy faith hath made thee whole; go in peace." A daughter, comforted, healed and sent forth into peace. Peace—that deep, divine rest that comes with the touch of God and is the richest part of the inheritance that faith brings.

It is not merely that peace comes into her. She goes into peace—a land so wide and fruitful that she never can know its boundaries or exhaust its precious things. And could one little act of faith for her body bring all this deep spiritual blessing? Yes, the most precious part of the blessing His healing gives is that it heals the whole being. It brings us into union with God with a fullness we never could have known without this living and human touch.

Indeed, most of the great spiritual blessings, experiences and revelations of God to His people in the Scriptures began with what we would call temporal blessings. Abraham became the father of the faithful by believing in God for a son. Jacob became the prince of Israel by claiming a temporal deliverance. Daniel saw the coming of Jesus while asking for the restoration of the captives. The Syro-Phoenician woman won her transcendent victory while pleading for a suffering child. And so still, the things we call little and commonplace are the very pivots on which the greatest spiritual experiences turn. Trusting God for a headache or a dollar may teach us to trust Him for all the fullness of His grace and holiness.

## The two blind men

The short story of the healing of two blind men (Matthew 9:27–31) illustrates several important principles.

Mere prayer will not heal the sick. These blind men followed Jesus from the house of Jairus crying, "Have mercy on us." And yet their petitions brought no reply. "I have been praying for my healing for 40 years," someone occasionally says to me, "and I am no better." Well, little wonder. If the person had prayed in faith, he or she would not have prayed so long.

Mere coming into the presence of Christ will not heal us. They came to Him—into the house—but still they were not healed. So people go to meetings, try to come under spiritual influences and seem to think that these things will bring healing. Perhaps they even present themselves definitely to Jesus for His help and healing, and yet they are no better.

All this is of no avail unless we definitely believe that He does do for us what we claim. "Believe ye?" Jesus asked the blind men, and then He uttered the great law of faith that determines for every one of us the measure of our blessings. "According to your faith be it unto you." Then His touch brought sight and healing, and the men went forth into the glorious light of day.

There is a secret in everything. There is a secret that opens heaven—commands all the forces and resources of the throne. It is not agonizing prayer. It is not much labor. It is simply this: "According to your faith be it unto you."

## The Syro-Phoenician woman's child

The Syro-Phoenician woman (Matthew 15:21–28) offers us

another example of faith when there was little light or opportunity. It is doubtful if this woman in all her life had ever heard a promise of Scripture or seen an inspired teacher. She belonged to an alien race, and everything was against her.

When she came to Jesus, He seemed against her, too. To her pitiful cry for help, He answered her not a word. His disciples appealed to Him to send her away—that is, to grant her request and dismiss her. He replied in language that seemed to exclude her from any right to His mercy. And when at last she came to His very feet and implored His help, He answered in words so apparently harsh and repelling that it seemed like courting insult to approach Him again. He had even called her a dog—in the East a name for the unclean and unfit for fellowship. Yet in the face of all this, the woman's faith only grew stronger until at last she drew out of His very refusal the argument for her blessing.

Difficulties cannot injure true faith. They are the very stimulus of its growth. We see the Lord's design in dealing with us and sometimes seeming to refuse us. All through that struggle Jesus loved the woman and saw the trust that would not be denied. He was only waiting for its full manifestation. Indeed, He tested her faith because He knew it would stand the trial and come forth at last as gold. So He keeps us at His feet and even seems to refuse our cry in order to call forth all the depths of our trust and earnestness.

Another purpose, too, He had for her. He was bringing the woman to the death of self and to a sense of sin. And when at last she was willing to accept His judgment of her and take her place as a worthless sinner—yes, even a "dog," which to her meant the basest of sinners—then she could receive all. Faith is a descent as well as an ascent, a death as well as a life.

The woman's great faith consisted not only in her persistency in holding on but in her ingenuity in finding in His own Word some ground on which to claim the blessing. Faith is a process of logic, an arguing of our case with God. Faith is always looking for something to rest upon. The woman seemed at first to lean upon Jesus' grace and love. She somehow felt it instinctively. Something told her that the One with that calm, gentle face could not refuse her. But still she had no word from Him. Only one little word, one whisper, one faint concession would do. But He had spoken nothing but words of exclusion. And then He spoke the word that seemed to close the door forever. Not only a Gentile, but a dog.

Could she surmount that? But that word became the very bridge on which she crossed. A dog—that gave her a place. Even a dog had some right. She would claim hers.

Only a crumb. The thing she asked for was but a crumb to Jesus, who was so great that mighty deeds of power and love dropped from His fingers. But, oh, it meant so much to her. *Lord, I accept it. I lie down at Thy feet, at Thy children's feet. I ask not their fare, but that which is but their leaving. It will not diminish their share. This I humbly claim for myself and child, and Thou canst not say no.*

Jesus could not say no. Filled with love and wonder, He answered, "O woman, great is thy faith: be it unto thee even as thou wilt." And the mighty deed was done.

"As thou wilt." Here again, we have the same element of decision, of fixed and concentrated will that is essential to all strong faith and action. It was the same determination, in negative form, that overcame at Peniel, 16 centuries before (Genesis 32:24–30). These two instances, both for a temporal deliverance, are companion pictures of overcoming faith.

### The demon-possessed child

Immediately after His transfiguration, Jesus was brought face to face with the power of Satan. A demon-possessed child (Mark 9:14–29) had resisted all the efforts of Jesus' disciples. The cause of their failure was a lack of faith. The reason for their unbelief was their contention over personal ambition. When Jesus came to the multitude, He rebuked the unbelief that He perceived and then called the father and child into His presence.

The moment the father began to speak about the difficulties he had had with his son, he fell into an attitude of discouragement. "If thou canst do any thing, have compassion on us, and help us." The Lord's answer quickly brought him to see that it was not a matter of Christ's power, but of his own faith. "If thou canst believe, all things are possible to him that believeth." He at once recognized the tremendous responsibility this placed on him and met it. "Lord, I believe; help thou mine unbelief."

These two words together—the Lord's great word to him and his word to the Lord—are among the most wonderful teachings of the Bible about faith. The first tells us the possibilities of faith—"all things." It signifies God's omnipotence, for the only one to whom all things are possible is God. Faith does, indeed, take and use God's own omnipotence.

The second defines the possibility of faith. It tells us how far we can believe. Many spend their lives wondering if they can believe. Others, like this man, more wisely put forth the effort and then throw themselves on God to sustain them and carry them through.

Had the man said "Lord, help my unbelief" without first saying "Lord, I believe," it would have been vain. Had he said "Lord, I believe" and stopped there, it would have been equally vain, for it would only have been his own willpower. He put forth his will, and then he depended on Christ for the strength. This is faith. It all comes from Christ and is, indeed, His own faith in us. But it must be taken by us and used with a firm and resolute hand.

The healing power now comes, but it seems at first only to make matters worse. There is such desperate resistance from Satan that in the conflict the child is thought by the spectators to be dead. So, often, when God begins to heal us, we really seem to get worse, and the world tells us that we have destroyed ourselves. But death must precede life; demolition, renovation. Let us not fear, but trust Him who knows, and all will be well. Jesus took the child by the hand and lifted him up. The demon had left him forever.

## The blind man at Bethsaida

The first thing Christ did with the blind man at Bethsaida (Mark 8:22–26) was to take him by the hand and lead him out of the town. He thus separated him from the crowd, giving him time to think. He taught him to walk hand in hand with Himself and to trust Him in the dark. So Jesus first leads us out alone with Himself, long before we look in His face or know that He is leading us.

Next, Jesus began the work of healing the blind man by a simple anointing, as a sign. He put His hands upon his eyes. The result was a partial healing. Sight was distorted and unsatisfactory. Thus would He teach us that sometimes our progress will be partial and by successive stages. Many never get beyond the first stage.

There is a third stage: perfect sight. It comes from one cause: a look at Jesus. "I see men," the man said the first time. And while he saw only men, he saw nothing clearly. But the second time the Lord made him "look up." Then he saw clearly. That one look at Jesus, even through the dimness, made all things clear and whole.

## The blind man at Jerusalem

The question of sin in connection with sickness receives a very important illumination in the incident of the blind man at Jerusalem (John 9). Christ teaches His disciples that there are cases of infirmity where there has been no special iniquity beyond the common guilt of all men. The trouble has been permitted to afford God opportunity to show His love and power in restoration.

In the healing of this man, the Lord again used a simple sign. He anointed his eyes with saliva and clay. None will say that this could have had any medicinal effect to cure eyes blind from birth. Indeed, it did not cure. It was simply a sign of Jesus' touch. He then sent the man to wash in the pool of Siloam. And he was able to see.

This pool of Siloam was a type of Christ and the Holy Spirit. Siloam, or Shiloh, means the Sent One. The water typified the Holy Spirit, the One sent by the Father and Son.

The subsequent testimony of this man was glorious. With keen sarcasm he exposed the inconsistencies of the Scribes and Pharisees who came to see him. These had hoped to draw out of the man some evidence against Christ, who had again broken the Sabbath by this act of healing. But the humble peasant was more than a match for them, and the controversy that follows is intensely sharp and interesting. Unable to gain their purpose, they at last excommunicated the man from the synagogue. Soon afterward, Jesus appeared to him again and revealed His divine identity. The former blind man became a living disciple.

### Blind Bartimaeus

There was a deep insight in the cry of blind Bartimaeus (Luke 18:35–43). "Thou son of David," he called. Jesus was now coming to claim His throne, and the title by which He was to be known was "The Son of David." It was strange that His own people should be blind to His claim and that a blind man should be the first to see it. So still, the wise are frequently the blind.

We see persistent faith in Bartimaeus. He cried aloud. When people rebuked him, he cried the more. He threw away his garments in his eagerness to get to Jesus. So we must put all hindrances out of the way. Bartimaeus had but one request. His earnest faith summed up all its intensity: "Lord, that I may receive my sight." There can be no strong faith without strong desire. The languid prayer has not motive power enough to ascend to God.

Bartimaeus's healing was simple and glorious. There was a pause, a call, a question, an earnest reply. Jesus spoke the word, the work was done. Bartimaeus gazed on the beautiful scene: the people around him and the face of the Lord. Looking no farther, he sent up a shout of praise and followed the Lord in the way.

### The withering of the fig tree

The cursing of the fig tree (Mark 11:12–14, 20–22) was a miracle of judgment, not a miracle of healing. It would seem to be, therefore, an unpromising theme of faith and comfort. We look at it here because Christ made it the occasion of His highest teaching about faith. It is indeed a symbol of the deepest and tenderest operations of His grace. The greatest principle of Scripture is salvation by destruction, life by death.

The life of the world is the destruction of Satan, sin and death. The sanctification of the soul is the withering up of the natural life. The healing of the body is the death stroke at the root of evil disease. There are things that need God's fire and God's holiness. There are times when we want more than mercy and gentleness, and the spirit longs for the keen sword that slays the foul thing that is crushing life. How glorious at such a time is the consuming holiness of the living God! This is the meaning of the withered fig tree.

"If ye have faith, and doubt not," Jesus told His disciples, "ye shall not only do this which is done to the fig tree, but also if ye shall say unto this mountain, Be thou removed, and be thou cast into the sea; it shall be done" (Matthew 21:21). Yes, we can speak the word of faith, and, the flesh withers and dies. We can speak it again, and the poison tree of sickness is withered. Although leaves and branches may for a while retain their form and color, we know that the death blow has been struck at the root. The real work is done.

The secret is this: "Have faith in God." Literally, "Have the faith of God." The faith *of* God is as different from faith *in* God as Christ's faith is different from that of the disciples who were laboring with the demon-possessed boy. Jesus means to teach us that no less than such a faith as His own will do these things, and we can have it and may take it.

## The lame man at Gate Beautiful

The first recorded miracle of the Holy Spirit after Christ's ascension was the healing of a lame man begging by the temple gate called Beautiful (Acts 3:1–10). It is marked by the repudiation of all human power or glory and the most emphatic recognition of the name of Jesus only as the source of power. The apostles used that name as their first word to the crippled man. And when the people came crowding around them and the rulers summoned them, they again and again disavowed any personal part in the miracle beyond representing the mighty name and power of Him who had been crucified. He was not then a present but an absent Lord, represented by His ministers invoking His name.

Again, the very faith through which the miracle had been performed and received was as distinctly disavowed as in any sense their own power or the man's. They declared, "Yea, the faith which is by him hath given [the former lame man] this perfect soundness in the presence of you all" (3:16). Both the faith and the power were simply the Lord Jesus Himself working and believing in them.

Again, the miracle was only valued as a testimony for the Lord and an occasion for more widely and effectively spreading His Word. The apostles did not wait to wonder over it. They did not let it monopolize their attention. But they quietly pressed on with their greater work: the preaching of the gospel. The healing of the sick was simply accessory to the great work of the gospel, although it ought always to be associated with it.

The lame man was an unanswerable argument for the gospel, a very buttress in the walls of the young church. "Beholding the man which was healed standing with [the apostles], [the rulers] could say nothing against it" (4:14). We need such testimony still. The world, the infidel and the devil cannot answer them. I have seen the proudest infidel put to shame by a poor woman coming up before the people who knew her and telling how God had made her whole.

### Aeneas at Lydda

The healing of Aeneas by the hands of Peter (Acts 9:32–35) has the same features as the healing of the lame man at Gate Beautiful of the temple. Peter is most careful to recognize only the power and name of the Lord. "Aeneas, Jesus Christ maketh thee whole." Peter is wholly out of sight and ever must be.

The effect of the healing is to bring sinners to God. It is not to set people wondering, but to set them repenting. "All that dwelt at Lydda and Saron saw [the healed Aeneas], and turned to the Lord." The true effect of a gospel of supernatural power is always spiritual. It results in the salvation of men and women. The prophet Joel tells us that through these mighty signs and wonders will come the last great outpouring of the Spirit upon the world and the awakening of men before the Lord's return.

### The lame man at Lystra

One of the most instructive instances of healing in the Bible is that of the lame man at Lystra (Acts 14:8–10). Lystra was a purely heathen community. The people there had no prejudices. Paul preached "the gospel" to them (14:7). No doubt he told them of the healing and redeeming work of the Lord Jesus.

As Paul preached, he perceived the light of faith and hope irradiating the face of one of his most helpless hearers. God gives the spiritual mind instincts of discernment. He did it for Paul; He does it yet.

Paul evidently would not have gone further unless he had "perceived" that this man had "faith to be healed." It is no use trying to force someone to receive Christ who has not even the desire to do so. It was not Paul's faith that healed the man; it was the man's faith.

But the man must be helped to act it out. "Stand upright on thy feet," Paul cried. There must be no halting and half-believing. A bold step like this must be carried through audaciously. And lo! the man responded. He not only stood up, but he began to leap and walk. By works, his faith was made perfect.

The effect of the miracle and the self-renouncing spirit of Paul needed no additional word. Paul gave God all the glory, and God was glorified.

## Paul's own experience of healing

It was not long until the great apostle had occasion to prove his own faith. The excited people first worshiped Paul and then stoned him. The mob, infuriated by Jewish agitators, dragged him out of the city, and he was left for dead in the midst of the little band of disciples (Acts 14:11–20). But did Paul die? No.

"As the disciples stood round about him, he rose up, and came into the city: and the next day he departed with Barnabas to Derbe"—where he also preached the gospel. Could there be anything more simply sublime or sublimely simple? Not a word of exploitation, no utterance even of surprise, but a quiet trust and deliverance. Then Paul went on about his work in the strength of the Lord.

In Second Corinthians 4, Paul gives us the secret of his strength: "We which live are alway delivered unto death for Jesus' sake"—

that was what happened at Lystra—"that the life also of Jesus might be made manifest in our mortal flesh" (4:11). That was the secret of the wondrous restoration at Lystra. Later Paul gives it to us again: "For which cause we faint not; but though our outward man perish, yet the inward man is renewed day by day" (4:16).

In Second Corinthians 1, Paul gives us another instance of his healing. A great trouble came to him in Asia and pressed him above his strength so that he despaired even of life. And, indeed, when he looked at himself, his condition and his feelings, the only answer he could find was death.

But even in that dark hour his confidence was in the resurrection life of Christ and "God which raiseth the dead" (1:9). This trust was not in vain. Christ did deliver him from death. Christ since then had been delivering him. And Paul was sure He would deliver him to the end. Paul simply adds his thanks to the Corinthians for their prayers that had so helped and comforted him. Those prayers gave occasion for wider thanksgiving on his behalf, to the glory of God.

## *Our Savior's experience of physical life*

Our Lord Himself has left to us the great lesson of living physically, not on natural strength and support, but on the life of God. This was the very meaning of His first temptation in the wilderness (Matthew 4:3–4). It was addressed directly to His body. Weakened and worn by abstinence, Jesus heard the tempter suggesting that He should resort to a miracle to supply the means of sustenance and strength. He should make some earthly bread.

The Lord answered that the very reason of His trial and abstinence was to demonstrate that life can be sustained without earthly bread—by the life and Word of God Himself. The words have a deep significance when we remember that they are quoted from Deuteronomy. They were first directed to God's ancient people, to whom God says He had tried to teach this same lesson that "man doth not live by bread only, but by every word that proceedeth out of the mouth of the Lord" (8:3).

So it was not only the Son of man who was thus to live as a special evidence of God's divine power. The lesson is for every Christian believer. We must all learn to receive our life for the body as well as the soul not by the exclusion of bread, but by God's Word. This is exactly what our Savior meant when, two years later, He said in the synagogue at Capernaum, "As the living Father hath sent me, and I live by the Father: so he that eateth me, even he shall live by me" (John 6:57).

Our Lord refused the devil's bread and overcame in His body for us. The next two temptations were addressed to His soul and His spirit. They were, in like manner, overcome. And so He became for us the Author and Finisher of our faith.

Such are some of the glorious precedents of faith. In the words of Hebrews 12:1–2, "Seeing we also are compassed about with so great a cloud of witnesses, let us lay aside every weight, and the sin which doth so easily beset us, and let us run with patience the race that is set before us, looking unto Jesus the author and finisher of our faith."

# CHAPTER

## 7

# *Personal Testimony*

A ll that I know of divine healing and all that I have written in the preceding pages, the Lord Himself had to teach me. I was not permitted to read anything but God's own Word on this subject until long after I had learned to trust Him for myself and, indeed, had written much that is in this book.

For more than 20 years I was a sufferer from many physical infirmities and disabilities. Beginning a life of hard intellectual labor at the age of 14, I broke hopelessly down with nervous exhaustion while preparing for college. For many months I was not permitted by my doctor even to look at a book. During this time I came very near death. On the verge of eternity, I gave myself at last to God.

## A successful pastor

After my college studies were completed, I became at age 21 the ambitious pastor of a large city church. Plunging headlong into my work, I again broke down with heart trouble and had to go away for months of rest, returning at length, as it seemed to me at the time, to die. Rallying, however, and slowly recovering in part, I labored on for years with the aid of constant remedies and preventives. I carried a bottle of ammonia in my pocket and would have taken a nervous spasm if I had ventured out without it. Again and again, while climbing a slight elevation or going up stairs, an awful and suffocating agony would come over me, and the thought of that bottle as a last resort quieted me.

Well do I remember the day in Europe when I traveled to the top of the Righi in Switzerland by rail, and again when I tried to climb the high Campanile stairs in Florence. As the paroxysm of imminent suffocation swept over me, I resolved never to venture into such peril again. God knows how many hundreds of times in my earlier ministry, when preaching in my pulpit or ministering by a grave, it seemed that I must fall in the midst of the service or drop into that open grave.

Several years later, two other collapses came in my health. They were of long duration. Again and again during those terrible seasons did it seem that the last drops of life were ebbing out.

I struggled through my work most of the time and often was considered a hard and successful minister. But my good people always thought me "delicate." I grew weary of being sympathized with every time they met me. The parishioners excused many a neglected visit because I was "not strong." When at last I took the Lord for my Healer, I asked Him to make me so well that my people would never sympathize with me again. I wanted to be a continual wonder to them through the strength and support of God.

I think the Lord has fulfilled this prayer, for in these recent years they often have been amazed at the work I have been permitted to do in God's name.

It usually took me until Wednesday to get over the effects of the Sunday sermon. About Thursday I was ready to begin to prepare for the next Sunday. Thanks be to God, the first three years after I was healed I preached more than a thousand sermons and held sometimes more than 20 meetings in one week. I do not remember once feeling exhausted.

A few months before I took Christ as my Healer, a prominent physician in New York insisted on speaking to me about my health. He told me that I had not constitutional strength enough to last more than a few months. He required my taking immediate measures for the preservation of my life and usefulness.

During the summer that followed, I went for a time to Saratoga Springs, New York. While there, one Sunday afternoon I wandered out to the Indian campground, where the Jubilee Singers were leading the music in an evangelistic service. I had been deeply depressed. All things in life looked dark and withered. Suddenly I heard the chorus:

> *My Jesus is the Lord of lords:*
> *No man can work like Him.*

Again and again, in the deep bass notes and the higher tones that seemed to soar to heaven, they sang that line:

> *No man can work like Him . . .*
> *No man can work like Him . . .*
> *No man can work like Him.*

The song fell upon me like a spell. It fascinated me. It seemed like a voice from heaven. It possessed my whole being. I took Jesus to be my Lord of lords and to work in my behalf. I knew not how much it all meant. But I took Him in the dark and went forth from that rustic, old-fashioned service, remembering nothing else, but strangely lifted up forevermore.

### Old Orchard Beach

A few weeks later I went with my family to Old Orchard Beach, Maine. I went chiefly to enjoy the delightful air of that loveliest of all ocean beaches. I lived on the very seashore while there and went occasionally to the meetings at the campground. But only once or twice did I take part in the services. Up to that time, I had not committed myself in any full sense to the truth or experience of divine healing.

Just the same, I had been much interested in divine healing for a long while. Several years before this I had given myself to the Lord in full consecration, taking Him for my indwelling righteousness. At that time I had been very much impressed by a remarkable case of healing in my own congregation. I had been called to see a dying man given up by all the physicians. I was told that he had not spoken or eaten for days. It was a most aggravated case of paralysis and softening of the brain. So remarkable was his recovery that it was published in the medical journals as one of the marvels of medical science.

His mother was a devoted Christian. The man had been converted in his childhood, but now for many years had been an actor and, his mother feared, a stranger to the Lord. She begged me to pray for him. As I prayed I was led to ask not for his healing but that he might recover long enough to let his mother know that he was saved. I rose from my knees and was about to leave, leaving my prayer where we too often leave our prayers—in oblivion. But some of my people arrived, and I was detained a few minutes introducing them to the mother.

Just then I stepped up to the bed mechanically, and suddenly the young man opened his eyes and began to talk to me. I was astonished and still more so was the dear old mother. And when, as I asked him further, the man gave satisfactory evidence of his simple trust in Jesus, we were all overwhelmed with astonishment and joy.

From that hour he rapidly recovered and lived for years. He called to see me later and told me that he regarded his healing as a miracle of divine power. The impression produced by that incident never left me.

Soon afterward I attempted to take the Lord as my Healer. For a while, as long as I trusted Him, He sustained me wonderfully. But being entirely without instruction and advised by a devout Christian physician that it was presumption, I abandoned my position of simple dependence on God alone and floundered and stumbled for years. But as I heard of isolated cases of miraculous healings, I never dared to doubt them or question that God did sometimes so heal. For myself, however, the truth had no really practical or effectual power, for I never could feel that I had any clear authority in a given case of need to trust myself to God.

## I had to settle the matter

In the summer I speak of, I heard a great number of people testify that they had been healed by simply trusting the Word of Christ, just as they would for their salvation. These testimonies drove me to my Bible. I determined that I must settle the matter one way or the other. I am glad I did not go to man. At Jesus' feet, alone, with my Bible open and with no one to help or guide me, I became convinced that this was part of Christ's glorious gospel for a sinful and suffering world—the purchase of His blessed cross for all who would believe and receive His word.

That was enough. I could not believe this and then refuse to take it for myself. I felt I dare not hold any truth in God's Word as a mere theory or teach to others what I had not personally proved. And so one Friday afternoon at three o'clock, I went out into the silent pine woods. There I raised my right hand to heaven and in view of the judgment day, I made to God, as if I had seen Him there before me face to face, these three eternal pledges:

> 1. *As I shall meet Thee in that day, I solemnly accept this truth as part of Thy Word and of the gospel of Christ. Thou helping me, I shall never question it until I meet Thee there.*
>
> 2. *As I shall meet Thee in that day, I take the Lord Jesus as my physical life for all the needs of my body until my life work is done. Thou helping me, I shall never doubt that Thou dost so become my life and strength from this moment and wilt keep me under all circumstances until Thy blessed coming and until all Thy will for me is perfectly fulfilled.*
>
> 3. *As I shall meet Thee in that day, I solemnly agree to use this blessing for Thy glory and the good of others. I agree to speak of it or minister in connection with it in any way in which Thou mayest call me or others may need me in the future.*

I arose. It had only been a few moments, but I knew that something was done. Every fiber of my soul was tingling with a sense of God's presence. I do not know whether my body felt better or not. I did not care to feel it. It was so glorious to believe it simply and to know that henceforth, God had it in hand.

## My faith was tested

Then came the test of faith. The first struck me before I had left the spot. A subtle voice whispered, *Now that you have decided to take God as your Healer, it would help if you should just go down to Dr. Cullis's cottage and get him to pray with you.* I listened to the suggestion for a moment without really thinking. Suddenly, a blow seemed to strike my brain that made me reel as a stunned man.

"Lord, what have I done?" I cried. I felt I was in some great peril. In a moment the thought came, *That suggestion would have been all right before this, but you have just settled this matter forever and told God you will never doubt that it is done.* Immediately I understood what faith meant. I understood what a solemn and awful thing it was to keep faith with God. I have often thanked God for that blow. I saw that when a thing was settled with God, it was never to be unsettled. When it was done, it was never to be undone or done over again in any sense that could involve a doubt of the finality of the commitment already made.

In the early days of the work of faith to which God later called me, I was as much helped by a holy fear of doubting God as by any of the joys and raptures of His presence or promises. This little word often shone like a living fire in my Bible: "If any man draw back, my soul shall have no pleasure in him" (Hebrews 10:38). What the enemy desired was to get some element of doubt about the certainty and completeness of the transaction just closed, and God mercifully held me back from it.

The following day I started for the mountains of New Hampshire. The next test came on Sunday, just two days after I had claimed my healing. I was invited to preach in the Congregational church. I felt the Holy Spirit pressing me to give a special testimony. Instead, I tried to preach a good sermon of my own choosing. But it was not the word for that hour, I am sure. God wanted me to tell the people what He had been showing me. Instead, I tried to be conventional and respectable, and I had an awful time. My jaw seemed like lead, and my lips would scarcely move. I finished the sermon as soon as I could and fled into an adjoining field, where I fell to the ground before the Lord and asked Him to show me what He meant and to forgive me. He did—most graciously. And He let me have one more chance to testify for Him and glorify Him.

That night we had a service in our hotel, and I was permitted to speak again. This time I told what God had been doing. Not very much did I say, but I tried to be faithful. I recounted how I had lately seen the Lord Jesus and His blessed gospel in a new way as the Healer of the body. I had taken Him for myself and knew that He would be faithful and sufficient. God did not ask me to testify of my feelings or experiences but of Jesus and His faithfulness. And I am sure He calls all who trust Him to testify before they experience His full blessing. I believe I should have lost my healing if I had waited until I felt it.

I have since known hundreds to fail just at this point. God made me commit myself to Him and His healing covenant before He would fully bless me. I know a dear brother in the ministry, now much used in the gospel and in the gospel of healing, who received a wonderful manifestation of God's power in his body and then went home to his church but said nothing about it. He was waiting to see how it would hold out.

In a few weeks he was worse than ever. When I met him the next time, he wore the most dejected face you could imagine. I told him his error and it all flashed upon him immediately. He went home and gave God the glory for what He had done. In a little while his church was the center of a blessed work of grace and healing that reached far and wide, and he himself was rejoicing in the fullness of Jesus.

I am very sure that Sunday evening testimony did me more good than anybody else. Had I withheld it, I believe I should not be writing the pages of *The Gospel of Healing*.

## The third test

The next day, the third test came. Nearby was a mountain 3,000 feet high. I was asked to join a small group who were to ascend it.

At once I shrank back. Did I not remember the dread of heights that had always overshadowed me? Did I not recall the terror with which I had resolved in Switzerland and Italy never to attempt high places again? Did I not know how ordinary stairs exhausted me and distressed my poor heart?

Then came the solemn, searching thought: *If you refuse to go, it is because you do not believe that God has healed you. If you have taken Him for your strength, need you fear to do anything to which He calls you?*

It was God's thought. I knew my fear would be, in this case, pure unbelief. I told God that in His strength I would go.

I do not wish to imply that we should do things just to show how strong we are or without any real necessity. I do not believe God wants His children needlessly to climb mountains or walk miles just because they are asked to. But in this case—and there are such cases in every experience—I needed to step out and claim my victory sometime, and this was God's time and way. He will call and show each one for himself or herself. And whenever we are shrinking through fear, He likely will call us to the very thing that is necessary for us to do to overcome the fear.

And so I ascended that mountain. At first it seemed as if it would almost take my last breath. I felt all the old weakness and physical dread. I found I had in myself no more strength than ever. But over against my weakness and suffering I became conscious that there was another Presence. There was a divine strength reaching out to me if I would have it, take it, claim it, hold it and persevere in it.

On one side there seemed to press upon me a weight of death; on the other, an infinite Life. And I became overwhelmed with the one, or uplifted with the other, just as I shrank or pressed forward, just as I feared or trusted. I seemed to walk between them, and the one that I touched possessed me.

The wolf and the Shepherd walked on either side, but the blessed Shepherd did not let me turn away. I pressed closer, closer, closer to His bosom, and every step seemed stronger. When I reached that mountaintop, I seemed to be at the gate of heaven, and the world of weakness and fear was lying at my feet. Thank God, from that time I have had a new heart in this body, literally as well as spiritually, and Christ has been its glorious life.

A few weeks later I returned to my work in New York City. With deep gratitude to God I can truly say, hundreds being my witnesses, that for many years I have been permitted to labor for the dear Lord in summer's heat or winter's cold without interruption, without a single season of protracted rest, and with increasing comfort, strength and delight. Life has had for me a zest and labor and exhilaration that I never knew in the freshest days of my childhood.

## *The subsequent years*

A few months after my healing, God called me into the special pastoral, evangelistic and literary work that has since engaged my time and energy. I may truthfully say it has involved four times more labor than has any previous period of my life. And yet it has been a continual delight. It has been very much easier in every way than the far lighter tasks of former years.

All the time, however, I have been conscious that I was not using my own natural strength. I would not dare to attempt for a single week on my own constitutional resources what I am now doing. I am intensely conscious, with every breath, that I am drawing my vitality from a directly supernatural source and that it keeps pace with the calls and necessities of my work. Hence, on a day of double labor I will often be aware, at the close, of double vigor and feel just like beginning over again. Indeed, I am almost reluctant to have even sleep place its gentle arrest on the delightful privilege of service. Nor is this a surge of excitement to be followed by a reaction, for the next day comes with equal freshness.

I have noticed that my work is easier and seems to draw less upon my vital energy than before. I do not seem to be using up my own life in the work now, but I am working on a surplus of vitality supplied from another Source. I am sure it is nothing else than "the life . . . of Jesus . . . made manifest in [my] mortal flesh" (2 Corinthians 4:11).

Once or twice since I took the Lord for my strength, I have felt so wondrously well that I began to rejoice and trust in the God-given strength. In a moment I felt it was about to fail me, and the Lord instantly compelled me to look to Him as my continual strength and not depend on the strength He had already given. I have found many other dear friends compelled to learn this lesson and suffer until they fully learned it. It is a life of constant dependence on Christ, physically as well as spiritually.

I know not how to account for this unless it be the imparted life of the dear Lord Jesus in my body. I am surely most unworthy of such an honor and privilege, but I believe He is pleased in His great condescension to unite Himself with our bodies. I am persuaded that His body, which is perfectly human and real, can somehow share its vital elements with our organic life and quicken us from His living heart and indwelling Spirit.

I have learned much from the fact that Samson's physical strength was through "the Spirit of the LORD" (Judges 14:6). Paul declared that although he was daily delivered to death for Jesus' sake, yet the very life of Christ was being made manifest in his body. I find that "the body is . . . for the Lord; and the Lord for the body" (1 Corinthians 6:13). Our "bodies are the members of Christ" (6:15), and "we are members of [Christ's] body, of his flesh, and of his bones" (Ephesians 5:30).

I do not desire to provoke argument, but I give my simple, humble testimony. To me it is very real and very wonderful. I know "it is the Lord." Many of my fellow Christians have entered into the same blessed experience. I only want to consecrate and use this divine life more and more for Him. What a sacred and holy trust it is! I so wish that my weary, broken-down, overladen Christian friends could also taste its exquisite joy and its all-sufficient strength.

To my brothers in the ministry I would like to add that I have found the same divine help for my mind and brain as for my body. Having much writing and speaking to do, I have given my pen and my tongue to Christ to possess and use. God has so helped me that my literary work has never been a labor. He has enabled me to think much more rapidly and to accomplish much more work and with greater facility than ever before. It is very simple and humble work; but such as it is, it is all *through* Him and, I trust, *for* Him only.

With all its simplicity, I believe it has been more used to help His children and glorify His name than all the elaborate preparation and toil of the weary years that went before. To God be all the praise!

# CHAPTER
## 8

---

# *Testimony of the Work*

Let me add a few words about the beginning of the ministry of divine healing in New York City and some of the instances that I have known.

As I have already stated in the previous chapter, one of the pledges I made to the Lord concerning my own healing was that I would use this truth and my experience of it for the good of others as He should require and lead me.

This was no small thing for me. I had a large amount of conservative respectability. I had high regard for my ecclesiastical reputation. I knew intuitively what it might cost to be wholly true in this matter. At the same time, I shrank unutterably from the thought of having to pray with anyone else for healing. I feared greatly that I should involve God's name in dishonor by claiming what might not come to pass. I almost hoped that I might not have to minister personally in this matter. I was intensely glad that God had already raised up other ministers for this work, and I would gladly strengthen their hands.

My first public testimony in New York to the truth of divine healing, made in the course of a sermon to my own people, then a Presbyterian church, awakened little or no opposition. A few weeks later I was asked to speak at the anniversary of the Fulton Street Prayer Meeting—the day of President James Garfield's funeral. The Lord led me to speak frankly and refer to the true scriptural method of prayer for the direct healing of the sick in the name of the Lord Jesus. At the close of my address there was only one who gave me a word of response. He was a Methodist presiding elder. He thanked me very cordially and said he believed every word I had said.

## *A family crisis*

Soon after, a test came in my own family. My little daughter became suddenly very ill with diphtheria. Her mother, not then believing at all as I did, insisted upon having a physician. She was much distressed when I simply took the little one to God and claimed her healing in the name of the Lord Jesus. That night, with a throat as white as snow and a raging fever, the little sufferer lay beside me alone. I knew that if the sickness lasted until the following day, there would be a crisis in my family and I should be held responsible.

The dear Lord knew it, too. With trembling hand I anointed her brow. She was the first or second person I had ever anointed. I claimed the power of Jesus' name. About midnight my heart was deeply burdened. I cried to God for speedy deliverance.

By morning my daughter was well. I shall never forget the look my wife gave me when she saw the ulcers gone and our child ready to get up and play.

About that time the Lord led me to commence the special work of faith that has since engaged my life. This was not by any means to teach divine healing but to preach the gospel to the neglected masses by public evangelistic services. For several years no single word about physical healing was spoken in those meetings, our supreme object being to lead men and women to Christ and not to prejudice them by any side issues.

But the facts about my own healing and the healing of my child spread quietly among my little flock. One and another came to me to ask about it and whether they could be healed also. I told them they could if they would believe, as I had done, and I sent them to their homes to read God's Word for themselves and to ponder and to pray.

The first inquirer was a dear sister, then widely known in Christian work, who afterward became a deaconess in our

Berachah Home. She had suffered from heart disease for 20 years. She took about a month to weigh the matter. Then in her calm, decided way she came to have her case presented to God. Instantly she was healed. For several years she worked untiringly, hardly knowing what weariness even meant. At length she finished her work and fell asleep amid great peace and blessing.

Others began to come and ask about physical healing. At length the Friday Meeting grew up as a time and place where all who were interested in this special theme could gather, be instructed and strengthen each other by mutual testimony. This meeting has since grown in size to several hundred people from all the evangelical churches and many different homes.

## The blessing is for all

The cases of healing that have come under my notice in these years would fill many volumes. They have represented all social extremes, all religious opinions, all professions and callings and all classes of disease. I have had spiritists come, broken down at length by the service of Satan and seeking deliverance from their sufferings. I have never felt free even to pray with such without a complete renunciation of this snare.

I have had Roman Catholics come as if they were consulting some oracle. And when they have been patiently instructed and led to the true Savior, I have seen them healed. I have had men come and offer large sums if they or their dear ones could be prayed back to health. I have never dared to touch such cases except to send them directly to Christ and tell them that at His feet only, in true penitence and trust, could they expect deliverance.

I have had poor sinners come seeking healing and go having found salvation. Many people have been led to Christ through their desire to escape disease. I have never felt that I could claim the healing of anyone until he or she first accepted Jesus as Savior. But I have several times seen the soul saved and the body healed in the same hour.

I have never allowed anyone to look to me as a healer. I have had no liberty to pray for others while they placed the least trust in either me or my prayers—or in anything or anyone but the merits, promises and intercessions of Christ alone. My most important work has usually been to take myself and my shadow out of people's way and set Jesus fully in their view.

I have seen very humble and illiterate Christians suddenly and gloriously healed and baptized with the most wonderful faith. I have seen intellectuals and Christians who had great reputations unable to touch even the border of Christ's garment. I saw a brilliant physician once rise in the meeting and make a learned speech about healing. And I saw a humble girl who, when I first met her, did not seem to have capacity enough to grasp the idea, healed by his side of the worst stage of tuberculosis and her shortened limb lengthened two inches in a moment.

I have seen this blessed gift of Christ bring relief and unspeakable blessing to the homes of many of the poor. I have seen it take from worn and weary working women a bondage like Egypt's iron furnace. And I have also seen it enter the homes of many of the refined, the cultivated and the wealthy who have not been ashamed to witness a good confession and bear a noble testimony to Christ as a complete Savior.

I have seen the theologian often answered after his most logical assaults upon it by the healing of some of his own people in a way he could not answer or explain. Sometimes I have taken one of these simple persons to a boasting infidel and asked him or her to testify to the person concerning what God has done. I have seen infidels overwhelmed, silenced and sometimes deeply impressed.

Often have I seen women of the world break under deep conviction of sin and seek a true and devout religious life by the simple, genuine testimonies of the Friday Meeting. I have seen many a clergyman accept the Lord Jesus in His fullness for soul and body. Some of the most devoted and distinguished servants of Christ are glad to own Him as their Healer. But I have also noticed that the ecclesiastical straitjacket is the hardest fetter of all, and the fear of man the most inexorable of all bondages.

Not a few physicians of the highest standing have taken Jesus as their Healer, and when their patients are prepared for it, they love to lead them to Christ's care. Many of the most consecrated Christian workers and city missionaries have found this precious truth. Some have faced a bitter ordeal of prejudice and opposition in their churches and organizations. But when they have been wise, true and faithful, God has vindicated them in the end.

I have found that the most spiritually minded men and women in the various churches are usually led to see and receive this truth. When Christ becomes an indwelling and personal reality in the soul, it is hard to keep Him out of the body.

## What about medical remedies?

I have not found any serious practical difficulty in dealing with the question of remedies. Where a person sets any value on them or is not clearly led of the Lord to abandon them, I never have advised him or her to do so. There is no use in giving up remedies without a real personal faith in Christ. And when a person really commits his or her case to Christ and believes that Christ has undertaken, he or she does not want, as a rule, any other hand to touch it. He or she does not see that anything else is necessary.

Where people have real faith in Christ's supernatural help, they will not want remedies. And where they have not this faith, I have never dared to hinder them from having the best help they can obtain. I have never felt called to urge anyone to accept divine healing. I have found it better to present the truth and let God lead them. Often when urging them most strongly not to attempt it unless they were fully persuaded, the effect has been to impel them to it more strongly and to show that they had real faith. I have never felt that divine healing should be regarded as the gospel. It is part of it, but we labor much more assiduously for the salvation and sanctification of the souls of men and women.

The cases of healing have been varied. One of the most remarkable in the early days was a woman who had not bent her joints for eight years. She used to stand in our meetings on her crutches, unable to sit down during the whole service. She had not sat for eight years. She was healed in a moment, and all in the house were filled with wonder.

Another was cured of spinal curvature. A great many have been delivered from fibroid tumors and a few from malignant and incurable cancers. We have seen broken bones restored without surgical aid. We have seen God heal severe heart disease, tuberculosis and hernia, when it would have been death to walk forth as they did if Christ had not sustained. Paralysis and softening of the brain, epilepsy and St. Vitus' dance—even a few cases of dangerous insanity—all have been markedly cured through believing prayer. The numbers of such healings will reach to thousands.

## *Consecrated lives our chief joy*

Our chief joy has been in the consecrated lives thus redeemed from destruction and given to the work of God and the needs of mankind. These are blessed and glorious. One person is in charge of a mission where hundreds are led to Christ. Another, refused by her mission board on account of illness, was healed by the Lord and is again in India with her husband, preaching Christ. Some are in Japan, some in Africa, some in South America, some in England. Many are in the streets and lanes of New York City and in the most earnest work of our land. God be thanked for the blessings they have received, and the blessing they have become.

During these years the Lord has opened our Berachah Home and allowed us to meet hundreds of His dear children within its walls. We have seen them go forth in strength and blessing. Other homes of healing are scattered over this and other lands. Already a great multitude are joining hands and singing together these verses from Psalm 103 as they journey home:

> *Bless the LORD, O my soul: and all that is within me, bless his holy name. Bless the LORD, O my soul, and forget not all his benefits: who forgiveth all thine iniquities; who healeth all thy diseases; who redeemeth thy life from destruction; who crowneth thee with lovingkindness and tender mercies; who satisfieth thy mouth with good things; so that thy youth is renewed like the eagle's.*

## Abiding and Confiding

I am crucified with Jesus,
And He lives and dwells with me;
I have ceased from all my struggling,
'Tis no longer I, but He.
All my will is yielded to Him,
And His Spirit reigns within;
And His precious blood each moment
Keeps me cleansed and free from sin.

All my sicknesses I bring Him,
And He bears them all away;
All my fears and griefs I tell Him,
All my cares from day to day.
All my strength I draw from Jesus,
By His breath I live and move;
E'en His very mind He gives me,
And His faith and life and love.

For my words I take His wisdom,
For my works His Spirit's power;
For my ways His ceaseless presence
Guards and guides me every hour.
Of my heart He is the portion,
Of my joy the boundless Spring;
Savior, Sanctifier, Healer,
Glorious Lord and coming King.
—A. B. Simpson

Other books by Christian Publications on divine healing:

*Breast Cancer and Me* by Lois Olmstead

*Christ Our Healer Today* by Drake Travis

*Coping with Cancer* by John E. Packo

*Divine Healing: The Children's Bread* by Keith M. Bailey

*The Gospel of Healing* by A.B. Simpson

*The Lord for the Body* by A.B. Simpson

*Understanding Divine Healing* by Richard M. Sipley